The Goddess Obscured

The Goddess Obscured

Transformation of the Grain Protectress from Goddess to Saint

Pamela Berger

Beacon Press   Boston

Beacon Press
25 Beacon Street
Boston, Massachusetts 02108 2892
www.beacon.org

Beacon Press books
are published under the auspices of
the Unitarian Universalist Association of Congregations.

First digital-print edition 2001

Cover illustration: *Hours of the Virgin: The Flight into Egypt.* Photograph courtesy of the Bibliotèque Nationale, Paris.

Library of Congress Cataloging-in-Publication Data
Berger, Pamela C.
The goddess obscured.
p.   cm.
Includes bibliographical references and index.
ISBN 0-8070-6723-7
1. Grain goddesses. 2. Goddesses. I. Title.
BL473.5.B47
291.2´11   85-47524

For Laurel, Noah, and Alan

Contents

List of Illustrations

Acknowledgments

I wrote this book to satisfy my own curiosity about the endurance of old customs; to understand the syncretism that fuses pagan figures and Christian saints; and to seek out the influence of dreams and visions in the transformation of gods and goddesses into saints or demons.

I am indebted to Boston College for supporting this project through the faculty research grant program.

My thanks to those colleagues and friends who have read and criticized various parts of the manuscript: Professors Matilda Bruckner, Michael Connolly, Patricia De Leeuw, Jeanne Guillemin, Emily Hanawalt, and Andrew Von Hendy. And special thanks for important bibliographical material to Professor Proinsias Mac Cana of University College, Dublin.

I am grateful to those who helped with the typing of the manuscript and the gathering of the photographic materials: Donna Gold, Charles Connor, Patricia Thomas, Kathi Mirza, and Lucia Trevino. I also thank the libraries, museums, and scholars who have so generously allowed photographs of their holdings to appear in this publication. Specific acknowledgments appear in the list of illustrations.

I wish to thank my husband and children for their critical advice and loving encouragement.

And special thanks to my editor at Beacon Press, Joanne Wyckoff, who saved me from the pitfall of making those things that were merely *obscura* . . . absolutely *occultissima*.

Introduction

For millennia the image of a sacred grain protectress persisted in the human imagination. Invoked when the earth was broken up to receive the seed, she was associated with the growth of the crop and thus with the survival of humankind. Let it be understood from the start that we are not dealing with one goddess; we are discussing diverse realizations of a single magico-religious idea. This idea is embodied in figures that are not identical but somewhat equivalent, having evolved from the same generative impulses among disparate agrarian peoples. The grain goddess figure and the form of her rite differed according to geography, ethnic-religious group, and epoch. With various cultural successions, she was transformed and sometimes radically metamorphosed. Sometimes her particular features were changed while her essential meaning remained the same. At other times the exteriors of her form remained constant while her meaning was significantly altered. Such a figure cannot be cataloged in detail. Goddesses merge into one another with the ease of the three shape-shifting Celtic Morrigan, who transform from eels into heifers into crows while we impatiently insist that they stand still to be described. Sacred figures change their meanings and powers not only with the passage of centuries and with geographical areas but also with different seasons and especially with different recorders. Mythology becomes mercurial when we attempt to force it into patterns or molds. Nonetheless, there is archeological, textual, art-historical, and anthropological evidence that points to the ongoing veneration in a variety of cultures of a protectress of grain, a figure propitiated by special rites when the earth was loosened and the seed planted.

This book focuses on the different manifestations of the grain protectress and the rituals associated with her at the moment the hoe or plow was put into the earth and the seed committed to the soil. The calendrical demarcations of this event differ with latitude, altitude, climate, and topography. In Greece the plowing and sowing festival took place in the fall when the dead land, burned by the heat of summer, was about to revive under the fall rains. In Western Europe the major plowing and seeding took place in late winter or early spring, when the ground was first "awakened" and the seed placed into the "belly" of the earth. This first spring hoeing and plowing was fraught with magical danger as well as economic importance, and ancient farmers sought to mark the event by propitiating the goddess whose growth-engendering powers would cause the grain to sprout. We know that the ritual practiced in her honor in Roman times, included an invocation for protection of the fields from dangers and sometimes an animal offering or a libation. The fields were "purified" by either a procession around them or a symbolic passage of the goddess through them or near them. Sometimes the

1

procession and the passage of the goddess were combined. The importance for European mythic history of the various manifestations of this personified protectress cannot be underestimated. Human survival depended on the spontaneous produce of the soil and ancient agriculturalists stood in awe of that life-producing power. When the hoe or plow entered the womb of the earth and the seed was sown, a new process of creation was initiated, all under the protection of the grain mother.

The grain protectress appeared in various guises, from the ancient Near East to the classical world, from the Mediterranean to the Celtic and Germanic north, from paganism into Christianity, from the Middle Ages into the Renaissance, and still survives in folksongs and village celebrations of the modern world. Her earliest manifestations can be studied by investigating the figurines, statuettes, cultic objects, and household or communal shrines of Upper Neolithic and Chalcolithic sites.[1] Though no specific farming rituals can be attached to her at this early period, it is possible that some of the Neolithic figurines of the grain goddess were put to ritual use. Though the grain goddess remained part of the substratum of religious conceptions passed down to the Minoans and early Greeks, much of the Neolithic goddess imagery was lost, since the texts and archeological material preserved from ancient Greece and the Near East were set down or fashioned in a patriarchal social context.[2] The Greek grain goddess Demeter is only a shadow of the earlier great vegetation goddess. Thus, scholars must ferret out traces, in fragmentary form, of the earlier matrifocal patterns of veneration, for these beliefs and practices were often obscured as they were assimilated with elements from later cultures.

Texts record two seeding rites dedicated to a grain goddess in the Roman world — one early in the spring and the other in the fall. In Rome as elsewhere the commencement of seeding depended on the rains and temperatures of the season; however, toward late January or early February, a purification and seeding festival was held in which a manifestation of the plowing and sowing goddess was venerated with a prayer as well as with an offering of porridge and a pregnant sow. The boundaries of the field were purified so that the newly sown seeds would be protected. The Roman records of this early spring rite are few, but that does not necessarily reflect a dearth of veneration for the grain goddess. The sources that record agrarian attitudes and customs cannot be counted on to reflect accurately the practices of those who tilled the soil. Though many Roman writers attest to a great nostalgia for the rural life, they did not actually participate in many agricultural activities. For those leisured scholars or poets who provided our written documents, the first spring plowing and sowing would have been an event to remark on and to use poetically, but for those writers who would not have plowed or strewn the seed, sowing time was simply not fraught with the potential of life and death that it was for the farmer.

As is the case with the written sources, art-historical documents relating to rural life and particularly to the crucial acts of plowing and sowing are few. The materials used by rural peoples to fashion deities and cultic objects were limited to wood, straw, and other perishable stuffs. Stone statues and reliefs relating to agrarian life are limited in number and often show evidence of an unpracticed hand. Unlike the aristocracy or, later, the church, the people who planted had little access to training as artists, and there were few patrons to provide rural artists with the necessary leisure and the resources for acquiring precious or permanent materials. Thus, our understanding of the scope or importance of the deities venerated by agrarian peoples in the Roman world is limited both by the dearth of surviving objects and by the perspective of the recorders.

The churchmen of the early Middle Ages regarded the idea of the vegetation protectress with opprobrium. Since the vast majority of texts from that period was written by ecclesiastics, and since most of the surviving artworks were commissioned by them, our knowledge of practices or events that the church opposed derives from hostile or deprecating sources. The literate, Latin, clerical culture was consistently opposed to ceremonies dedicated to the grain goddess. Practiced by unlettered peasants, these rites and other agrarian customs were nevertheless vigorously maintained.[3] The language churchmen used to describe the peasants taking part in these rites is derogatory. The participants were described as "stupid," "foolish," "unenlightened." The clerics' unremitting castigation of the grain goddess and her rites served as an ironic proof that she continued to be venerated.

Reluctant to abandon such a deeply rooted mythic figure, early medieval peasants sought ways to retain the grain protectress while rendering her innocuous to the church hierarchy.[4] In some cases the earth mother became part of folk pageants celebrated at seeding time. In other areas popular imagination invented new forms of the figure or syncretized her — that is, attempted to see her as, or combine her with, a Christian saint. Christianity was successful in part because it allowed and even encouraged syncretism.

Accordingly, some of the earliest female saints—Radegund, Milburga, Macrine, Wilpurga—as well as the Virgin Mary, were mythically to take the place of the grain goddess in one locale or another. At some undetermined time, the nucleus of a legend developed in which a female saint, passing by a field at plowing and sowing time, demonstrated a great power over the growth energy of the seed. Her passage and her power effected a miracle and protected the plowmen as well as herself. Those participating in the event were protected from harm, the forces of evil were foiled, and an abundant harvest would assure survival for yet another year. The core of this legend reflects the topos, or major characteristics, of the sowing goddess ritual as revealed in ancient texts and artworks.[5] Though that topos was Christianized, the purpose and meaning of the Christian legend remained analogous to the purpose and meaning of the pagan rite.[6]

Ecclesiastical documents reveal the ways in which the church encouraged or discouraged this adaptation, but in most cases the process by which this particular new symbolic pattern was created is left to our imaginations. In some areas, the peasants may have merely rechristened the dedicatee of an ancient rite. Psychologists as well as historians have pointed to the role that dreams might have played in the re-creation of legends or heroes based on old prototypes.[7] In any case, as a Christianized figure linked to an event in the Christian tradition, the grain protectress could be preserved and eventually, in transmuted form, incorporated and celebrated in church-commissioned sculptures and paintings.

Chapters I and II set forth the ancient and late antique materials concerning the grain and sowing protectress; Chapters III through VII describe her perpetuation into the Christian and folkloric contexts. This book illuminates obscure but deep-rooted agrarian beliefs and practices; it also casts light on the underlying meaning of these grain protectress rites for those who worked the land. Until recently the isolation of art history from such disciplines as anthropology, folkloric scholarship, and psychology has prevented a composite view of such a figure from emerging. Traditional historians of medieval art have only just become interested in the folk tradition or the oral tradition. And folklorists, in turn, have been concerned mainly with recording rather than interpreting their material; they all too frequently lack a historical perspective, not to mention an art-historical perspective.

Most art historians have been uninterested in examining events or cults that have left no "significant" artistic remains. However, it is often the crudely wrought objects which reflect the lives of a majority of the people. If the cultic objects were not made of durable materials or if the practice left only crude evidence, that part of human history remained in limbo. However, with the present tools of scholarship one can more confidently attempt to explore the behavior and attitudes of those vast numbers of people who left us only fragmentary archeological or art-historical documents. In the cases in which written testimonies about rituals and practices have been preserved, the texts must be carefully interpreted, for they were usually written by individuals attached to the dominant culture. Thus the thoughts and hopes of the people who worked the land often reach us only through the distorting pens of unsympathetic intermediaries. This study is based on the premise that even though only limited historical or art historical records survive, a long-enduring figure crucial to rural culture can now be uncovered and brought to light.

Chapter I

The Goddess in the Ancient World

The Ancient Near East, Southeastern and Central Europe,
Egypt, and Crete

To a member of any ancient society, it was axiomatic that all phenomena of nature were regulated by the energies of mighty, humanlike forces. The division of the world into compartments, each governed by a manifestation of one of those forces, was a concept that could easily arise out of human experience. During the Neolithic period, when the importance of hunting as a means of subsistence diminished, the fertility of the soil and the regular growth of crops became the center of interest. Early farmers could not help noticing the cyclical changes of the seasons, as well as the biological rhythms of plants. In an effort to encourage the favorable outcome of these changes, communities directed their worship toward various personifications of these life-creating forces. Since women, like the land, were seen as the primary source of life, most early agriculturalists envisioned a female deity, an earth mother goddess, as the creative power behind all animal and plant fertility.

Different cultures had different appellations for this female personification of growth energy. In some areas she was known as the Great Mother, and though the figure represented more than just the image of motherhood, numerous modern scholars have used this term. It must be understood, however, that from the Upper Paleolithic onward (beginning about 35,000 years ago), the persona of the mother goddess splintered in response to the changing economy. She was envisioned as having a multiplicity of divine aspects and functions. As a multifaceted goddess she not only controlled the changing seasons but was sovereign over the underworld as well. It was, however, in the realm of birth, regeneration, and plant fertility that her cult was mainly centered.

Figure 1. Clay figure. Goddess giving birth to a child. Found in a grain bin at Çatal Hüyük.

Figure 2. The Venus of Lespugue. Mother goddess figure.

Artifacts from Neolithic and Chalcolithic settlements, wherein the economy was concentrated on intensive agriculture, offer a glimpse of how various agrarian communities conceived of their particular versions of this goddess.[1] At Hacilar and Çatal Hüyük in central Anatolia (present-day Turkey), numerous statuettes of the mother goddess type were discovered (figure 1).[2] Roughly modeled, many of them resemble their Upper Paleolithic prototypes, generally known as Venuses (for example, the Lespugue, Willendorf, and Laussel female figurines; see figure 2).[3] The breasts, belly, and navel are stressed, and an abundance of flesh characterizes the figurines. Frequently depicting a pregnant figure, the statuettes emphasize the goddess's capacity to procreate, as well as to sustain and nurture life.

Those who executed the Anatolian statuettes did not depict the act of sexual intercourse. It is questionable whether these early peoples connected intercourse with conception. There are almost no phallic or vulval symbols in the Anatolian Neolithic.[4] And no representations of male deities have been found at these sites;[5] this seems to accord with the diminished importance of the male as hunting grew less important in communal life.

The most prominent aspect of the Anatolian goddess figure was her role as nurturer and protectress of plant life. This divine power has been deduced from painted or sculpted design on the figures and the nature of the places where the statuettes were found. Some mother goddess statuettes, sculpted as if giving birth, were uncovered in heaps of grain or in grain bins (figure 1).[6] Such placement of a birthing goddess supports the notion that women's

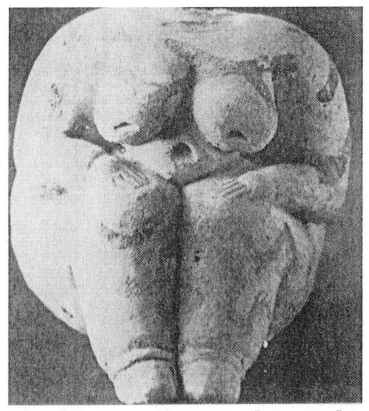

Figure 3. Clay statuette painted with cruciform flower patterns. From
Çatal Hüyük.

power to bring forth life was seen as analogous to the earth's miraculous
power to quicken the seed. In the imaginations of early farmers, these
analogous birthing powers not only linked women's fertility to that of the
soil but also made it inevitable that a female deity would be envisioned as
controlling vegetation.

Other statuettes from Çatal Hüyük and Hacilar further support the notion
that the mother goddess was conceived of as sovereign of plant life, for floral
and vegetable patterns frequently adorn them (figure 3). Dressed in these
patterns, the goddess had control over the leaves and stalks she wore. Furthermore, floral and vegetable patterns sometimes decorated the shrines
where mother goddess figures were found. Since there are no written texts
from this period, literature cannot help us interpret further the significance
of these figures, but the statuary does indicate that in the sixth millennium
B.C. this mother goddess of plant fertility was predominant in the religion of
Hacilar and Çatal Hüyük.

The statuettes' vegetal decoration and their places of discovery, as well as the overwhelming predominance of female over male statuary of this period, suggest that among early agriculturalists women may have taken a primary role, and that it was not until sowing and reaping expanded, involving heavy manual labor, that agrarian tasks were transferred to men.[7] Proponents of this theory cite numerous present-day tribal societies in which the tasks of hoeing the ground and sowing the seed devolve almost entirely on women. Women in those societies must observe particular rules when planting the seed or, it is thought, the crop will fail. Whether because of women's economic role as primary tillers of the soil or because of their mysterious capacity to produce life, the evidence from the early civilizations of Anatolia consistently attributes the control over agriculture to a female, to a great vegetation goddess personifying the earth's fecundity and the germinating energy of the seed.

Central Anatolia is not the only area that has yielded sculptural evidence of the primacy of a mother goddess. Excavations of Neolithic and Chalcolithic settlements in southeastern and central Europe reveal that inhabitants of those regions likewise venerated a mother goddess.[8] Though conquerors who infiltrated during the late Chalcolithic and early Bronze ages (4500–2800 B.C.) obscured much of this early goddess worship, figurines as well as cultic objects and shrines uncovered throughout the area enable one to form an idea of the persistence of goddess worship there.

As in Anatolia, the aspects of this great goddess manifest in statuettes and figurines were her fertility and her power over plant life.[9] Statuettes dating from the seventh to the fifth millennia B.C. display a rich repertoire of signs and symbols that challenge the interpretive powers of the archeologist. The specific sets of symbols or conventional signs incised on the mother goddess and on associated cultic objects intimate how early cultivators may have envisioned her domain. In some cases the goddess is decorated with lozenges, with a dot inside each one (figure 4). In a few cases the dot inside the lozenge was made by the impression of a grain seed. This ideogram of a dot or of a seed impression within a lozenge has been interpreted as a representation of the fertile field and the seed planted within it.[10] Since seed was recognized by primitive farmers as the cause of germination and growth, did its presence on the goddess's form within a shape reminiscent of a field allude to her power over the seed and her ability to impart fertility?

The dot and lozenge incised on the goddess figurines could be on the thighs, neck, or arms, but was usually and most significantly on the belly (figure 4). In some examples, the goddess is pregnant (figure 5), a figuration that supports the assumption that the womb of a woman was associated with the fertility of the land.[11] At times the goddess is exquisitely clothed; sometimes just her abdomen is bare. On occasion her exposed belly is encircled by a snake, a creature known to penetrate the earth and therefore thought to be privy to the secrets of fecundity. Though the lozenge and dot are abstract

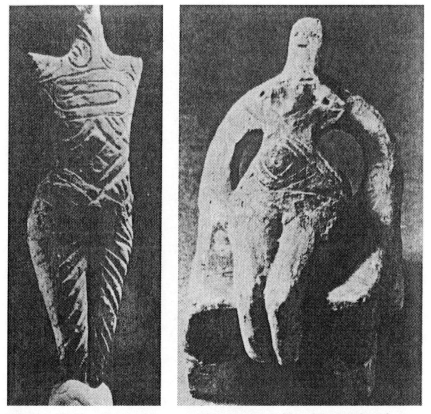

Figure 4. Goddess figure with quartered lozenge on belly and dot inside each quarter. Snake design on chest. Mid–fifth millennium B.C. From Cucuteni, northern Moldavia.

Figure 5. Goddess with multiple-lozenge design on pregnant belly. From Selo Kolekovets, central Bulgaria. Throne from another site.

and sometimes difficult to decipher, their repetition and placement on significant parts of the often-pregnant figurines, as well as their frequent association with the snake, support the interpretation that they symbolized the fruitfulness of the grain field, and that this figure could indeed be called a grain goddess. Furthermore, terra-cottas have been found that show what may be goddess figures involved in the ritual grinding of grain and the baking of sacred bread. [12]

Much of the archeological data compiled in recent studies of the southeastern European mother goddess indicate that the figurines may have played a role in the enactment of myths and seasonal dramas. [13] Some of the statuettes are wearing animal masks or are dressed in ritual garb; others are dancing or leaping, or are juxtaposed to musical instruments; some shrines and shrine

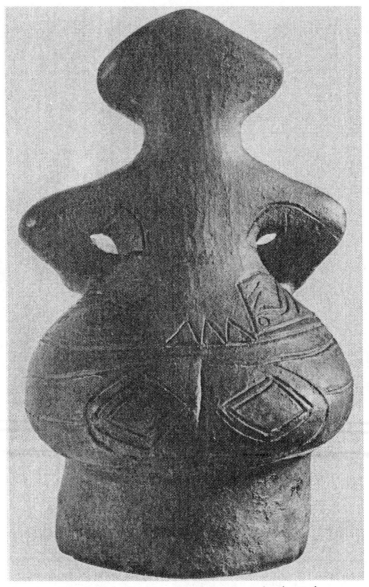

Figure 6. Vessel-shaped goddess with lozenges on her buttocks.

equipment that have been uncovered point to the possibility of sacrifices being performed in connection with the figurines. Some of the goddess figures were fashioned in the shape of vessels for libations or crop watering (figure 6). These may likewise have been used in early ritual drama, perhaps enacted to ensure the cyclical renewal of life. It has been suggested that the goddess figures in the shape of vessels might have been ceremoniously carried around the field as a watering implement to irrigate the crops at certain prescribed stages of their growth. In any event, the figurines and their attributes, their postures and decor, as well as the places they were found all point to one important aspect of the mythological world of our Neolithic and Chalcolithic ancestors, a world characterized by the worship of one manifestation of the mother goddess as a grain goddess, a figure who emerged with the inception of agriculture and who was seen as symbolizing fertile fields and the germination, sprouting, growing, and ripening of grain. [14]

Modifications of the dominant mother-goddess religion occurred during the fifth millennium B.C. and coincided with the incursion of nomadic herders from the Eurasian steppes into the Near East and the Mediterranean. [15] They brought with them an economic, social, and religious organization that focused on masculine functions. The invasion marked the patriarchalization of agrarian culture. The earliest extant written sources demonstrate that these invading patriarchal peoples accommodated their divinities to those of the indigenous goddess-worshiping cultures, and they did not immediately denigrate the importance of the Great Mother. Instead, the literature from the third millennium B.C., recorded after the invasions, demonstrates the fusion of the goddess-worshiping with the god-worshiping culture.

The earliest evidence of the melding of matrifocal with patrifocal traditions is in Sumerian documents from Mesopotamia. Humankind's first written religious ideas are copiously inscribed in cuneiform on these clay tablets. [16] Among the myths is one that tells of the sky god inseminating the earth mother in an act of intercourse that results in the birth of plant life:

Smooth, big Earth made herself resplendent, beautified her body joyously,
Wide Earth bedecked her body with precious metal and lapis lazuli
Adorned herself with diorite, chalcedony, and shiny carnelian,
Heaven arrayed himself in a wig of verdure, stood up in princeship,
Holy Earth, the virgin, beautified herself for Holy Heaven,
Heaven, the lofty god, planted his knees on Wide Earth,
Poured the semen of the heroes Tree and Reed into her womb,
Sweet Earth, the fecund cow, was impregnated with the rich
    semen of Heaven,
Joyfully did Earth tend to the giving birth of the plants of life,
Luxuriantly did Earth bear the rich produce, did she exude
    wine and honey. [17]

Though principally a personification of earth, this Sumerian goddess, like the Neolithic-Chalcolithic goddesses before her, was multifaceted. She was a leader in combat as well as an advocate in the assembly. But as Inanna, the

goddess of procreation, she inspired the Sumerian mythographers to com-
pose some of their most beautiful poems. The ritual marriage between the
king of Sumer and this fertility goddess was essential for the productivity of
the soil, the prosperity of the land, and the well-being of the people. Early
Sumerian texts (from the third millennium B.C.) recount that the union of
the king with the goddess was celebrated with joyous music and ecstatic love
song.[18] The myth recounts that after selecting the king and making him
divine, the goddess mated with him and their cohabitation brought forth the
vegetation all around them.[19] Thus, the earliest known writings confirm
what we know to be true from the prehistoric archeological record: that
early agriculturists conceived of the earth in the form of a female goddess
and that one of the most potent aspects of that great goddess was her power
over vegetation; for, by having sovereignty over plant life she was responsible
for the well-being of humankind.

The concept of the mother goddess was likewise strong and prevalent in
the Syro-Palestinian region.[20] Almost every major excavation of middle
Bronze Age through early Iron Age sites (2000–600 B.C.) has produced
terra-cotta plaques impressed with the nude female holding plant forms and
standing in such a position that she can be identified as a goddess.[21] Some
are specifically mother figurines, pregnant, sometimes with a child or nursing, and often with navel and breasts emphasized.[22] Others are depicted as
holding their breasts.[23] In one group the goddess is clutching stalks of
plants, possibly lotus or papyrus.[24] The figurines and plaques are so numerous that they could not have belonged only to shrines, but must have been
the possessions of private households (figures 7–8).

The literary sources and inscriptions from the Syro-Palestinian region
mention three major female deities: Asherah, Ashtart, and Anat. Ashtart
seems to have been known in this region as the woman of the horse and
chariot, as well as the deity associated with the fecundity of flocks.[25] Anat,
the virgin goddess, was one of the consorts of Baal and exhibits a warlike
character.[26] Asherah was popular throughout the Near East and is mentioned
in documents far more frequently than the other two. She is called the
mother of the gods, and she plays the role of consort to the chief god, El.[27]
She is also called the progenitor of the gods, who in turn are seen as the
seventy children of Asherah.[28]

The word asherah also occurs many times in the Old Testament. In rab-
binic commentaries, as well as in the King James Version, asherah is translated "grove." Though the meaning of the term has been a point of contention, most scholars agree that the term asherah applies in some way to a
goddess.[29] And it is clear that whenever an asherah is set up by the Israelites,
they anger the Lord Yahweh.[30] A study of the verbs used with the word
asherah indicates that the asherah was often made of wood.[31] An asherah can

Figures 7 and 8. Plaques with fertility goddesses holding stalks of vegetation. Late Bronze and early Iron Age.

be built, planted, erected, constructed. It is placed near the altar and can be destroyed by chopping it down and burning it. The object is never described in the Old Testament, but scholars conclude that one should probably picture the *asherah* as a rude wooden pillar representing the goddess, or as an actual statuette of her.[32]

Moses had warned against the *asherahs (asherim)* of the Canaanites and advised the Israelites that they should cut them down,[33] but through various periods of their history the Israelites apparently did not heed the warning. Maacah, the mother of King Asa (1 Kings 15:13), built an abominable image for Asherah and was thus removed from the position of queen mother.[34] Elijah vanquished the four hundred prophets of Asherah who "dined off Jezebel's table."[35] The final case of royal worship of Asherah was when Manasseh erected a statue of her in the Temple.[36]

Though often we have the impression that the cultic sites associated with Asherah were outdoors, on hills, or in groves of trees,[37] she may also have been worshiped in a temple, for at one point women were castigated for weaving clothes for Asherah, possibly in the form of hangings for a tabernacle or indeed for a clothed statue of the goddess herself.[38] In Deuteronomy 16:21 prohibition is given against placing an *asherah* beside the altar of the Lord, which indicates that at times Asherah was worshiped along with

Yahweh. During the religious reforms of the eighth and seventh centuries B.C., the adoration of this apparently widely venerated mother goddess was totally suppressed.[39]

Clearly, the worship of Asherah (or of any of the goddesses) was considered an abomination by those of the Israelite nation who left us written sources. The prophet Micah even associates Asherah with witches and soothsayers (Mic. 5:14). Though both the extra-Judaic texts and the biblical sources establish the existence of the cult of Asherah in Palestine before about 1500 B.C., the Old Testament gives no indication of what the people imagined to be the powers of the goddess, or of her association with the chief god El.[40] Nor is the extent of her cult discernible in the biblical textual sources. Wooden representations of Asherah or her "pillar" would have decayed over the millennia and metal images would have been melted down. Thus, perhaps the terra-cotta plaques of the nude goddesses preserve a final witness to the worship of the female deities so frequently mentioned with opprobrium in the Old Testament. And perhaps the stylized plant stalks represented in her hands and the emphasis on nurturing breasts and pregnant belly indicate that here as elsewhere one aspect of this mother of the gods was her sovereignty over human and plant fertility.[41]

The Hittite pantheon was populated by many gods and goddesses.[42] The major goddess in this culture was Arinna, the sun goddess, queen of heaven and earth.[43] She stood at the head of the Hittite pantheon along with the sun god of heaven. There was also a specific Hittite earth mother or vegetation goddess, Lilwani, venerated during a spring festival celebrating the resurgence of plant life.[44] Lilwani's role, like that of the other vegetation goddesses, was to invigorate the earth so that plant life could flourish and sustain humankind. Unfortunately, there is a dearth of both textual and archeological material about this Hittite vegetation goddess.

Among the Egyptians (and later among the Greeks and Romans), Isis was worshiped as the great divine mother of all nature.[45] The most ancient Egyptian documents reveal that she was identified as the goddess from whom all becoming arose.[46] She was also the female embodiment of the Nile's reawakening, the embodiment of the flood waters that annually revived the land. Under the power of Isis the river that had seemed dead during the dry season was reborn as living, life-producing waters.

Isis was also known as a deity of the earth, or rather of the soil fructified by the Nile. Though her powers were envisioned as vast, tradition held that the sowing of wheat, barley, and flax was among the skills Isis taught to humankind, and she was consequently known as the woman of bread, beer, and green fields.[47] A regulator of the Nile's cycles and mistress of farming, she was responsible for the rebirth of vegetation and the prosperity of Egypt.

During the course of Egyptian history, her personality grew more and more potent.[48] That Isis was the primary goddess by the time of Herodotus

Figure 9. Cretan seal with figures of goddess, officiants, and sacred trees.

is incontestable, and by Ptolemaic and Roman times she was conceived of as the universal power or, as she is evoked in Apuleius's *Metamorphoses*, "the Mother of Nature, the mistress of all the elements, the first offspring of time, highest of deities, queen of the Underworld, foremost among the gods of Heaven, in whose divine appearance all gods and goddesses are fused."[49]

Though numerous material remains document the religious life of ancient Crete, texts to assist and control interpretation are lacking. Nevertheless, it is possible to distinguish certain features of Minoan religion, in particular the dominance in Cretan culture of the female deity. The Minoan as distinct from the Mycenean phase of Cretan religion was dominated by a goddess, one of whose manifestations was linked to a sacred tree.[50] Palaces, shrines, and sanctuaries have produced votive offerings, frescoes, and seals that suggest a tradition of vegetation worship dominated by a goddess sometimes associated with a young male. The cult not only centered on sacred trees and plants, but also was connected with axes, stones, and pillars. The goddess's name is not presently known. But she is represented with animals, birds, snakes, and pillars, as well as with sacred branches and sacred trees (figure 9).[51] She is both a vegetation goddess and a household or palace goddess, a mother as well as a maid. Her meaning can be partially discerned by studying the symbols accompanying her: The snake that casts its slough and renews itself symbolizes immortality; the poppy may relate to her initiates' ecstatic

Figure 10. Cretan hairpin. Vegetation goddess encircled by stylized plants. Found in Mycenaean tomb.

Figure 11. Roman terra-cotta relief. Greek goddess Demeter, worshiped by Romans as Ceres, has serpents around her arms, holds up severed wheat stalks.

visionary experiences; the lily may suggest traditions of herbal magic; boughs and stylized leaves and flowers link her with vegetation (figure 10), and the double axe may relate to the cutting and death of that vegetation. Though inferences derived from the monuments do not constitute proof, one thing seems clear from the mass of visual evidence from the Cretan world: Though the male element may have been prominent in the realm of government, during the first half of the second millennium B.C. a female deity was supreme in Minoan civilization.

Greece

The deified earth in Greek mythology was Gaia, universal mother of humankind. According to Hesiod she came into being after Chaos, and brought forth of herself the sky (Uranus), the mountains, and the sea. In Homer she was especially honored as the mother of all, who nourishes her creatures and pours rich blessings upon them. She was commonly identified with other goddesses such as Themis, Demeter, and Hera, all of them maternal deities expressive of the creative, sustaining earth. Though their specific characteristics differed according to period and geographical milieu, these female personifications of the earth express the common principles of abundance, protection, and nourishment.

In ancient Greece, Gaia came to be most often syncretized with Demeter, goddess of grain, who created plant life, conserved it, and dissolved vegetation in order to renew it again (figure 11). In the *Odyssey* she is said to have made love to Iasion in a furrow three times plowed — in other words in a field prepared for sowing.[52] Demeter gave grain seed and a plow to Triptolemus and sent him over the world to teach the arts of agriculture.[53] The major plowing and sowing festival in Greece, the Thesmophoria, was dedicated to Demeter.[54] Observed in the month of Pyanopsion (October/November), it was one of the most famous and widespread of Demeter's festivals and was celebrated by women alone. The meaning of the name *Thesmophoria* and of Demeter's epithet Thesmophoros has been much discussed.[55] The most cogent explanation is that the title alludes to Demeter's gift of mystic rites, not only the mystic rites of Eleusis, but also all of those traditional women's rituals whose correct performance was first revealed by Demeter.

The most complete description of the ceremonial of Thesmophoria is found in a scholium (a commentary or annotation) to Lucian's *Dialogues of the Courtesans*.[56] The festival was marked by processions, purification rites, and sacrifices. Men were excluded from all ritual activities and it was incumbent upon women to participate. At some point before Thesmophoria it was customary to throw the bodies of piglets into the chasms of Demeter and Kore, her daughter. Next to the piglets were strewn pine cones and wheat cakes in the shape of male genitals. The high point in the Thesmophoria ceremonies came when women called drawers, who had purified themselves for three days, descended into the innermost sanctuaries of the chasm, carried up the rotted remains of the piglets, and laid them on the altar of Demeter and Kore. Snakes in the chasm had eaten most of the piglets' flesh, but what remained was mixed with the seeds to be sown that year. The piglets' remains, the pine cones, and the wheat cakes were believed to increase the capacity of the seed to germinate, and those who could secure some of the rotted flesh to mix with their seed were assured of a good crop.

The phallus-shaped pine cones and the wheat cakes were obvious symbols of fertility. The snakes were seen as guardians of the inner sanctuaries and were generally viewed in the ancient world as being privy to the mysteries of the underground. At the time of sowing the powers of regeneration were assumed to pass from the fertility symbols to the piglets and to the seed. In this way, the Thesmophoria ritual was expected to aid vegetal as well as animal and human fertility.

What is the origin and meaning of the Thesmophoria? The scholium linked it to that moment in the Demeter/Kore/Pluto myth when Pluto seized Kore and carried her down the chasm: "At that place a swineherd named Eubouleus was tending his swine, and they were all swallowed up in the chasm of Kore [that is, the chasm into which she was carried by Pluto]. In honor of Eubouleus, piglets are thrown into the chasm of Demeter and Kore. . . . The piglets, because their fertility is a symbol of the generation of animals and men, are a thanks-offering to Demeter, since by providing Demetrian [cereal] crops, she civilized the race of men." Thus , according to this text, Thesmophoria was celebrated in gratitude for Demeter's providing humankind with the capacity to grow crops, especially grain, thereby civilizing the race. And if we take this scholium literally, the piglets were thrown into the chasm in honor of the swineherd Eubouleus.

A more adventurous explanation of the origins of Thesmophoria was proposed by James Frazer in *The New Golden Bough*.[57] Frazer suggested that piglets were thrown into the chasm not in remembrance of the herder or the swine, but as part of a dramatic representation of Kore's descent into the underworld. The piglets were cast into the deep as her representative. According to this interpretation, Kore is the anthropomorphic representation of an ancient grain spirit who had been envisioned in the form of a pig. Frazer believed that a trace of this old conception survived in the legend that relates how when Demeter was searching for traces of her vanished daughter, the footprints of the girl were obliterated by those of a swine.[58] The link between Kore, the grain spirit, and the pig are further hinted at by the legend of Eubouleus, the brother of Triptolemus, to whom Demeter first gave the secret of grain cultivation. According to one version, it was the swineherd himself who, along with his brother Triptolemus, received the gift of wheat from Demeter as a reward for revealing the fate of Kore.[59] Whether the piglets were a thanks-offering in honor of Eubouleus or whether they represented the ancient totem of Demeter/Kore, during both Neolithic and Greek times the pig was linked to the sowing goddess.

It is notable that Thesmophoria, as well as many other fertility festivals dedicated to Demeter, was celebrated by women alone.[60] The Greek reliance on women for fertility magic reflects a mentality that continued to link women's fertility with that of the land. Either because of their agrarian role as planters or because of their biological endowment, women as bearers of the secrets of birth were considered to be better equipped than men were to carry out fertility rituals, particularly at those moments like sowing time crucial to the growth of the crops. This perspective is certainly advanced by the text of the scholium in which it is clear that women, to the exclusion of men, were called upon to perform those rites required to promote the germination of the seed.

The Demeter/Kore/Pluto myth, which on one level deals with the agricultural process, can also be interpreted as a metaphor for the events in a woman's life.[61] Kore's abduction turned into a rape/marriage; her sexual awakening occurred when she ate the pomegranate;[62] and her "death" to the world of light corresponded to her captivity as the wife of Pluto. Her "rebirth" alludes to the birth of vegetation, which in the ancient world was compared to the birth of the fetus as well.[63] The adventures of Kore could thus teach something of the life cycle of the woman as well as the events of the agrarian year. We should not forget that the festivals of Demeter were concerned not only with the cultivation of a plentiful crop, but also with fruitful progeny in general, both animal and human. This may explain the central role of women in all of Demeter's fertility rituals, particularly those practiced at the moment of sowing, when all life hangs in the balance.

Rome

Tellus (Terra Mater) and Ceres were two of the female deities in the Roman pantheon. Though generally the female had little significance in the patrifocal world of the Romans, the great preoccupation with agriculture in early Roman religion explains the importance retained by these two major goddesses.[64] The Romans conceived of the earth mother goddess as the protectress at the various stages in the growth of the grain. She was invoked in one form or another at specific agrarian ceremonies throughout the year: at Feria Sementiva, the time of plowing and sowing; at Fordicalia and Cerealia in the spring, when the farmers sought to promote the fertility of the ground before the critical formation of the grain in its sheath; at Floralia, when the gardens and fields were mature; and at the sacrifice of Porca Praecidanea, when the grain was actually harvested and thanks were given for the first fruits.[65] On some of these occasions, a *lustratio* (purification or lustration) was performed by circling around the fields. Part of the purification was a sacrifice to the earth mother goddess.

One of the Roman grain goddess festivals, the Feria Sementiva, was celebrated in the very early spring, when the earth was broken and the first seeds of the new agricultural cycle were sown.[66] The oldest textual account of this Roman plowing and seeding rite appears in Ovid's poetic treatise on the Roman calendar, the *Fasti,* composed in the first decade of the first century A.D.:

> Three or four times I searched the record of the calendar, but nowhere did I find the Day of Sowing. Seeing me puzzled, the Muse observed, "That day is appointed by the priests. Why look for movable feasts in the calendar? And while the day of the feast may shift, the season is fixed: it is when the seed has been sown and the field fertilized." Ye steer, take your stand with garlands on your heads at the full crib: with the warm spring your toil will return. Let the swain hang up on the post the plough that has earned its rest: the cold ground shrinks from every wound inflicted by the share. Thou bailiff, when the sowing is done, let the land rest, and let the men who tilled the land rest also. Let the parish keep festival; purify the parish, ye husbandmen, and offer the yearly cakes on the parish hearths. Propitiate Earth and Ceres, the mother of the corn, with their own spelt and flesh of teeming sow. Ceres and Earth discharge a

common function: the one lends to the core its vital force, the other lends it room.[67]

At this point, Ovid inserts a poeticized prayer to the two goddesses and a rumination on war. Then he concludes: "Yoke the ox, commit the seed to the ploughed earth. Peace is the nurse of Ceres, and Ceres is the foster-child of Peace."

The festival described here is Sementiva, the day of sowing.[68] The precise day of the feast was not fixed, but depended upon the rains and weather conditions. In Ovid's poem Sementiva is recorded among the events of late January. The ceremonies took place just before and after the seed had been put into the ground, in the late winter or early spring.[69] The poet tells us that at that time a marking of the time must take place, for the share has "inflicted wounds" on the cold ground. The language (line 667) reflects the idea that the plow cutting into the land wounds the earth. The words *volnus (vulnus)* ("wound") and *reformidat* ("shrinks from, dreads") may be allusions to the notion that the delving into the belly of the earth mother goddess demanded some act of propitiation, some sacrifice, in order for the seed implanted in the "womb" to quicken and be born.

In celebration of Sementiva the farm steward allowed both the land and the men who worked it to rest. The whole district celebrated the festival by performing a purification of the fields.[70] The husbandmen offered flat cakes at the rural altars and, in propitiation of Tellus and Ceres, they sacrificed some of their own grain and a pregnant sow. Ceres and Tellus were one: The former lent her "vital force" and the latter her space for the growing grain.[71]

After describing Sementiva in broad outline, Ovid poeticizes the farmer's prayer to the goddesses (lines 675–694). The farmer asks that boundless crops ensue from the seeding and prays for the eventual sprouting shoots of grain. He requests the goddesses' protection in keeping the fields free from the dangers of birds, ants, mildew, foul weather, and weeds. Though the prayer is more poetic than liturgical, Ovid states that he saw and participated in many of the rites he recorded, and no doubt the themes of protection and bountiful harvest originated in actual rural supplication at this time of year.

Though poetic in form, this text provides a vivid picture of the plowing and seeding festival. The main elements of the event are clear: It was celebrated by the farmers of the countryside to invoke from Ceres/Tellus protection of the seed. A major part of the festival was a purification rite, probably including a circuit of the field. The peasant made offerings of grain cakes, seed, and a pregnant sow. Coming as they did at a decisive point in the vegetation cycle, the Sementiva rites were an attempt to assure, in spite of meteorological risks, the fruition of the grain, and to stimulate the forces of growth as spring approached.

In the sixth century Joannes Lydus provided some slightly different information about Sementiva.[72] Lydus, like Ovid, wrote that the Sementiva festival (which, for Lydus, occurred at the beginning of sowing) did not fall on a fixed day, because not every time was suitable for sowing: The time would depend on the weather. Lydus, writing in the Greek-speaking East, noted that the festival was celebrated on two different days, separated by an interval of seven days. On the first day one sacrificed to Demeter, and at the end of seven days to Kore, who was seen as the protectress of grain. His text indicates that the first sacrifice was made at the time of sowing, and the second, a week later, just as the seedlings began to sprout.[73] Demeter and Kore, the two goddesses named by Lydus, obviously corresponded to Ovid's Tellus and Ceres, Demeter standing for Tellus, the earth that received the grain, and Kore for Ceres, who gave it the creative force or energy.[74]

Another author whose text has been interpreted as referring to the Sementiva is the first-century B.C. poet Tibullus.[75] Tibullus characterizes this festival as a time of repose after seeding, when the field is pregnant with the new grain and the tiller rested (2.1.5–8). Tibullus begins by describing a lustration rite in which the wheat crop and the fields are cleansed. Ceres is again invoked, but in this case along with Bacchus, the god of wine. The festival is to be kept by tillers of the soil. They are not to plow or do hard labor on that day, nor are women to spin. Purification standards are invoked: Those who have had sexual intercourse the night before cannot be part of the ceremonies, and all participants must have clean hands and clean clothing. The actual rite consisted of the sacrifice of a lamb and a lustration of cattle and field. The invocation entreats Ceres and Bacchus to provide abundant grain and protection from danger. Entrails are consulted and wine is consumed.

Some information about Sementiva emerges from these texts. It was a movable feast and varied somewhat with the weather conditions of the particular year. Ceres or the earth goddess was invoked, sacrifices were made, and protection against a variety of evils was sought. Tibullus refers specifically to the sowing of grain and to the performance of a lustration. Though Tibullus's text differs somewhat from Ovid's elaborate description (Bacchus, not Tellus, is associated with Ceres; a lamb rather than a sow is sacrificed), both authors describe a seeding festival that included an animal sacrifice, an invocation to the mother goddess of grain to provide abundant growth and protect the fields, and a purification of the fields by making a sacred circuit around them.

A celebrated passage of Virgil elucidates more fully the ancient lustral procession around the fields:

> . . . But chiefly pay
> Fit worship to the gods. Make sacrifice
> Each year to sovereign Ceres, when the grass
> Is green and glad, the winter making end
> And gentle Spring is in the air, when lambs

Are fattening, when the wine grows smooth and mild,
And sweet is slumber in cool hillside shade.
Let all the country youth of manly prime
On Ceres call, bearing her tribute due
Of honey mixed with milk and sweet, new wine.
Three times around the freshly bladed corn
The blessed victim guide, while all the choir
In gladsome company an anthem sing,
Bidding the goddess to their lowly doors.
And let no reaper touch the ripened corn
With sickle keen until his brows bind
With twine of oak-leaf, while he trips along
In artless dance with songs in Ceres' praise.[76]

Virgil begins this section by recommending that the farmer renew his sacrifices to Ceres each year. The succeeding lines are difficult to understand in the Latin, but the poet seems to be advising that Ceres be invoked at three different moments in the grain cycle: when the grains are young shoots ("when the grass is green and glad," "laetis in herbis," line 336); when there is to be a new harvest ("freshly bladed corn," "novas fruges," line 345); and when the ear of grain is mature ripened corn ("maturis aristis," line 348).[77] Virgil's repetition of the name Ceres throughout this passage signifies that she was the goddess venerated at each of these rites. The texts indicate that at least one of these festivals, if not all three, involved a "going around the field," "ambarvalia" (lines 47–50), the purification or lustral procession mentioned by Ovid and Tibullus.[78] The passage around the field is explicitly dedicated to the earth mother goddess, here in the form of Ceres. It was both apotropaic and cathartic: The magic circle created by the procession formed a barrier against the various evils to which the grain could still succumb.[79] The sacrificial victim in Virgil's lustral procession is the sow, the same animal that had been linked with the earth mother goddess since Neolithic times.

The agricultural festivals that included the purification procession out into the fields and around the crop were not limited to Rome. The practice also occurred in Gaul. There is specific evidence of one of these lustration processions, the Robigalia, originally celebrated in Rome to preserve the sprouting crop from blight. Perpetuated into postpagan Gaul, it was transformed in the fifth century into the Christian ceremonies of Rogations, celebrated on April 25.[80] In the Rogations ceremony, the farmers filed into and around the field late in spring to protect the growing grain. The rite was supposedly instituted by Mamertius, bishop of Vienna, around 470 and extended to all Gaul by the first Council of Orleans in 511. Mamertius, however, did not create this ritual. He Christianized a deep-rooted pagan practice by attaching it to the Christian calendar and giving it a fixed date. He also substituted a

Christian liturgy for the pagan hymns traditionally recited at the event. Sidonius Apollinarus, a contemporary of Mamertius, informs us that the processions around the fields when the grain approached ripeness existed before Mamertius (*Epistle* 5.14); the bishop merely gave them a "greater solemnity."

The festivities associated with Sementiva and other rural pagan celebrations were very difficult to extirpate; many of the practices lasted well into the Middle Ages.[81] Peasants would have been reluctant to abandon customs so intimately connected with the growth of vegetation, and therefore with the very process of life itself. The Christianization of the early spring seeding ritual (as well as the later spring ripening festival) was one way that the church could redirect peasant veneration from pagan deities to Christian figures and, as we shall see, from the pagan earth mother goddess to early medieval female saints.

Chapter II

The Goddess
in the North

People's dependence on vegetal life led to the development of agrarian ceremonies that marked significant moments during the annual growing cycle. Beginning with the rites associated with plowing and seeding (Thesmophoria in Greece and Sementiva in Rome), a series of observances were undertaken to appease those forces that influenced the mysterious life of the plant. The earth mother goddess in one manifestation or another was an object of veneration at these ceremonies, as communities sought to energize the seed and protect the impregnated land. The peoples of the north, like those of the ancient Near East and Mediterranean, tried to encourage the yearly rebirth of food plants by focusing their worship on various female personifications of fertility.

Germania

In the Celto-Germanic world, the agrarian year was marked by seasonal rituals. We lack written sources from these tribal peoples who were encountered by the Roman armies on their marches northward. This dearth of sources hampers our search for evidence of specific plowing and seeding rituals. The work of one classical author, Tacitus, and several Christian texts are our only written accounts of a Germano-Celtic earth mother goddess associated with plowing, seeding, and protection of the newly sown crops.

Tacitus published his *Germania* in 98 A.D. A Roman senator and son of a knight, he gathered his information about the customs of the northern peoples from the soldiers and merchants who spent time among the various tribes. In *Germania*, Tacitus reported on a cultic festival of the goddess

Nerthus, a festival participated in by seven tribes in the neighborhood of the lower Elbe. The tribes ". . . revere in common Nerthus, or the earth mother, and they believe that she intervenes in human affairs and that she rides among their peoples. In an island of the ocean is a sacred grove, and in it a consecrated chariot covered with a cloth. One priest is permitted to touch it. He senses that the goddess is present in the inner sanctum and he follows with great veneration as she is drawn away by cows. Days of joy follow, and holidays, in all places that she honors with her arrival and stay. No one goes to war and no one takes up arms. . . . When she has had enough of the society of mortals, the priest brings the goddess back to her temple. Afterward, the cart, the cloth, and, if you believe it, the goddess herself are cleansed in a secret lake. This rite is performed by slaves who are immediately afterward drowned in the lake."[1]

The festival is not named, nor is the time of its celebration explicitly indicated, but there are elements in this text that connect Nerthus with the Greco-Roman manifestations of the grain goddess. Tacitus himself sees her as such a figure, for though he gives her Germanic name as Nerthus, he translates the term as well: ". . . Nerthum, id est Terram matrem," "Nerthus, that is, the earth mother."[2] According to Tacitus, the tribe members believe that Nerthus interests herself in human affairs and periodically rides among their people in a cart. During most of the year the cart stands draped with cloth, which only the priest can touch. At some unspecified point in the agricultural year, the priest knows that the deity is present in the inner recesses of the cart, ". . . is adesse penetrali deam intellegit,"[3] and that the ceremony can begin. Then the priest, with great veneration, accompanies the goddess as her cart is drawn by cows through the lands. Tacitus reports that the goddess was conceived of as visiting a variety of places in this cart, and her presence in an area was marked by merrymaking and peace. When the goddess is brought back to her temple, the cart, the cloth, and, it is believed, the goddess herself are bathed in a secluded lake. The slaves who attend her in her bath are then drowned in the lake.[4]

From Tacitus's text we can infer that the tribal people thought the cart housed the actual deity or some symbolic representation of her. In areas under Greco-Roman influence the cart may have contained a sculpted image covered by a cloth, but in the Celto-Germanic area, where naturalistic figurative sculpture was rare, the goddess would more likely have been represented by a rough-hewn wooden statue or perhaps a rudely crafted stone (figure 12).

Though the text does not mention the season during which this yearly event occurred, there are hints that the procession took place in the late winter or early spring, when the priest saw the first signs of the imminent revival of vegetable life. Perhaps it was the changes in plant life that enabled the priest to *intellegere* (to know or intuit) that the goddess was present in inner sanctum, her "penetrali." If we take Tacitus's account as a description

Figure 12. Fragment of stele. Germano-Roman or Celto-Roman goddess seated on throne, holding basket of fruit on her left knee and two stalks of grain in her right hand. Reverse of stele is incised with low-relief geometric designs. Found in Miltenberg, West Germany.

of an actual event, incorporating a cart drawn by cows, even a small procession on the goddess's island would probably not have been possible in this region in the middle of the winter. However, in the very late winter, before the ice melted, it would have been possible for the priest to begin a procession off the island, with cart and cows, onto the frozen lake. Then the procession could have returned after the ice melted to perform the goddess's bath and drowning of the slaves.

What Tacitus recorded, then, was a tribal vegetation rite: First a goddess is carried over the land, with the implication that her presence will afford protection and bring vegetal prosperity. Then she is bathed in the lake to produce, by a kind of sympathetic magic, sufficient rain for the timely sprouting of the seed.

The bathing of Nerthus introduced a new element into the characteristics of the vegetation goddess, for the Greek and Latin texts describing Sementiva did not allude to immersion. The major features of the Nerthus cult — the procession of the goddess in a cart drawn by cows and the bathing of her symbolic statue — were also very close to a rite associated with the goddess Cybele, a deity known as Magna Mater or the Great Mother, whose worship was introduced into Rome from Asia Minor in 204 B.C.[5] Part of the Roman rite associated with Cybele was an early spring procession to a stream where the statue of the goddess would be bathed.[6] Ablutions such as those prescribed for Cybele and Nerthus were a feature of many popular festivals in which the participants attempted to purify the land or produce rain by immersing the goddess in water.[7]

There is evidence that the Nerthus cult survived for a long time in various forms. Place names indicate that she was worshiped in Sweden, and medieval Icelandic literature reveals that a name linguistically identical to Nerthus, Njordh (or Niordr), designated a major Norse fertility god who was responsible for human prosperity.[8] The Icelandic mythology reveals, however, that it was Njordh's son Frey, and to some extent Frey's sister Freya, who took over the functions associated with the Nerthus rite; for like Nerthus, Frey and Freya made journeys through the land in a wagon to spread their fructifying influence.[9]

The passage of the Terra Mater through the countryside to promote crop fertility was one of those pagan observances that could not be effaced. It became part of folkloric pageant and was even recorded in a twelfth-century description of a rural festival.[10] Though with the coming of Christianity the human sacrifices to the pagan goddess were forbidden, certain aspects of the cult continued, purged gradually of those elements most repellent to the new faith.

Celto-Roman Gaul

From about 600 B.C. until the Roman invasion of the first centuries B.C. and A.D., most of Western Europe, from Austria to the Atlantic, was occupied by tribes who were sufficiently similar to be thought of as culturally one people and who probably referred to themselves by a name that sounded like Keltoi when translated into Greek. Those Celts inhabiting the area west of the Rhine and north of Italy were called Gauls. These Celtic inhabitants of Europe were eventually assimilated with the conquering Romans (thus the terms *Celto-Roman* and *Gallo-Roman*), as well as with later invading tribes. The only places where a Celtic civilization survived were Scotland, Wales, Brittany, and Ireland.

We have seen that textual sources as well as figurative imagery from the classical Mediterranean and the Germanic regions testified to the veneration of an earth mother goddess of vegetation. But though the continental Celtic peoples likewise venerated such a figure, they did not commit their histories and beliefs to writing; with each generation, a few gifted apprentices were chosen to spend long hours memorizing Celtic law and lore that, for the most part, remained unwritten.[11] Consequently, for information about pre-Christian Celtic culture, one must rely on archeological remains (often without accompanying inscriptions); classical texts (which interpret Celtic culture from a Greek or Roman perspective); medieval Irish writings (which were recorded centuries after Celtic Ireland was Christianized); and

Figure 13. Statue of veiled goddess holding several stalks of grain in her left hand. From Roman Gaul. Found at bottom of Corent Mountain in La Sauvetat, the Auvergne.

Figure 14. Relief of the goddess Cybele holding a small lion and bunch of grain stalks. On her head rests a mural crown enclosing an unusual attribute, the eagle, symbol of the sky. Flute, horn, and tambourines, musical instruments played by those in her procession, adorn the relief below. Provenance unknown, perhaps Rheinish.

some early Christian Latin texts that describe and decry pagan Celto-Roman practices in second- to fourth-century Gaul.

In Gaul, the cult of a mother goddess can be traced back as far as the Neolithic period. [12] When the Celts moved into Western Europe, they inherited elements of the earlier, Neolithic belief systems, elements that included the belief in a mother goddess, protectress of vegetation. As Roman influence took hold in the Celtic regions, the Celts began to fashion their mother goddess images in stone and in other permanent materials. Consequently, from the period of the Roman incursions, images of the mother goddess appeared throughout Gaul and Germania as well as in the British Isles. Some seem to have been crafted before Roman influence took firm hold (figure 12); many others were fashioned under the influence of Roman naturalism (figure 13). Sometimes two or three mother goddesses were grouped together, at other times the figure was alone. As is evident from their attire and the attributes they hold, these mother goddess figures were syncretized with Demeter, Tellus/Ceres, and the Great Mother Cybele (figure 14).

Many are small and were probably used as household goddesses, occupy-

Figure 15. Relief depicting ceremony in veneration of mother goddess at boundary of field. Libation is being poured on altar, and animals are being led up to it for sacrifice. The veiled goddess sits in the center. From Beaujeu, France. Gallo-Roman.

Figure 16. Goddess supporting tray and standing in center of bronze cart. From Strettweg.

ing niches in domestic shrines. Others served as the focal point of a community procession or ceremonial (figure 15). Lightweight and portable ones were probably used in processions, when the goddesses' presence at or

Figure 17. Plaque from Gundestrup caldron. Bust of goddess depicted between two abstracted wheels.

around a certain area was required. The condition of many of the mother goddess figures reveals the fate of their cult. With the coming of Christianity, the vast majority of the statues were mutilated: Their heads were struck off or their bodies otherwise defaced with a blunt instrument.[13] Many were found in pieces at the bottom of Roman wells, and some were recovered from building foundations where they had been used as masonry blocks. As the early medieval texts corroborate, the struggle against this ancient deity was ferocious.[14]

Female deities positioned on a cart or wagon (as described by Tacitus) also appear in Gallo-Roman material. Though there is no surviving Celtic textual account of this or any other pre-Roman Celtic ritual, archeologists have unearthed precious examples that suggest that the topos of the goddess in the wagon was well known in Celtic tradition as far back as the early Iron Age (about the seventh century B.C.).[15] The bronze Strettweg cart with a goddess standing in the center appears to be an early example of this theme (figure 16). Men on foot and on horseback are riding in the cart along with a stag.[16] The goddess dominates: She is at least twice the size of the other figures and her central position and priestlike stance convey her importance. The tray on her head might have been meant to support some tiny ritual object or symbol.

Another example of a goddess figure on a cart appears in abstracted form on the Gundestrup caldron (figure 17).[17] The bust of a female flanked on both sides by animals adorns one plaque of this Iron Age vessel. On either side of the goddess are circular forms that can be read as six-spoked wheels. The configuration of the female flanked by two wheels has convincingly

Figure 18. Ritual wagon. From Dejbjerg, Denmark.

been interpreted as a goddess seated or standing in a cart.[18] This kind of abbreviated abstraction for wheels and a cart is stylistically consistent with other works of art from this period. Though neither the archeological contexts nor the surrounding figures or attributes provide a clear indication of the meaning of the cart goddess topos, the Gundestrup and Strettweg goddess figurations might be related to Nerthus, described by Tacitus as the earth mother whose procession in the cart took her over the countryside to render the land fertile.

Two other ritual wagons discovered in Denmark can also be linked to the theme of the cart goddess. Found in the bog at Dejbjerg, the wagons have bronze decorations that indicate they must have been made during the first century B.C. (figure 18).[19] They are full-size wagons with thronelike constructions occupying the center. It has been suggested that this "throne" may have been intended as a seat for a lay figure representing a deity or for a cultic statue.[20] With such a statue in the center, the cart and its occupant would resemble the image on the Gundestrup caldron.

A still later representation of the same theme is a small statuary group found at the village of Essey in eastern France.[21] A wagon built like a throne carries the mutilated forms of three mother goddesses, with only the middle one clearly visible. In the Celtic world the mother goddess was frequently depicted in groups of three.[22] Though partially destroyed, the wagon with large wheels still retains some of its built-up rear section, a sign of comfort and stateliness, and the rigid bodies of the goddesses still have their dignified allure.

Thus, though the archeological materials are scarce, the evidence points to the probability that the mythic idea of a cart goddess, extending far back in the Celtic tradition, was part of the Celto-Roman and Germanic pantheons. In spite of the fact that this deity was primarily worshiped in rural areas and very likely was fashioned in crude, impermanent materials; and in spite of the rampant image smashing of the Christian period when so many statues of the pagan deities were destroyed, at least some archeological material has survived to suggest the existence of a cart goddess topos. This archeological material alone, however, does not provide insights into the purpose and meaning of the topos. Fortunately, a series of texts stemming from the centuries of conversion describes the pagan practice surrounding this cart goddess — the practice of parading with her statue in a cart into the countryside for the protection of the crop.

In considering the following texts from the third to the sixth centuries, three strata should be kept in mind: the ancient Celto-Germanic practices of the north; the pagan Greco-Roman religion that came into the area with the invading Roman armies; and the relatively new Christian layer whose partisans, hostile to what they saw as demonic rural practices, provided our only textual records of the pre-Christian vegetation goddess ceremonials. It is these Christian texts that, in railing against rural rites, testify to the very tenacity of those ancient practices. [23] Everyday rural life, revolving around agriculture, exhibited a basic sameness, and even though the conquering Roman and eventually Christian cultures came to dominate, syncretism was common. Newly arriving groups or religions were rarely able to supplant completely the local folk religions or folk customs, especially when those customs were seen as protecting the crops and, by extension, as securing the survival of the community. [24] Even though, as we shall see, the Christian observers of the mother goddess ceremonies adopted a Romano-Oriental name for the mother goddess (Berecynthia, from Mount Berecynthia in western Anatolia, a site sacred to Cybele), that appellation was merely superimposed on a deeply rooted figure that had probably been venerated in some form for millennia — a figure whose paradigmatic meaning for rural people had changed very little, even with the Roman (and eventual Christian) overlay.

One precious record from early medieval Gaul provides a description of a rural ceremony at Autun in France, where a statue of the earth mother goddess in a wagon is drawn around the fields by oxen to ensure that no harm would befall the crops. The description is supplied by Gregory of Tours (c. 538–594) in his *Liber in Gloria Confessorum:*

> They say that in this city there once existed a statue of Berecynthia [another name for the Great Mother, Cybele] just as the history of the passion of the holy martyr Symphorian makes clear. The bishop Simplicius was present when, according to the wretched custom of the pagans, they were drawing this [statue] about in a cart, for the prosperity of their fields and vineyards.

Not very far off, Simplicius saw them singing and dancing before the idol. And emitting a groan to God for the foolishness of the people, he said: "Enlighten, I ask O Lord, the eyes of these people in order that they know that the idol of Berecynthia is nothing." And when he made the sign of the cross against it, immediately the statue tumbled down to the earth. And the animals who were drawing the cart in which the statue was carried were struck motionless, and could not be budged. The huge crowd was stupefied and all the group exclaimed that the goddess had been hurt. Victims were sacrificed and the animals were beaten, but they were not able to move. Then four hundred men of that foolish multitude, gathered together, said to one another: "If the deity has any value let her set herself erect without the aid of others, and order the oxen, who are not able to move, to proceed. Certainly, if she cannot move herself it is clear that there is no divinity in her." Then, approaching and immolating one of their animals, when they saw that their goddess could by no means move, they abandoned their error of paganism, and, having gone to find the bishop of the locale, converted to the one church and recognized the greatness of God, and they were consecrated by holy baptism. [25]

Gregory of Tours, the writer of this account, was a bishop who had spent his entire life in an upper-class religious milieu. As a zealous ecclesiastic, he recounts everything from the viewpoint of the church. [26] On the surface, the story relates Simplicius's destruction of the goddess Berecynthia as she is being drawn in a cart through or near the fields or vineyards. [27] Gregory writes about this event in the context of other miracles associated with the life of Simplicius. He begins his account with "Ferunt," "they say," because he had gathered his information from oral ecclesiastical sources. [28] The incident recorded here takes place outside the city walls of Autun during the bishopric of Simplicius in the late fourth century; Gregory gives us a description of what Simplicius witnessed. Hundreds of pagans escorted the goddess's cart, singing and dancing before the statue ("cantantes atque saltantes"). Animals, to be sacrificed at the appropriate moment, formed part of the cortège.

In its general outlines, Gregory's description of this agrarian rite parallels many others before and since. These Gallo-Roman peasants, confronted by a potentially hostile world, were seeking to ensure that no harm would befall their crop. They were seeking to assure themselves that recalcitrant nature could be tamed if the community adhered to the inherited ancient rites. It was precisely these long-established observances that the church tried to abolish. The pagan singing and dancing were especially despised by the ecclesiastical observer. [29] We might imagine that the words of the chants that Simplicius heard, as well as the gestures of the crowd, were directed to the goddess: invocations for her protection, solicitations for appropriate weather, and so forth. There probably was a chant leader and companions who sang the refrain or mimed specific movements.[30] Such a crowd might even intone snatches of mythical narratives about the goddess and her powers.

The inimical perspective of the church pervades this account. Gregory writes of the miserable custom of the heathens ("misero gentilitatis more"). On viewing the scene, Simplicius lets out a groan and prays for the enlightenment of the foolish people ("pro stultitia plebis"). His prayers and his making the sign of the cross are said to have the effect of immediately dashing the statue to the ground in ruins. The celebrating peasants straightaway protest Simplicius's act, and cry out in dismay that their goddess might be hurt. They are fearful lest the protective powers of the deity be turned away from them. They twice immolate animals, unable to believe that "simulacrum Berecynthia nihil est," the image of Berecynthia was destroyed. These are not the urban middle and lower classes who, by the fourth century in a place like Autun, would already have been Christianized. These are the rural people who worked the fields and vineyards and had always depended on the powers of a vegetation goddess.

The clerical culture and the culture of the common people in Gregory's anecdote had a certain attitude in common: Both groups believed in supernatural interventions in daily and seasonal events.[31] Both were ready to believe that spiritual forces could intervene in the material world. The people believed that sacrificing the animals would cause the cart to move; Simplicius (and presumably Gregory) believed that prayer and the sign of the cross could cause the statue to tumble down and the cart to get stuck.[32] Whatever conversions took place that day, the underlying similarity of beliefs expedited that process.

Yet conversion in instances like these was no simple process. What Simplicius was attempting to extirpate was a manifestation of that figure who, under many names and through many cultural overlays, had been venerated in the countryside since the beginning of agrarian life. Even if the bishop had immobilized the cart and toppled the statue, such an act could hardly have convinced all the people to convert so swiftly. An acculturation had to take place. In rural areas that process took generations or even centuries; rarely were the old observances completely abandoned. The ancient ritual continued in some form, and eventually it was linked with a new myth to give it a raison d'être in the Christian context.[33] The grain protectress once again would have to undergo a metamorphosis.

Hundreds of peasants participated in the ritual activities described by Gregory. The act of following the mother goddess in the cart into the fields was crucial for communal protection. The event described by Gregory was not an isolated occurrence. Two other texts from Roman Gaul also refer to the ritual procession with the statue of the Great Mother, again called Berecynthia. In both, the pagan rite is again recounted from the antagonistic perspective of the church. One account is recorded in a life of Saint Symphorian (c. 180–280 A.D.).[34] In that account, Autun is described as a city of diverse temples filled with idols; Berecynthia, Apollo, and Diana are especially venerated. On a certain day, a multitude of people gather at the "unholy" solemnities dedicated to "Berecynthia, mother of demons" ("matris daemonum"). The statue of Berecynthia is carried in a cart by a multitude as the people crowd together in procession. Symphorian refuses to adore the statue. He is asked by the Roman consul why he does not want to worship the statue of the mother goddess. He answers that he is a Christian and will not adore the statue of the demon.

This account from the life of Symphorian provides even earlier evidence than Gregory's account of a Gallic procession in honor of the cart-drawn mother goddess Berecynthia. The text does not specify if the procession took place inside or outside the city gates, though it seems to have had its origin within the city walls. Considerable epigraphic and archeological evidence corroborates the fact that, in the second and third centuries, Cybele/Berecynthia was particularly venerated in the cities of Gaul; many Roman functionaries, as well as Oriental slaves, were devotees of her cult.[35] Peasants were slower to adopt her, but eventually they assimilated Berecynthia/Cybele with the pre-Roman, Celtic protectress of the crop.

It was just such a group of peasants that Saint Martin, in the fourth century, thought he saw as he was making his way through Gaul on his missionary voyage. Saint Martin's story is told by his biographer Sulpicius Severus.[36] Once, as Saint Martin was making his way through the countryside in his campaign to convert pagans, he spied, about five hundred feet away, a crowd of peasants in a procession. He had difficulty seeing just what they were carrying on a litter, but he did notice that it was covered by a cloth. Martin thought he was witnessing a pagan sacrificial ceremony ("profanos sacrificiorum ritus") of a type that, Sulpicius tells us, Gallic peasants used to practice.[37] In their "miserable foolishness," they would carry about their fields the statue of a "daemon" covered by a white cloth.

Martin was mistaken. He mistook a funeral cortège for the procession with the statue. He mistook the shroud that covered the body for the ritual veil that covered the pagan idol. But his mistake indicates that it was a familiar sight to see peasants in procession accompanying the statue of a goddess drawn in a cart or carried on a litter around their fields. For this was one of the ceremonies associated with the ancient earth mother goddess, venerated in Neolithic Europe, traceable in the Celto-Germanic world, and assimilated with Roman and Romano-Oriental goddesses during the Roman Empire. Protectress of the crop, she was revered under various names in various cultural strata. She appears in these Christian texts as the mother of demons, and will undergo further transformations in the Christian era.

Chapter III

The Mother Goddess in Art from Antiquity to the Middle Ages

Gregory of Tours's description of the destruction of images of the earth mother goddess Berecynthia is just one of many early Christian writings that report the defacement or outright smashing of pagan statues in early medieval Gaul. Particularly in rural areas, such images — whether of Ceres, Cybele, or other pagan gods and goddesses — posed a great threat to ecclesiastical authority. A majority of the hundreds of mother goddess statues uncovered in modern times in the areas that made up Gaul and Germania either have their heads struck off or bear other evidence of purposeful disfigurement.[1] Their frequently mutilated condition supplies dramatic evidence of the destruction described by Gregory. Though a principal objective of fourth- to fifth-century missionaries like Saint Martin was to destroy such statues, ninth-century church fathers were still inveighing against their worship, an indication of the statues' lingering presence.[2]

During the era of conversion, from the fourth through the eighth centuries, some rural pagans no doubt hid their statues, perhaps even buried them. Legends concerning the finding of statues of stately females, immediately christened the Virgin, abound throughout Europe. The sites of the discoveries have often been what archeologists now know to be ancient mother goddess shrines.[3] The legends explain the discoveries of the statues as part of a divine plan to render certain sites sacred and worthy of ecclesiastical notice; some of the legends even reflect furtive attempts to retain the old sacred figures by rededicating them with a new appellation.

When the figurative image of the mother goddess was not destroyed

Figure 19. Statue of Augustus of Prima Porta.
Figure 20. Detail of breastplate depicting mother goddess (Terra Mater) with cornucopia, stalk of grain; and children nestled in her lap.

outright or rechristened, it was transformed. Beginning in the fourth century, the earth mother, once the focus of veneration, gradually became in Christian art a mere personification of the earth, similar to embodiments of air and water. Eventually, during the tenth and eleventh centuries, the mother goddess was juxtaposed to the seductive mermaid (an association that sullied her image) or was tied to the negative principle of materiality (as opposed to the spirituality implicit in the earth's opposite, air). In this way the female image of the once-revered goddess came, by the twelfth century, to stand for one of the worst sins of Christendom, female sensuality. This chapter traces Terra Mater's metamorphosis in the official art of church and state.

The image of the mother goddess as Tellus remained positive throughout the time of the Roman Empire. Tellus had been firmly entrenched in Roman iconography since the reign of Augustus in the final decades of the first century B.C. A symbol of dominion and prosperity, she appeared on the breast plate of the statue of Augustus of Prima Porta (figures 19–20).[4] On the breast plate, the earth mother reigns below and heaven above. The imperial events occur in the center, while Sol and Aurora above, along with Apollo and Diana below, complete the cosmic framework. The symbolic function assigned here to Terra Mater is evident; she symbolizes the world throughout which Roman peace and prosperity were supposed to prevail.[5]

Terra Mater had also come to symbolize fruitfulness and fecundity in Roman imperial art. On the silver ceremonial dish from Aquileia in northeastern Italy, datable to the first century A.D., Triptolemus (the prince) stands in the center offering incense at the altar of Ceres, whose image

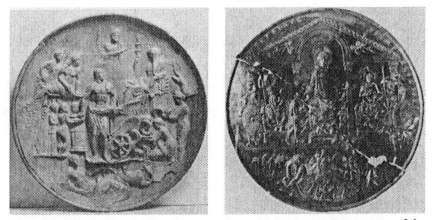

Figure 21. Silver plate. Prince in center offers incense at altar of Ceres (one of the Roman manifestations of the mother goddess). Ceres herself seated to right under tree. At bottom of plate is another manifestation of the mother goddess, Terra Mater, with a cow at her feet. Found at Aquileia, Italy.

Figure 22. Missorium of Theodosius. The Emperor, surrounded by palace guards, is handing down document of appointment to official. Terra Mater (surrounded by grain stalks and holding a cornucopia), symbol of prosperity of the realm, is reclining in the lower portion.

appears on the right under the tree (figure 21). His snake-driven chariot is attended to by two personifications of seasons. Two other seasons look on from the ledge on the left. Three children act as altar ministrants. Terra plays a leading role, dominating the scene from below with a cow resting at her feet. The allegory is of the earth's fecundity under imperial rule, particularly as a result of the emperor's concern for agriculture.[6] This generalized image of Terra survived into the Christian period and was employed as a symbol of prosperity.

In the works executed during the fourth and fifth centuries for the urban aristocracy and the court, images of the earth mother, as well as of other pagan deities, were retained as part of the Christian pictorial repertoire.[7] Divested of all religious content, antique pagan figures such as Terra Mater were used as symbols of temporal sequences or of qualities, or as topographical-cosmological signs. For instance, on the missorium (ceremonial plate) of the Christian emperor Theodosius (388 A.D.), Terra Mater reclining among fruits, flowers, and children is employed as a symbol of the prosperity of the world state under the rule of the emperor (figure 22). And, on the sixth-century Barberini ivory (figure 23), earth, raising her hand to support the emperor's foot, symbolizes the universality of imperial power. Thus Terra Mater, not as a deity but as a personification of fruitfulness and dominion, had passed into early Christian art.

Ninth-century Carolingian artists frequently used late antique Christian and pagan imagery as models. With the courtly aristocracy and the rich

Figure 23. Barberini ivory. Terra Mater, with fruits in her lap, supports foot of emperor.

Figure 24. Ivory book cover. The Crucifixion is depicted above the three Marys at empty tomb of Christ. Resurrection below. Though the snake beneath the cross has become the symbol of evil, Terra Mater in the lower right retains it as an attribute; it is nursing at her breast.

monastic foundations as patrons, Carolingian artists, particularly ivory carvers, copied antique representations in which Terra Mater, along with other pagan figures, were sometimes included (figures 24–26). A generalized, allegorical form of the mother goddess, devoid of all pagan religious content, gained prominence in church- and court-sponsored art. Among these lofty patrons, emperors and archbishops, the emblematic appearance of Terra Mater did not even suggest her former threatening status; here she merely signified a topographical or geographical allusion. Whatever meaning the concept (or indeed the rustic statue) of an earth mother goddess had among the peasants, her inclusion in official Christian iconography at the courts and monasteries presented no problem. Thus through the costly ivories and illuminated manuscripts of the courtly and ecclesiastical establishments, the image of Terra Mater was projected into the aristocratic art of the early Middle Ages, even though it was barred from the countryside, where it may have connoted dangerous practices.

During the Carolingian period the image of Terra Mater had remained close in type to its late antique forerunner: With long, flowing hair or a crown of grain, she was usually depicted supporting a cornucopia and welcoming children at her side (figures 24–26).[8] Juxtaposed to Oceanus, she most often sat on the ground, and sometimes held up a sheaf or branch.

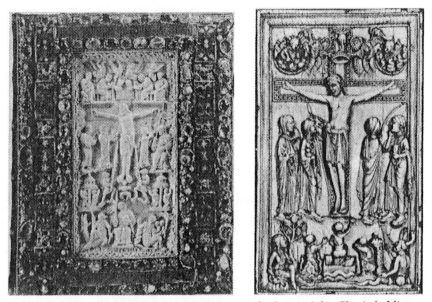

Figure 25. Ivory book cover. Terra Mater is in the lower right. She is holding a branch and a snake, with two children at her arm. She is seated opposite Oceanus, who is on the Leviathan, the monster of the deep.

Figure 26. Ivory book cover. Terra Mater is in the lower left-hand corner. She is holding foliage and a snake is nursing at her breast. The Crucifixion is depicted above. To right, a personification of the ocean, with lobster claws coming out of his head like horns, reclines on vessel of water.

On occasion she was portrayed nursing an animal or a snake at her breast (figures 24, 26). Though the image of Terra Mater nursing is rare in Roman works, its frequent occurrence in medieval art indicates that it must also have been firmly established in antiquity (figure 30).[9]

The ninth-century Terra Mater, though similar in type to her antique model, takes on a subtle new meaning. For instance, on the Munich ivory (figure 24), she and Oceanus, along with personifications of the sun and moon in the upper corners, frame scenes of the Crucifixion and Resurrection. Terra is no longer the symbolic source of the prosperity of the realm; she becomes a witness to the cosmological significance of the Christian events. Far from her classical role as a figure to be propitiated or as a symbolic source of the prosperity of the world state, in Carolingian art Terra is merely one part of a larger spiritual cosmography. The snake, in ancient art her frequent companion and a guardian of underground secrets, now appears not only as her nurseling but also in a more conspicuous new symbolic role: It coils at the foot of the cross, usually in the center of the composition, as a symbol of evil and death, which Christ, through the Crucifixion, vanquishes. The malevolent connotation of the snake implicit in Judeo–Christian as opposed to Greco–Roman culture foreshadows a series of changes in the import of Terra's attributes and characteristics — changes that ultimately resulted in the total transmutation of the meaning of her image.

In tenth- and eleventh-century art, the figure of Terra and the pictorial attributes associated with her were placed even more firmly within the Christian biblical and patristic context. With a subtle shift in meaning, she came to represent the material as opposed to the heavenly or spiritual. This shift in meaning resulted from her personification within the rubric of the four elements: [10] the sun and the moon were associated with fire and air; land and sea were represented by Terra and Oceanus. In this way a dualistic principle crept in. Earth came to be associated with materiality and corporealness, to which men and women are condemned after the fall. Air, on the other hand, was linked with spirituality, purity, and the soul. Thus, Terra was viewed in counterdistinction to Heaven, paradise, spirituality, and salvation. As a corpulent, full-breasted female, she was, to the medieval mind, a particularly apt image in this context. Woman and anything relating to her sexuality represented the carnality that was partially to blame for the fallen plight of the human race.

This transmutation in meaning had significant ramifications for Ottonian imagery of the tenth and early eleventh centuries. Now when Terra was portrayed, the children nestled in her lap could be interpreted as Adam and Eve; the branch she held as the forbidden tree; and her companion snake as the cursed demon of paradise, the great tempter (figure 27). Though still recognizable, Terra Mater began to be associated with sin, and in particular with the sin of Eve, shown picking the fateful fruit. Though in some cases Terra continued to be represented as simply the earth mother, the image of Terra ultimately came to represent the female sinner par excellence. The Terra Mater figure inherited by artists of the late eleventh and twelfth centuries was already tainted by the allusions implicit in her attributes: the diabolical snake and the wicked children, now seen as Adam and Eve. The eleventh-century artist who viewed such a figure, whether contrasted to the more spiritual elements of air and fire or serving as a lap for Eve and Adam, no doubt perceived in her a negative connotation.

By the early Romanesque period (the twelfth century), another juxtaposition served to tarnish further the image of Terra Mater. As the symbolic representation of land, she was set next to the figure of sea, which, during the twelfth century, was frequently personified as a mermaid, emblem of carnal temptation. [11] The myth of the seductive mermaid derives from an ancient tradition going back to Ulysses' adventures, where mermaids were portrayed as demonic temptresses. Water, primary substance of human life, is, in dream life, also the carrier of death. [12] In this respect, mermaids as personifications of water connote not only seduction but also life-threatening danger.

Figure 27. "Bernward Gospels," from Hildesheim, fol. 174r. Above,
Christ in Majesty. Below, Terra Mater to the right with Adam and Eve
in her lap and her companion snake interpreted as the serpent of Eden.

The motif of the mermaid became very popular in the art of the Middle
Ages. The church fathers had made her a symbol of the mortal passions that
must be resisted by good Christians. [13] Following their example, clerics like
Maximus of Turin, commenting on the adventures of Ulysses, were prone
to associate Ulysses with the Christian and the mermaid with vice. [14] In the
second half of the twelfth century, the monk Honorius of Autun, denounc-
ing the temptation of the mermaid, recommended that Christians follow the
example of Ulysses. [15] No doubt Romanesque sculptors were aware of the

seductive connotations that surrounded the mermaid: Her long hair, her undulating movements, and especially her close association with music—all spelt lascivious activities. Thus the mermaid, associated as she was with semibestiality, temptation, and music, had become for the Middle Ages a symbol of culpable sensuality and was frequently included among the images of vice.

The representation of a mermaid was, on occasion, substituted for the figure of Oceanus, especially in monumental sculpture and in wall painting. [16] She came to symbolize the waters of the earth as opposed to the land. It is in this connection that the mermaid came to be pictured next to Terra, both figures used as geographical or topographical symbols (figure 28). [17] The proximity to the mermaid, the most dangerous of seductresses, set Terra in a context where she could be viewed as equally dangerous and malevolent, and thus both figures could be seen as incarnations of vice.

This derogatory image of Terra Mater with her snake and her sinful children along with her juxtaposition to the mermaid has been linked to the development of a still more radically transformed figure, that of Luxuria. [18] The long, flowing hair typical of antique and early medieval representations of Terra Mater came to be interpreted as a sign of wildness and profligacy; the children were eliminated and her bare breasts were seen as a sign of sensuousness and promiscuity; the snakes were no longer sucking her nipples but biting them. In this way, the meaning of the image of Terra was recast and her figure came to symbolize Luxuria, sexuality. The image that had remained voluptuously rendered through late antiquity and the Carolingian period was bound ultimately to suggest unlawful sensuality to an age that regarded the human body with opprobrium. During a period when women wore their hair tightly braided or covered with a cloth, the long, flowing tresses typically found on the models of Terra could easily connote a temptress. Though the nursing snakes in Greco-Roman artistic tradition were meant to allude to the nourishment provided by the earth for all creatures, by the twelfth century the snake was firmly equated with the demon; and the seminude figure suckling snakes was, to twelfth-century clerical sensibilities, reinterpreted as lust personified. In this nude form, with snakes at her breasts, Terra was seen by clerics and artists throughout Romanesque Europe as a primary symbol of sexual sin (figure 29). A monk from Saint-Victor interpreted the image: "The courtesan dies like all the rest. She who divides her long tresses with golden combs, who colors her forehead and face, who decorates her fingers with rings, . . . look at her, who herself became the victim of worms and the food of the snake. The snake twists around her neck and the viper crushes her breasts." [19]

Luxuria, a transformed image of Terra, symbolized the horrible punishment awaiting women who engaged in illicit sexual practices. Though certain aspects of the Terra figure remained constant, a profound alteration in the meaning of the image had taken place. The innocuous symbol of the

Figure 28. Capital. Terra Mater suckling two serpent-like creatures, and placed next to two mermaid seductresses. In nave, church at Urcel, France.

Figure 29. The Devil and Luxuria, personification of sexual sin punished. Twelfth century. Sculpted figures on south porch, west flank, abbey church of Moissac, France.

earth had given birth to a new iconographic type. Unbeknownst to the clerics who commissioned the works or the artists who executed them, the ancient mother goddess had undergone a metamorphosis: She was now the victim of devouring reptiles that had previously been her beneficent companions and a sign of her secret powers. Her former significance was transmuted, and she was now a symbol of one of the worst vices to which a Christian woman could succumb: sexual sin. An image that in other times elicited respect now became an object of horror. In the form of Luxuria, the image was to have a life of its own, and in the late twelfth and thirteenth centuries it would undergo its own evolution.[20] But in that radically altered form it is no longer discernible as Terra Mater, and thus passes out of the purview of this book.

Though rare, the traditional representation of Terra was still visible in eleventh- and twelfth-century works. Less and less was she pictured nursing infants; animals were progressively substituted (figure 30).[21] In a few instances, in the works of mythographers and encyclopedists, a form of the earth goddess was depicted under one of her Greco-Roman or Romano-Oriental names (figure 31).[22] Sometimes her image was used as a model for the nursing Mary. Several of the Gallo-Roman mother goddess figures could easily have been employed in this manner. No doubt some of those statues of the goddess holding an infant were rechristened the Virgin and Christ.[23] It is not necessary, however, to accept the thesis that mother god-

Figure 30. Exultet roll. Terra Mater nursing serpent and cow.

dess images were used as models for Mary nursing. The nursing mother is a familiar image in everyday life, and even the most secluded monk probably witnessed the scene at one time during his life. One can, however, explore a related question: Was the role of the earth mother goddess as a symbol of nurturance and protection taken over in medieval imaginations by Mary and by other female Christian figures?

The following chapter will address that question. We will explore one way in which the pagan mother goddess of vegetal life, newly transformed, manifested herself as a Christian saint of plowing and sowing, and as such was perpetuated in the art and literature of Europe down to modern times.

Figure 31. Manuscript drawing. Cybele above riding in her cart, stylized vegetation depicted to her left. Eleventh century. From Regensburg.

Chapter IV

Metamorphosis:
From Goddess to Saint

Over the centuries from antiquity to the late Middle Ages, the pictorial image of the mother goddess was gradually denigrated. In popular imagination, however, the figure of this vegetation protectress was not destined for such a fate. Instead, she underwent a metamorphosis that enabled her to live on in the new, Christian context.

An earth mother goddess was still worshiped in the countryside during the fourth and fifth centuries. This is clear from Gregory of Tours's account of a procession in honor of the mother goddess Berecynthia and Sulpicius Severus's biography of Saint Martin in which the saint mistakes a funeral cortège for a mother goddess procession, as well as from archeological evidence. Yet eventually it became impossible to venerate the mother goddess as she had been venerated throughout the Mediterranean since Neolithic times. During the third century, as Christian writings were sorted and judged by the leaders of Christian communities, judgments were made by the church fathers as to which to include and which to reject. Among the texts excluded from the canon as heterodox were those that contained feminine symbolism for the deity.[1] Once this process was completed, feminine imagery for the deity had been almost completely effaced.[2]

The exclusion of any female images from the Christian concept of the deity was particularly hard on agricultural people whose experience with the growth- and life-producing forces had been connected with the female principle for millennia. By the fourth century, Christian doctrine was devoid of all imagery incorporating a female aspect in the divine. New modes had to be found for those deep-rooted habits of venerating a protectress of seeds and plant life. One method of doing this was to transform the goddess into a Christian saint with attributes that were identical or similar. This transformation would, of course, have to be fashioned within the Christian matrix, so that although a female saint was seen as accomplishing the sacred act, ultimate power was usually ascribed to Christ, God the Father, or the Trinity. However, underneath the façade of this attribution, it is possible to uncover a hidden allusion to a female power.

Throughout the early Middle Ages, any ostensible veneration of a vegetation protectress was seen by ecclesiastics as part of the vast body of protective magic that threatened the new faith. The church set itself the task of undermining all such vestiges of paganism. But disposing of those beliefs and practices proved to be a prodigious task. In rural areas in particular conversion took place gradually. Many of the converts were content merely to pay lip service to the new faith while finding ways to continue the older rites.[3] Even in locales that were Christianized quite early, ancient beliefs and rituals continued for generations.

The letters of Pope Gregory the Great provide an insight into the methods adopted by missionaries going out to convert new populations. In a letter of 601 to Saint Augustine, Gregory expounded his policy. He specifically advised Augustine not to destroy the temples of the pagan idols, but rather to adapt them to Christian worship. Quoted by the English monk and historian Venerable Bede, these were the pope's instructions to Augustine: "He is to destroy the idols, but the temples themselves are to be aspersed with holy water, altars set up, and relics enclosed in them. For if these temples are well built, they are to be purified from devil-worship, and dedicated to the service of the true God. In this way, we hope that the people, seeing that its temples are not destroyed, may abandon idolatry and resort to these places as before, and may come to know and adore the true God."[4] Gregory ordered the pagan temples to be made into Christian temples so that the people would not have to change their meeting places. Whereas worshipers used to go to a pagan temple to sacrifice cattle to demons, now they were urged to go to the same place on a local saint's day. The people were now to slay an animal not as a sacrifice but for a social meal in honor of Christ.

Gregory's instructions indicate that Christian missionaries were ideally to change beliefs with as little dislocation of popular practice as possible.[5] This policy of adaptation proved to be wise from the point of view of the church because, for the most part, people hold on to cultic practices, that is, to what they feel obliged to do by virtue of their relations to transcendent powers. Cultic practice is inevitably more lasting than belief, the latter being a culture's speculative or mythological articulation of its relation to the divine.[6] If the missionaries could uproot what they considered to be the essential beliefs of paganism, they were willing to overlook the accidentals of the modes of worship until the practices could be Christianized over time.[7]

As long as this kind of policy governed missionary activities, the old worship left many traces in medieval Christianity. The Venerable Bede's writings contain an example of how persistently pagan habits lingered on. He gives an account of the behavior of King Redwald of East Anglia, converted to Christianity and baptized early in the seventh century: ". . . but to no good purpose; for on his return home his wife and certain perverse advisers persuaded him to apostatize from the true Faith. So his last state was worse that the first, for, like the ancient Samaritans, he tried to serve both Christ and the ancient gods, and he had in the same temple an altar for the holy Sacrifice of Christ side by side with an altar on which victims were offered to the devils."[8] This kind of dual allegiance, to Christ and to a pre-Christian deity, continued for generations. Ecclesiastical texts record similar instances of pagan practices well into the Middle Ages.[9]

A kind of catalog of forbidden pagan activities is found in a seventh-century sermon by Saint Eligius of Noyen (588–659).[10] The very fact that Eligius inveighs against these practices indicates that in varying degrees most of what he mentions must have been current in Gaul at that time. Eligius exhorts the people not to observe any of the sacrilegious customs of the pagans: Do not pay attention, he said, to auguries or "special" days; do not look to the moon as a guide for the proper moment to undertake a task; do not disguise yourself as a calf or deer at the Kalends festivities of January; do not dance or sing diabolical songs at festivals of the solstice; do not invoke the names of Neptune, Pluto, Diana, or Minerva; do not light fires or make vows at pagan temples, or at rocks, fountains, or trees, or at road crossings; do not suspend charms from your neck; and on and on. Whoever engaged in any of the above behaviors was guilty of demonism.

One section of Eligius's sermon relates particularly to the ceremony of the lustration, the purifying procession around the field for the protection of the crops. The sermon warns: "No one should presume to make a lustration or to say a magic formula over the vegetation."[11] Like other pagan practices still observed in seventh-century Gaul, a lustration of the fields associated with a prayer over the crops still occurred in some areas.

With respect to this custom, as with many others during the centuries of conversion, there had to be an osmosis, an exchange between the peasant and ecclesiastical cultures.[12] Cultural osmosis occurred in various ways: Some of the pagan heroes, legends, and ceremonies passed quietly into folklore and folk observances peripheral to the realm of religion.[13] Some gods and goddesses became characters in folk songs, chants, pageants, or folk drama.[14] The osmosis process also occurred in reverse — when the church assimilated pagan personae with Christian figures by linking Christian feasts with the cyclical observances of the pagan world. The Celts and Germans, as others before them, had celebrated the solstice, the equinox, or the first of the lunar month. After Rome brought north the Julian calendar (established in 46 B.C.), many Celto-Germanic seasonal customs were assimilated into the Latin pattern. Celtic celebrations and the figures to whom they were dedicated were not suppressed but were syncretized with the Roman ones.[15] Christianity was responding to this Celto-Germanic/ Roman cycle of festivals when it tried to ensure that the dates of significant events of the church calendar coincided with the old festal days, be they Celto-Germanic or Roman.

As the church established fixed dates for events in the gospel, a new cycle was grafted onto the old seasonal cycle: By the fourth century, the date of Christ's birth was placed on December 25,[16] and accordingly, the feasts of the Annunciation, Circumcision, the Presentation in the Temple, and the Purification of the Virgin were calendrically placed.[17] Thus, for instance, the birth of John the Baptist automatically fell six months before Christ's birth, and could be assimilated with the Celto-Roman summer solstice celebrations on June 21. Saint Eligius inadvertently describes the uneasy syncretism of the summer solstice and Saint John's Day by admonishing his flock: "At the festival of Saint John at the solstice, do not engage in dances, leaps, . . . or diabolical songs (cantica diabolica)."[18] These dances, leaps, and songs were undoubtedly part of a pre-Christian summer solstice rite. When the Christian calendar was superimposed on the Celto-Roman festal cycle, the solstice celebration continued, but Saint John was substituted for whatever pagan god had formerly been honored.

In some instances the substitution of a Christian saint and ceremony for a pagan figure and rite was initiated by the ecclesiastical hierarchy; at other times the process was initiated by the lower clergy, who were in closest contact with the people. These churchmen, not very well educated, often came out of the same semipagan environment as the majority of the population. It was often these lowly churchmen who were ready to absorb pagan elements into the ritual or liturgy.[19]

One of the reasons the church was successful in syncretizing the old practices with the new religion was that it was often able to incorporate those pre-Christian cultic practices that specifically related to the agrarian cycle and were thus linked to people's everyday tasks. It was most important to fuse the agrarian ceremonial activities into the new religious construct, since people were reluctant to forsake practices directed at a transcendent power and designed to ensure the sustenance of the family or community. Whatever belief system was in place, people were bound to hold on to the notion that, if properly propitiated, guardian forces could keep them and their families from harm. That mental habit and the ritual activities associated with it could not be easily discarded.[20]

In this atmosphere ancient rites and legends were transformed and ancient deities became either Christian saints or "deviant" folk figures. The predisposition to seek guardianship from a grain protectress could not be suppressed. It was too intimately connected with everyday life. A Christianized figure had to be created to carry on her symbolic function, to reassure the planter at sowing time that the earth would quicken the seed and that the crop would begin its growth to maturity. A new rationale for the old mental habits had to be invented. As long as people could continue to project their hopes for protection onto some personification of the transcendent powers, they were willing to disregard the name given to the figure or practice and to substitute the Christian saint for the pagan paradigm.[21]

This substitution was common during the early Middle Ages. People often created tales that assimilated the attributes and powers of the old gods with personae of the new religion.[22] Art historians have uncovered much evidence of pagan models being used for Christian figures.[23] Sometimes the substitution took place subtly, as when a belief in a certain god was forbidden, although the cultic practice associated with the deity continued and a Christian saint became the dedicatee. The saint, instead of a pagan deity, became associated with the desired outcome of the cultic practice: good health, prospering flocks, or fertile crops.[24]

Uncovering these pagan figures is not an easy task, for the substitution took place in a rural milieu among people who, for the most part, were preliterate, and the various changes that took place in their belief systems were not adequately recorded.[25] Whether in literature or art, traces of the old themes inimical to the literate clergy were unlikely to survive. Lingering pagan elements were camouflaged or suppressed in order to make their way into Christian sources. Only the nucleus of the idea could remain intact in the remodeled legend. Only if the figure was sufficiently devoid of pagan content in the transformed legend could she find her way into written texts or into enduring ecclesiastically sponsored artworks.

Given the evidence for the continued veneration of the grain goddess during the centuries of conversion, when peasants went on regarding her as a protectress of the fields and a promoter of growth, we ask: What Christian female figures were substituted for the pagan goddess of sowing, and what legendary reasons for the transference were invented? For a female saint to be substituted for the grain goddess in a legend or myth, several criteria had to be met. The saint, like the goddess, had to be placed in an agrarian environment; she had to be moving around or passing by a grain field; the event had to occur at the sowing season; she had to be seen as a protectress against evil and malicious forces; and she had to be connected with an abundant harvest and with forces symbolizing the perpetuation of life. All these criteria are met in the nucleus of a legend that was applied to various female saints and passed down orally through the centuries. The legend preserves, in allegorical form, all the elements of the sowing goddess topos:[26] (a) At plowing and sowing time, a peasant is seeding or is about to seed his field; (b) a female saint in flight from hostile pursuers passes by, through, or around the field; (c) she tells the peasant to tell anyone who comes in pursuit that he saw her pass by when he was sowing the seed; (d) miraculously, the saint's passage has caused the seed to develop great growth energy, so that it not only sprouts instantly, but grows to maturity straightaway, assuring a bountiful harvest; (e) the hostile pursuers arrive and ask if a woman has passed. They are duped when the sower replies truthfully that he saw a woman pass when he was sowing the seed for the crop that they now see full grown.

Though various rural raconteurs took the theme and gave it their own characteristic twists over the centuries and in different geographic areas, the structure of the tale, the order of events, the roles of the personae, the rural milieu, and theme of the instantaneous harvest all fall into the same consistent pattern. In this way, a Christianized legend embodying the grain goddess topos was perpetuated in rural culture. In each instance, the female saints lived during the early centuries of conversion, but written or visual evidence of the substitution process—vernacular texts or rustic artworks in rural settings—sometimes only appeared centuries later.

Scholars have suggested that dream life might have played an important part in the transfer of roles and power from pagan deities to Christian saints.[27] Gods, heroes, and, later, saints were a part of dream life, though only a few ancient and medieval texts are concerned with or reveal the influence of dreams. The appearance of Asklepios of Hygieia in a dream was a crucial part of the therapy administered at the Greek healing sanctuary at Epidaurus. Medieval texts recount the appearance of saints and the Virgin Mary in people's dreams. In the twelfth century, dreams were recognized as means for the soul to know "occulta Dei," the secrets of God.[28] Though pagan propensities were repressed, Christian censorship could not prevent the long-venerated figures from returning in the realm of dreams.

Certain preconditions might have promoted this oneiric transference: fears for the welfare of the crop which haunt all farming societies; reluctance of agrarian communities to discard the mental habit of linking the earth's fertility with the female's; and deep-seated rituals that were associated with female personifications of the land. One also wonders to what extent the tensions and struggles between the church and the populace over retaining suspect attitudes could have promoted syncretism in dream or in revery. Perhaps it was in dream that the old pagan grain protectress emerged as a female saint, thus keeping alive the ancient topos.

The rest of this chapter illuminates how, in different regions and at various times, the ancient rituals and beliefs surrounding the sowing goddess either were assimilated (officially or unofficially) to a Christian saint, or continued being practiced in altered forms in the countryside and emerged as part of the folk culture recorded in medieval and modern times. The materials that provide evidence for these metamorphoses are the noncanonical Christian vernacular legends, the rich collection of folktales now available, the medieval accounts of festal ceremonies and gestures, and the iconographic details in visual imagery. These tools enable us to penetrate, however obliquely, that alien mental world of the medieval peasant and to try to understand how mythic transformations might have occurred.

Radegund

One of the early saints who became a substitute for the ancient goddess of sowing was the sixth-century queen Saint Radegund, whose adult life was spent in Poitou in west-central France. Her assimilation with the goddess is evidenced by the vernacular legend in which Radegund's passage by a field at seeding time caused the seed to sprout and produce a miraculous growth, and by her early association with the February oat sowing. Two sixth-century Latin texts provide brief accounts of Radegund's life.[29] The virtuous Radegund had been forced to marry the brutal Merovingian king Clotaire. When Clotaire murdered Radegund's brother, she fled, became a nun, and undertook to minister to the poor and sick. King Clotaire determined to recover her, set out in pursuit, but never actually captured her, and she went on to establish monasteries and continue her life of good works.

Folklore preserved an embellishment of the story of the saint's flight from her husband. The tale developed at some undetermined date, and survived only in the oral tradition until it was recorded in Old French in the fourteenth century.[30] According to this vernacular tale, Radegund, hearing that the king was pursuing her, left Saix, where she had been residing. "As she went out of Saix she found a laborer who was sowing oats. She said to him, 'My friend, if anyone asks you if you have seen any person pass by here, say firmly that since the time when you sowed these oats, neither woman nor man has passed by here.' And, by the will of God, the oats in that very hour grew so tall that the saint hid herself in it with her two nuns named Agnes and Disciole. And soon after, King Clotaire arrived at that place and asked the laborer if he had seen anyone pass by. The laborer answered, No, not since he sowed those very oats."[31] The king, hearing the response and seeing the fully grown grain, decided to give up his pursuit and was foiled in his attempt to capture Radegund.

This vernacular tale transmits the figure of an illustrious female fleeing hostile forces, a saintly queen whose passage by or through a field at sowing time causes a bountiful growth of grain. The popular legend, though retaining the essence of the grain goddess topos, also transforms it by the inclusion of the magical, instantaneous harvest. However, the core of the phenomenon remains intact: The event occurs at sowing time and in a rural ambience; a female of importance goes by or around a field and stimulates the growth of the seed; a bountiful harvest ensues; the forces of evil are foiled; and human life is protected. Here in the Poitou region, when the early spring propitiation of the old protectress of grain was proscribed, a new female figure, Radegund, the earliest and most prestigious of female saints in this area, was evoked to take her place.

No specific record of this transformation exists, but seventh-century biographers of Radegund provide some evidence of the situation in which the

amalgamation took place. For instance, contemporary texts describe the
continuation of pagan rites and the worship of pagan statues specifically in
the milieu of Saint Radegund, in the area outside of Soissons and Orleans.
One day Queen Radegund passed near a temple in the wood where pagans
were worshiping the false gods. She ordered her servants to burn the edifice.
But the pagans and a considerable multitude of peasants tried to prevent the
execution of her order. They tried to defend their temple with swords and
cudgels.[32] In other words, like the peasants Gregory of Tours described,
these too continued to worship pagan statues and practice pagan rites, and
were fearful of forsaking their ancient gods. But Radegund did not back
down until the temple was reduced to ashes. The text tells us that ultimately
the pagans were calmed and charmed by the courage and majesty of
Radegund, but it does not say they were converted.[33]

This story of Radegund supports the conclusion that in the countryside,
people tried to continue their old worship and defend their old temples. No
doubt the peasants also made an attempt to retain the figure who, in their
eyes, protected the oats crop. When Christianity took firm hold, however,
and the old goddess had to be discarded, a Christian figure would have had
to take her place. The oats miracle legend suggests that the peasants of
Poitou regarded Radegund as the protectress of their oats crop, and that at
seeding time their thoughts, prayers, and even their ritual observances were
directed toward this new female guardian.

The church would have seen this substitution as dangerous. Radegund's
linkage with the miraculous growth of the oats was perhaps too reminiscent
of dangerous pagan precedents. Just as it took many centuries for idol-like
free-standing statues to become a fully accepted art form in the church (such
figures were installed mostly in crypts until the eleventh century), so too
those saints' legends that were linked too closely with paganism were often
not incorporated into Christian hagiography.[34]

The prayers directed to Radegund as a guardian of the crop were not
recorded in early church texts. Not until the tenth century did ecclesiastical
documents provide even a glimpse of Saint Radegund's association with
February sowing.[35] Though distant and fragmentary allusions to the miracle
of the oats appeared in church texts of the fourteenth century, the first
ecclesiastical writings to contain a version of the oats miracle appeared in a
fifteenth-century lectionary, the same time as Radegund's oats miracle was
depicted in church-approved art (figure 32).[36]

In 1627 the bishop of Poitiers officially sanctioned and consecrated a special festival, Saint Radegund of the Oats, to be celebrated February 28.[37] No
doubt the bishop was influenced by popular beliefs and customs relating to
Saint Radegund and the sowing of oats. The legend of the instantaneous
harvest was widespread and many areas boasted that the miracle had occurred in their locale.[38] Well before the feast was officially approved, an
anonymous author of a biography of Saint Radegund reported that those

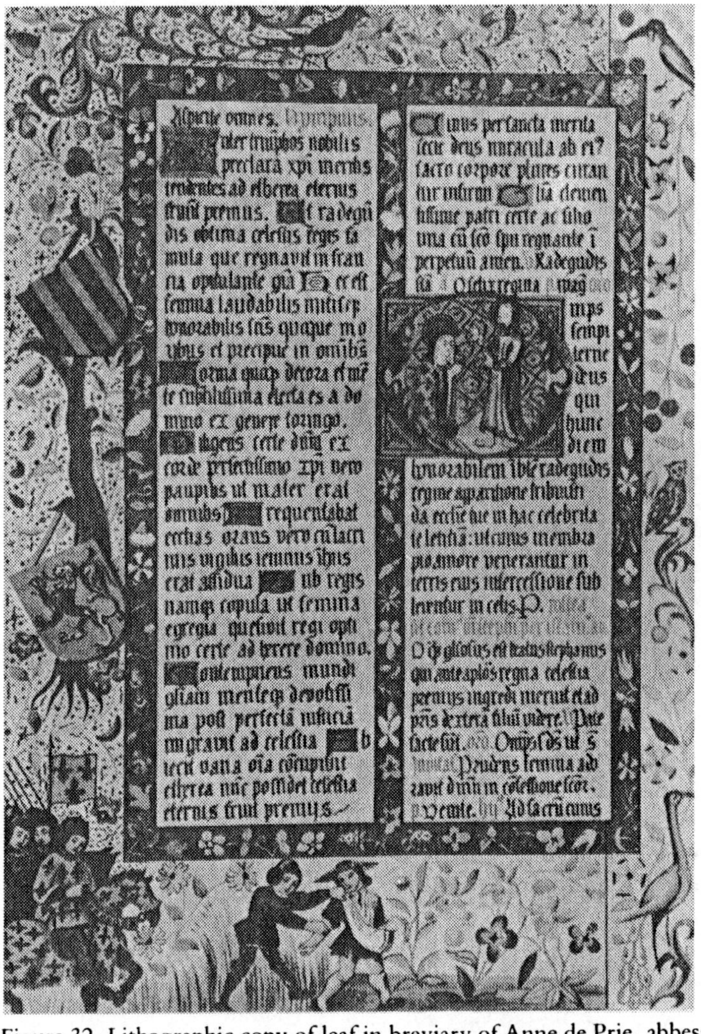

Figure 32. Lithographic copy of leaf in breviary of Anne de Prie, abbess of La Trinité at Poitiers, 1480–1505. Saint Radegund kneeling before Christ in the initial. Sower in lower border. Clotaire and his soldiers riding through the high oats on left. One soldier accosts the sower.

who invoked her carried to church little satchels of grain. And a man with a paralyzed arm is said to have been cured by offering her a coat sleeve full of oats.[39] The practice of offering oats to Saint Radegund continued until the twentieth century.

It is particularly telling that the date of Saint Radegund's oats festival was in February. Early spring plowing and sowing took place at various times in Western Europe according to latitude, altitude, and weather conditions.

Figure 33. Miniature painting in "Ruralium Commodorum Libri Decem," by Petrus de Crescentiis. Digging into the earth, early spring. Labor of the month of February. Late fourteenth to early fifteenth century.

Figure 34. Digging into the earth and the zodiacal sign of February — the Fishes. Relief from Parma Baptistry.

However, those records that exist from the Roman, Gallo-Roman, and medieval worlds indicate that February was the month in which these tasks were generally begun.[40] Many medieval calendars mark February as the beginning of spring, and calendar illustrations as well as sculptural reliefs frequently show plowing, tilling, or sowing as February or March tasks (figures 33–35).[41] Since Radegund's biographers did not specify at what season the saint fled her husband, the grain miracle was easily syncretized with the early spring plowing and seeding customs. And because the legend and customs associated with the grain miracle persisted over generations, the church eventually incorporated the February 28 date into the ecclesiastical calendar year.

Six hundred years before the bishop of Poitiers consecrated Radegund's February oats feast, tenth- and eleventh-century English calendars had recorded a Radegund festival on February 11 rather than on her official saint's day of August 13, the day of her death.[42] Though the February feast was not linked in the preconquest English calendar with grain, one early English calendar marks February 11 with "her originnad fugelas to singenne" ("at this time the birds begin to sing"), a phrase that indicates that in the mid-eleventh century Saint Radegund's Day was associated with the beginning of spring and thereby with the start of plowing and sowing.[43]

Figure 35. Illumination, Grimani breviary. Plowing, digging, and sowing. Month of March.

The English association of Radegund with February and early spring reflects a continental tradition alluded to by Jean Filleau of Poitou, writing about Radegund in 1643.[44] Describing the miracle of the oats, Filleau writes that the memory of the miracle had been passed down for many centuries and was preserved in the Royal and Collegiate Churches of Saint Radegund. He says that, in the abbey of Sainte Croix, the last day of February had long

been dedicated to the commemoration of the oats miracle, and the festival
was called Sainte Radegonde des Aveines, Saint Radegund of the Oats.
Thus, the seventeenth-century historian gives us further evidence that what
the church incorporated liturgically in 1627 had long been observed and
transmitted in the folk religion of the people of Poitou. Though Filleau did
not know how old the tradition was, preconquest English calendars and the
widespread vernacular folk legend indicate that, since the early Middle Ages,
feasts dedicated to Saint Radegund were celebrated at two different times in
the calendar year: one on August 13 to commemorate her documented death,
and one in February to commemorate her association with the sowing of
oats. Such a dual system of feast days was not uncommon and reinforces the
notion that one of the saint's days marked a pagan seasonal rite that was
subsequently Christianized.[45]

Macrine

In the marshy area near the mouth of the Sèvre River in western France,
popular tradition attached the name of the legendary Saint Macrine to
another version of the grain miracle. Macrine was a regional saint whose
persona was closely linked to local topography — at the mouth of the Sèvre
lay an extensive *marais* or marsh.[46] She was particularly venerated among the
maraichins, the people who cultivated the marshy terrain along the river. No
official church documents have preserved any record of Macrine; her legend
has been transmitted only in the oral tradition, compiled by hagiographers
of the nineteenth century, and it eventually found its way into the Bollandist
compilation of the lives of the saints.[47]

The Bollandist hagiographers record her existence as early as the first half
of the ninth century and relate the following about her life: Macrine and her
companions, the virgin saints Colombe and Pézenne, established a monastery in the environs of Niort in the Poitou region. Their solitude was marred
by the harassment and entreaties of "turbulent lords," one of whom "victimized" Colombe. The other two virgins quickly took flight. Saint Pézenne
expired en route and her remains were transported to the village north of
Niort that today bears her name (Pézenne/Pécine, the root of the word
implying bathing place or pond). Still fleeing, Saint Macrine came to the
little island of Magné. Here a version of the grain miracle similar to
Radegund's attaches to her legend.[48] She came to a field that had just been
seeded with oats; as she passed, the seed sprouted and grew miraculously;
her pursuers were told she had gone by at seeding time, and thus were
tricked into believing she had passed long before.

A colorful variant of this legend incorporates a late medieval tale about the
giant Gargantua.[49] In this variant the pursuer is a reflection of the ogre in
dream life. Peasants of the marshlands of the Sèvre tell the following story:

Saint Macrine, mounted on a mule whose horseshoes were on backward, was fleeing Gargantua. The weary animal stopped on the island of Magné. Nearby laborers were seeding oats in a field. Macrine bid them to tell anyone who came by that she had passed by their field the day they were seeding. To the great astonishment of the laborers, the next day the oats were ripe, and when Gargantua came they told him that the grain "was not yet born at the time of the passage of the saint." The giant abandoned the pursuit, "but before he departed he cleaned [the mud from] his clogs [and flung it on the countryside;] thus the hillock of the Garette and the other hillock, where the chapel of Saint Macrine now stands, appeared for the first time above the valley."[50]

Clearly, the inhabitants used this tale to explain local land formations. The "butte" or mound of Saint Macrine, a few miles east of Niort, is encircled by the waters of the Sèvre. A chapel, still discernible on the site in the mid-nineteenth century, was the focal point of a strong regional cult.[51] Every year thousands of pilgrims visited the site, which came to be known as the hermitage of Macrine.

Though the saint was never officially accepted into church records or granted a place in the ecclesiastical pictorial repertoire,[52] there were representations of her in folk art. In the popular tradition, Macrine was sometimes pictured as answering the prayers of peasants by healing the wounds of their animals. She was also represented by another iconographic tradition that has only one precious textual record. I quote from a description of what must have been an eighteenth- or nineteenth-century book of illustrations: "Macrine, in the form of an angel, floats in the middle of the air; kneeling at the doorway of their hut, a peasant family invokes the saint's protection over the eventual harvest, which, in the distance, the plow of the peasant laborer prepares. Macrine, drawing from her apron the fertile seed, throws them from her place in the sky into the furrow, which she blesses."[53]

Walpurga

A variation of the miraculous grain miracle legend is linked to the oral history about the life of the eighth-century nun Saint Walpurga. Walpurga, along with her brothers Willibald and Wynnebald, was one of the missionary saints who traveled from England to convert the Germans.[54] Very little about her life is documented, but apparently her brother Wynnebald appointed her his successor, and after his death in 751 she became abbess of the double monastery at Heidenheim in southern Germany. There is no precise documentation of the date of her death, but there is a tradition in nearby Eichstatt, where her bones are buried, that she died on a Thursday, and various historical considerations lead scholars to place her death in 779.[55]

By the time the first account of her life was written in 895, Wolfhard, her biographer, had woven into her life a series of miraculous healings. These accrued to one tradition that made Walpurga a healing saint. When her bones were moved to Eichstatt they were placed in a rocky niche. At some point, tradition has it, the rock began to exude an oil that had miraculous therapeutic powers. The healing powers of the oil from Walpurga's rock are emphasized in the ecclesiastical documents concerning Walpurga.

In addition to the healing tradition, there was a grain tradition surrounding Walpurga. The earliest representations of Walpurga, in the Hitda Codex, an early eleventh-century illustrated manuscript, show her holding stylized stalks of grain (figure 36).[56] This cryptic attribute, visible in other representations of Walpurga (figure 37), has been called a palm. But Walpurga was not martyred, so there is no reason for her to be holding a martyr's palm, unless the artist misunderstood his model. It has also been said that perhaps she is holding an olive branch, the source of her oil. But she had not yet even been buried in the oil-producing rock when she was first portrayed with this attribute. Thus it is likely that these artists were copying a Walpurga image in which she was holding a stalk of grain.

Walpurga has long been labeled as a Christian saint who replaced a pagan goddess.[57] Though the dates of her birth and death were not known, May 1 was designated Saint Walpurga's Day so that the pagan spring harvest festivities would have a Christian focus.[58] Yet a hagiographer writing shortly after 1075 was the first to record another important date associated with Walpurga, February 25. Though no date had yet been recorded for her death, February 25 became her official and primary saint's day. Like Radegund, Walpurga was honored in February, the month of plowing and sowing in southern Germany.

In the hagiographic tradition, Walpurga was known as the saint of good crops and the patroness of the peasant.[59] In the popular tradition, folk sayings preserved evidence of her relationship with the sowing and sprouting of grain.[60] Reflecting the affinities between fertile land and female fertility, she was also known as the patron saint of pregnant women.[61]

Though no early documents permit us to discover how the peasant farmers may have venerated this female grain saint, folklore has preserved a tale associated with her that is very similar in structure to the tale we have already seen linked with Radegund and Macrine.[62] One night a farmer who feared it was going to rain was bringing his harvest home on a wagon. Suddenly he encountered Saint Walpurga. She was fleeing and asked the peasant if he would hide her among his sheaves of grain, for her enemy was following close behind. The peasant accepted and "hid the saint in a sheaf. For that reason was Saint Walpurga fashioned [or modeled] in a sheaf."[63] Hardly was the saint hidden when the fiendish white rider came by. The peasant quickly made the sign of the cross and was happy when the danger was past. Saint Walpurga climbed out of the grain sheaf (or out of the wagon on which the grain sheaves were piled), thanked the peasant, and told him

Figure 36. Manuscript illustration, Hitda Codex. Saint Walpurga, with grain stalk in her left hand, receives a book from Abbess Hitda.

to watch carefully over his grain. The peasant continued home, and the next morning he was overjoyed to find that his grain had turned to gold.

The basic elements of the Radegund legend—the saint's passage by a field and the creation of a grain miracle—are here linked to Walpurga: The saint is pursued by evil forces, she appears before a peasant in a field and hides in the grain, and she is saved with the peasant's help. In this folkloric account, however, the peasant is not sowing; the sheaves have been cut and the peasant is bringing the crop to the barn. The ready sheaves allow the saint to hide in the grain.

The oral transmitter of this tale included another important element as a kind of explanatory phrase: "Daher wird die heilige Walburgis mit einer Garbe abgebildet" ("For that reason was Saint Walpurga fashioned [or modeled] in a sheaf [or in sheaves]"). Straw images of pagan agrarian deities existed in Celto-Germanic areas in the ancient world.[64] The fashioning of female puppets or dolls made out of the last sheaf of corn was particularly prevalent in Germanic areas.[65] In some places, the last sheaves were made into a doll that was dressed in women's clothing and carried home on a wagon. At times the doll was fastened to a pole that someone in the wagon kept moving so that the doll would seem to be alive. The figure was known as the wheat mother or rye mother, according to the crop of the region. In some parts of Germany, she was known as the Great Mother. Naturally these images were extremely perishable and therefore shortlived. A similar custom can be observed among farmers of Europe and North America even into the twentieth century (see figure 59 for an English example).

The farmer in the folktale takes for granted that the listener is familiar with the custom of fashioning a Saint Walpurga out of straw. Saint Walpurga, modeled of sheaves, was one of those figures that had become part of folkloric pageant. In these extra-ecclesiastical "popular" celebrations, Walpurga filled a role analogous to the former role of the ancient mother goddess of grain. Disguised in the tale as a wheat sheaf or placed among the wheat sheaves, the Walpurga figure shows that in some areas her persona was conflated with the lingering concept of the grain mother, the vegetation goddess. It is an eerie reminder of Tacitus's description of the veiled goddess statue carried on a wagon into the lands to assure their fertility and prosperity.

Milburga

In England there is evidence of the rural population's veneration of a plowing and sowing goddess, and of her later replacement by the sowing saint Milburga and by the folkloric "queen of the plow," Bessey. That Anglo-Saxon peoples invoked a mother goddess at plowing and seeding time is proved by an early medieval plowing charm recorded and preserved in a manuscript in the British Museum.[66] This Anglo-Saxon text provides a glimpse of an ancient preplowing ritual dedicated to a mother goddess. The ritual, though partially Christianized, has a profoundly pagan aspect. The Anglo-Saxon invocation is part of an elaborate ceremony for charming the land at plowing and seeding time. The text carries detailed prescriptions for chants, movements, and offerings. Though written down well into the Christian period, the charm incorporates decidedly pagan elements along with obviously syncretized material.

The Anglo-Saxon scribe who recorded the charm set out to relate how the farmer could promote the fertility of his land and protect it from malignant forces. The text offers a prescription for just how this should be done: Before dawn the farmers must remove four strips of turf from four quarters of the land and have masses said over them. A sacrificial libation of oil, honey, milk, parts of trees, worts, and holy water should be poured into the ground before the turf is replaced. Then the farmers must recite in Latin the formula "Increase and multiply and replenish the earth," as well as other Christian phrases.[67] After the prescribed prayers, songs, and turnings, the farmer must then take special seed and gather all the plowing apparatus together in preparation for the plowing and sowing. He must bore a hole in the plow beam and insert an aromatic resin, fennel, soap, and salt. Then before he makes the first furrow he is to put the seed on the body of the plow and address the following incantation to the earth mother.

> Erce, Erce, Erce, mother of earth,
> May the Almighty, the Lord everlasting, grant thee
> Fields growing and flourishing,
> Fruitful and reviving,
> Store of gleaming millet-harvests,
> And broad barley-crops,
> And white wheat-crops,
> And all the crops of the earth.
> May the Lord everlasting
> And his saints who are in heaven
> Grant him that his land be kept safe from all foes
> And may it be guarded against all evils,
> Witchcrafts sown throughout the land.
> Now I pray the Ruler who wrought this world
> That no witch be eloquent enough, nor any man powerful enough
> To pervert the words thus pronounced.[68]

Then the farmer is to drive forward the plow, cutting the first furrow, and say:

> Whole be thou Earth,
> Mother of men.
> In the lap of the God,
> Be thou a-growing.
> Be filled with fodder
> For fare-need of men.[69]

Then the farmer is to take meal and bake a loaf, kneading it with milk and holy water. And laying it under the first furrow, he is to say:

Acre full fed,
Bring forth fodder for men!
Blossoming brightly,
Blessed become;
And the God who wrought the ground,
Grant us gifts of growing,
That the corn, all the corn,
May come into our need. [70]

Then he is to say thrice, "Grow, in the name of the Father, be blessed," then amen and Paternoster thrice.

It is plain that here we have a pagan ceremony with Christian rites and names added to offset the pagan tone. Though some of the pagan chants are supplemented by Paternosters and Latin formulas, the text retains the ancient pre-Christian invocation "Erce, erce, erce, earthan môder." This poetic incantation addressed to the earth mother stands at the very beginning of the chant; the Lord is only addressed in the second line. The meaning of the word *erce* remains enigmatic, though it seems to be another name for earth mother, perhaps an ancient Germanic name;[71] it does not, however, appear in any other Anglo-Saxon text. It is clear that the personified earth, evoked before the Lord everlasting, must be ultimately responsible for the fertile acres and the crops of millet, barley, and wheat.

The farmer's second address—"hal wes thu folde, fira môder," "whole [uninjured, safe] be thou earth mother of human beings"—occurs as he is plowing the first furrow. He addresses the earth as if in propitiation for having to cut into her "belly"; though "furrowed," she is to remain "whole" or "uninjured." This propitiatory impulse to ask forgiveness for "breaking into" the earth mother may have been at the core of this as well as other ritual activity surrounding the first seasonal plowing. Since the time when the "belly" of the goddess was first "impregnated" with seed by Neolithic peoples, the preplowing ceremony may have been the farmer's way of seeking expiation for having "wounded" the earth mother. The second phrase, "fira môder," "mother of human beings," elevates still further the status of this earth mother. She is seen not only as the personified land from which produce comes forth, but also as the mother of all humankind.

The words of these charms personifying the earth and according her vast powers seem to hearken back to the beginning of settled agriculture. The charms give us an all too rare insight into the hopes and fears of early medieval farmers whose very lives depended on the propitious influence of nature. They reveal that in Anglo-Saxon England, as elsewhere, agrarian people were firmly attached to the concept of the earth mother protectress. Reluctant to cast aside such deeply rooted mental habits and practices, farmers settled a suitable Christian substitute, a saint who could be seen as a protectress at plowing and sowing time. [72]

In one area of England, Shropshire, there is an intimation of how the substitution of Milburga, an early English saint, for the mother goddess of plowing and sowing might have occurred. Like Radegund and Walpurga, Milburga, who died in 715, was born during the time of transition from paganism to Christianity.[73] Her father, a king, had been a pagan. As a princess claiming kinship with the royal houses of Kent, Mercia, and East Anglia, and as abbess of Wenlock, the most active center of Christianity in her father's kingdom, Milburga was a person of considerable importance and influence in the early days of Anglo-Saxon Christianity.[74] After her death, however, Christian religious life declined in the region; Wenlock fell into decay and was for a while completely abandoned. Christianity did not have a firm foothold in the area and with the death of important Christian leaders, the purely agrarian population vacillated between the old and new ways.

There is no contemporary record of Milburga's life; the earliest surviving sources are from the twelfth century.[75] They tell of her royal origin and her saintly sister, and relate an incident that happened in 1078 after Cluniac monks arrived from France to set up a new church in place of Milburga's now-abandoned monastery: ". . . A certain boy running violently along the pavement, broke into the hollow of the vault, and discovered the body of the virgin; when a balsamic odour pervaded the whole church, she was taken up, and performed so many miracles, that the people flocked thither in great multitudes. Large spreading plains could hardly contain the troops of pilgrims, while rich and poor came side by side, one common faith impelling all. Nor did the event deceive their expectations: for no one departed, without either a perfect cure, or considerable abatement of his malady, and some were even healed of the king's evil, by the merits of this virgin, when medical assistance was unavailing."[76] As the document relates, the miracles connected with the remains of Milburga were healings.[77] During the Middle Ages, churchmen were ever ready to testify to the therapeutic powers of saintly relics in their monasteries. This kind of reputation would bring flocks of pilgrims to the site and certainly enriched the monastery. It was in the interests of the monks to record such events.[78]

However, a slightly later medieval text preserves another tradition associated with Milburga's life: her power over waters and over forces threatening the seed. An account of Milburga's life written between 1325 and 1350 by John of Tynemouth provides an account of the miracles she supposedly accomplished during her lifetime.[79] John of Tynemouth traversed England and gathered his information not only from monasteries and cathedrals, but also from secular chronicles and other historical and contemporary sources. On occasion he appended legends, sayings, and anecdotes to his *vitae*. One might call him a fourteenth-century folklorist. His purpose was to record what was known and believed about the various saints, but not to aggrandize any particular one.[80] Two of Milburga's miracles recorded by John of Tynemouth are important for our purposes: One has to do with flowing water and the other with seed.[81] The first relates the flight of Milburga from a neighboring prince who lived outside her monastery and who "wanted to ravish her violently and take her in marriage."[82] Fleeing across a stream, Milburga checked his pursuit by causing the waters to swell enormously and block his passage. The second legend tells how, at sowing time, Milburga was able to keep seed-threatening wild geese and worms out of the fields.[83] By accomplishing these feats, she was able to ensure that the grain would grow and that the hungry would be fed. Peasants considered Milburga their patroness because of her extraordinary power over nature.

Two other miracles of Milburga were transmitted through the oral folklore of the Shropshire area and recorded by a folklorist in the late nineteenth century.[84] One miracle has to do with water and the other with arable land and seed. Saint Milburga's Well is a free-flowing spring on a hill above the village church in Stoke St. Milborough. People from the village explained the legendary origin of the spring with this story: When Milburga was fleeing from her enemy she was mounted on a white horse or a white ass—the villagers disagreed, some substituting the biblical animal (Judg. 5.10) for the more pagan steed. She was ". . . pursued by her foes with a pack of bloodhounds, and a gang of rough men on horseback. After two days' and two nights' hard riding she reached the spot where the well now is, and fell fainting from her horse. . . . On the opposite side of the road, some men were sowing barley in a field. . . . They ran to help the Saint. Water was wanted, but none was at hand. The horse, at St. Milburga's bidding, struck his hoof into the rock and at once a spring of water gushed out. 'Holy water, henceforth and for ever flow freely,' said the Saint."

In a few moments, a second miracle occurred, similar to the miracles associated with Radegund, Macrine, and Walpurga. Milburga passed by the newly planted field and endowed the earth with great fertility and the seed with miraculous growth energy. "Then, stretching out her hands, she commanded the barley the men had just sown to spring up, and instantly the green blades appeared. Turning to the men, she told them that her pursuers were close at hand, and would presently ask them, 'When did the lady on the white horse pass this way?' to which they were to answer, 'When we were sowing this barley.' She then remounted her horse, and bidding them prepare their sickles, for in the evening they should cut their barley, she went on her way. And it came to pass as the Saint had foretold. In the evening the barley was ready for the sickle, and while the men were busy reaping, St. Milburga's enemies came up, and asked for news of her. The men replied that she had stayed there at the time of the sowing of that barley, and they went away baffled."[85]

John of Tynemouth's fourteenth-century accounts that linked Milburga with the protection of seed and with the power over birds and insects already suggested the possibility that this saint was chosen to fill the role of grain protectress in Shropshire when the ancient pagan protectress could no longer be venerated. But the folkloric account provides convincing proof that in this region Milburga assumed this role. Not only does the tale contain the basic structural elements of the grain goddess topos (passage by an arable field; arrival at the time of plowing and sowing; instigation of amazing fertility and growth; protection not only of the seed, but also of human life), it is also juxtaposed to a miracle of "instantaneous water." Thus, the folktale attributes to the saint control over precisely those elements the farmer would have seen as essential in the production of grain: water and growth energy. In these tales the saint has not only the powers that would have been associated with pre-Christian agrarian water deities, but also the powers that formerly were associated with the mother goddess of seed and grain.

It is not possible to know when the Shropshire water/grain legends became part of Saint Milburga's story, though the water/grain legends in her *vita* must date from before the mid-fourteenth century. Even if popular rural culture had linked these legends of controlling water and germinating grain with Milburga in the early Middle Ages, the stories would have been judged too pagan in tone to be included in ecclesiastical documents. There are, however, several factors that argue that Milburga was viewed by the peasants as a seed protectress even during the first few centuries after her death. Though early accounts give her death date as May 25 and the translation of her relics as June 25, the oldest English calendars (beginning with the "Bosworth Psalter," written around 950) give her saint's day as February 23, a date that falls in the midst of the period of tilling and spring wheat sowing in Shropshire.[86] Thus one is prompted to ask: By making February 23 Saint Milburga's Day, was the tenth-century church trying to incorporate into the ecclesiastical calendar the pagan preseeding ritual of February along with its female dedicatee? Was the church trying to syncretize the pagan earth mother of sowing with a Christian sowing saint substitute? The evidence suggests that it was.

With this substitution, what the peasants could no longer venerate in pagan form they envisioned in Christian form. The ancient invocation of a protectress at plowing and sowing could be transformed to become part of a new mythic construct in which the Christian female figure is present at the field, going by or around it, protecting it with her proximity and causing a miraculous growth. Her passage, foiling the forces of evil, brings a bountiful harvest and actually saves human life. With this amalgamation, the peasants of the area, in spite of their ultimate conversion to Christianity, could maintain in their imaginations the notion of a powerful protectress, patroness of the farmer, guardian of fields and seed, and friend of the hungry. Her special day was February 23, in the midst of the spring sowing season. And at that time she mythically journeyed over the fields, controlling the magical precious waters and coaxing the barley seed to sprout.

Brigid

A February plowing and sowing festival associated first with an earth mother goddess and eventually with a female saint was also known in Ireland. Pagan Ireland was an amalgam of indigenous people, the Neolithic builders of the large stone tombs, and the Celts, who, having populated large areas of Europe during the seventh to first centuries B.C., expanded into England and then Ireland. They came in successive waves between the fifth century B.C. and the first century A.D. As Rome was occupying Gaul and Britain, the various Celtic migrations were coalescing in Ireland and an Irish Celtic civilization was emerging.

In pagan Celtic Ireland, the year was divided into four seasons according to a lunar calendar. The beginning of each new season was designated by an agrarian festival: Imbolc marked February 1; Beltaine, May 1; Lugnasa, August 1; and Samhain, November 1. These festivals were associated with particular agricultural tasks and with special customs and beliefs.[87]

The February festival, Imbolc, is the least well known of the four.[88] In Irish folk culture, it is generally regarded as the first day of spring, the day on which plowing and sowing begin.[89] Until modern times, to symbolize this, the farmer went to the tillage land at Imbolc and broke the sod with a spade.[90] The day was observed as a holiday and no work was done, least of all work such as carting, grinding, or spinning, which involved the turning of wheels. And, according to a medieval quatrain, it was also a day of feasting and ritual purification:

> Tasting every food in order,
> This is what behoves at Imbolc
> Washing of hand and foot and head,
> It is thus I say.[91]

The cessation from labor and the feasting are reminiscent of customs in ancient Rome and in other places, where after the sowing everyone was ordered to feast and to rest.[92] The instruction to wash has been related to another Roman activity undertaken in February, the purification ceremonies to rid both people and the fields of impurities before the new planting or before the new year (beginning March 1 in the old Roman calendar).[93] It has also been suggested that Imbolc relates to the root of the Celtic verb *folcaim*, "I wash," and that the sense of the ancient word has to do with ritual purification, like that undergone by the Romans in February.[94]

But another linguistic analysis of Imbolc suggests a different meaning for the root of the word: In Old Irish the prefix *im-* means "around" or "about," and *bolc* or *bolg* means "belly."[95] Thus, the word *Imbolc* could literally have meant "around the belly." With this etymology in mind, it is worth posing the question: Does the word *Imbolc* reflect an ancient ritual of going around the arable field (symbolic belly of the mother goddess), a ritual undertaken before the ground was first tilled and the seed sown? Could this have been part of a propitiatory or protective rite such as the one described in the Anglo-Saxon charm? This is an intriguing possibility, given the activities associated with the festival, the time of year when it occurred, and the figure to whom it was eventually dedicated. For Imbolc, long associated with first tillage and seeding, and with the date February 1, is a day that has been dedicated to Saint Brigid since the early Middle Ages, and is called La Fhéile Brighde.

Saint Brigid shows an incredible likeness to the Celtic goddess from whom she takes her name, Brigid, the great guardian of fertility and the land.[96] Though by the Middle Ages the ancient goddess was primarily associated with poetry, healing, and artisanship, etymology and scraps of mythology establish her as having been primarily a matriarchal deity.[97] Like most Celtic goddesses, Brigid was intimately connected with topography, particularly with sacred waters and wells.[98] Prayers and sacrifices would have been offered to Brigid (and to the other "topographical" goddesses), though the druidic liturgy and oral formulas were not set down by the medieval monks who recorded the mythology. Instead, they recast the pagan Brigid's legends and perhaps even some of her ritual (such as processions and pilgrimages) in a manner acceptable to the church.

Folk culture, however, preserved the links between Saint Brigid and her pagan forerunner. The folk traditions surrounding Imbolc highlight these affinities. Straw and grain from the previous harvest are central to Saint Brigid's Day celebrations: Until modern times, on Imbolc/Saint Brigid's Day, a small quantity of specially preserved seed grain was mingled with the first crop to be sown. The straw or stalks of the grain seed were used to make crosses and girdles that were blessed with holy water, hung up in houses, or set in the thatch of cottages (figure 38). A sheaf of oats, a cake of bread, or a dish of porridge was placed on the doorstep the night of Saint Brigid's Day as a grain offering to the saint, who was believed to be abroad.[99] Other cakes were placed outside the window to provision a hungry traveler.[100]

Brigid's associations with the grain plant and the seed must predate the Celts' conversion to Christianity. These customs connecting Saint Brigid with tillage and sowing at Imbolc surely reflect the linkage between the saint and the Celtic goddess from whom she got her name. The etymology of the word *Imbolc*, the agrarian customs and activities associated with it, and its date in the agricultural year all suggest that a pagan tilling and sowing

Figure 37. Manuscript illustration, hymn book. Saint Brigid in top
mandorla and Walpurga below. Each holds stalks of foliage.

ceremonial was transformed into the Feast of Saint Brigid, and that the
pagan mother goddess, whose symbolic "belly" or "womb" was envisioned
as producing the season's crop, was superseded by the Christian saint
who, until modern times, was honored at Imbolc/Saint Brigid's Day with
baked grain cakes and stalks of grain (figure 37). No doubt the farmer,

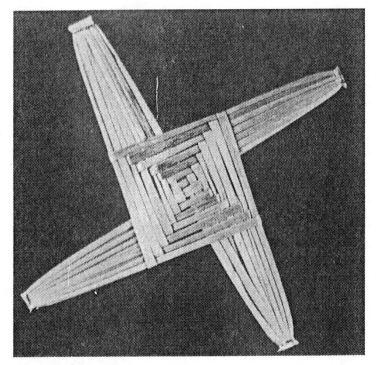

Figure 38. Straw Brigid's cross.

annually anticipating the rebirth of nature and the new growth in the field, continued to see the land and its growth energy as linked to a female transcendent power, a protectress around whose symbolic "belly" a preseeding procession at Imbolc might have taken place since the time when the Celtic language was first spoken on the island, or even before. [101]

Folk custom continued to retain the February 1 connection with seeding and tillage. However, when the Irish economy became centered on sheep and cattle Imbolc came to be linked with the beginning of the lactation of ewes and Saint Brigid's feast became associated with abundance of milk and milk products. [102] Though in the course of time some of the original sowing practices associated with this day disappeared or their symbolism was misunderstood, the ancient meaning of Imbolc is retrievable. Illuminating the roots of Saint Brigid's Day and the customs tied to it demonstrates how we can uncover those Celtic beliefs and practices that, though modified over time, were not completely destroyed. [103] The monks took the ancient figure of the mother goddess and grafted her name and functions onto her Christian counterpart, Saint Brigid. They made her a virgin, identified her as a second mother of Christ, and honored her as a kind of symbolic matriarch of all Ireland.

In our time, Saint Brigid's function continues to complement, in the folk traditions, those of the pre-Christian goddess Brigid, protectress of fertility and guardian of the lands. To this day pilgrims flock to wells, streams, and ancient ruins associated with Saint Brigid. One of the most important pilgrimages is to Brigid's shrine in Faughart, in northeastern County South.[104] Brigid is thought to have been born at Faughart, where she consecrated her virginity to Christ, founded a convent, and constructed a chapel. In the vicinity of the Hill of Faughart are large stone tombs, underground passages, and other prehistoric structures. It appears that as the old order passed away the Christian community reconsecrated the site, erected a stone cross, and set up a shrine with Brigid as the patroness and heroine. People still come to adorn the bushes around her outdoor shrine with mementos of her miraculous cures.[105]

Popular legends about the saint proliferate in the area. The most famous story concerns Brigid's flight from a determined suitor who was on horseback. As she fled, she knelt down by the bank of a stream and plucked out her eyes to avoid being recognized. To this day certain stones near the stream are named to recall various parts of the episode: the head stone, hoofmark stone, knee stone, waist stone, eye stone. These are focal points of the pilgrimage and provide the faithful visitor with tangible evidence of the saint's gruesome sacrifice.[106] The pilgrim who visits the site undergoes the prescribed ablutions in the stream and then makes a circuit around the large stones. The set movements more than hint at an elaborate pre-Christian ritual. Though a modern shrine complete with a replica of the Lourdes grotto and a canopied altar was erected in the area in 1934, there is still a private rite that brings the faithful to the stream where they can pray and make their circuit around the stones. Two pilgrimages occur each year: one in July and the other on the first Sunday in February.

Flight and Hunger

The grain miracle legend attached to Radegund, Macrine, Walpurga, and Milburga is multifaceted. Though it preserves the topos of the sowing goddess ritual, it also provides material for the analytic psychologist and social historian. From a psychoanalytic perspective the tale evokes one of the primal female fears, sexual violation. In her passage by the field, each of the female saints is fleeing from a hostile male or group of males who are determined to capture her and subdue her sexually. A woman unprotected, fleeing by a field alone or with a single companion, would predictably have been trying to escape sexual ravishment, and the texts and legends either explicitly state or strongly imply that these female saints were fleeing in fear of rape "violatio."

The fourteenth-century text regarding Milburga informs us that she had taken flight because a neighboring prince "wanted to ravish her violently and take her in marriage." The medieval practice of capturing and raping a highborn woman of property was common. By capturing a virgin, raping her, and forcing her into marriage, an adventurous lord could secure himself an estate or aggrandize his holdings. Though the raped virgin could try to prove that she was not complicit in the crime, painful tests by water and hot irons were employed to arrive at the "truth."

Macrine likewise was fleeing sexual violation. The hagiographic texts report that she and her companions, Colombe and Pézenne, were harassed in their cloistered solitude by the entreaties of "turbulent lords." One of the lords "victimized" Colombe; presumably the rape ended in a forced marriage or violent death for the nun. Macrine and Pézenne took flight from the lords. Pézenne did not survive the journey; only Macrine was able eventually to find solitude and peace on her island. The plight of the unprotected virgin, fleeing the rapacious lord, was indeed gruesome in the Middle Ages.

The married woman's flight from rape was no less terrifying. In the legend of Radegund King Clotaire had been awarded Radegund as booty during a tribal raid and had taken her as his wife. She fled him after he murdered her brother. The medieval texts imply that Radegund's flight from Clotaire was a flight from his continued sexual possession. Hagiographers have naively brought up the question of whether the young Germanic princess was able to keep her virginity when taken as booty by Clotaire. The hagiographers have been unable to resolve the question. Clotaire was known for what we would call his numerous sexual crimes, as well as for his many "wives," one of whom was Radegund. Rape has always accompanied inter-tribal warfare, and, during the rough and brutal Merovingian era, it is quite likely that Radegund too was victimized. The queen's flight and eventual seclusion in her cloister was no doubt her response to Clotaire's license to rape his booty/wife at will.

The folkloric account of Walpurga's flight is brief, but even here we are told that she was fleeing a "fiendish white rider." Saint Brigid was likewise fleeing from a determined suitor mounted on a horse. A man on horseback pursuing a running woman once again conjures up the image of violent rape.

In each of these cases the idea of a woman in flight was cast in terms of a female fleeing sexual violence. But these are special females, saints who harbored within them an element of the divine. They were heir to the ancient powers of the earth mother, and even as Christian figures, in people's imaginations they still maintained control over the earth's fertility. Using their magical powers, they were able to employ the best weapon a female has against rape — trickery. Not through force or through appealing to male protectors did these potential victims save themselves. These Christianized substitutes for the antique grain goddess called on their ancient linkage with the land, and together with the good male sower brought about a subterfuge that saved them and also benefited mankind.

Though it is impossible to know precisely what elements of the population formulated and transmitted a given folktale, the grain miracle legend was doubtless devised in an agricultural milieu. One could go still further and suggest that rural women played a large role in perpetuating the life of this legend. Cast as flight from sexual ravishment, the tale corresponds to the imagery of female dream experience—to be precise, nightmares of sexual assault. But the outcome of the pursuit in this legend is the denigration of the potential rapist, who is held up to ridicule, and the validation of the powers of the female, who is able to save herself and to increase the sower's crop.

The grain miracle tale not only reveals a link to the flight-and-pursuit theme; it also alludes to one of the most basic problems of the peasantry, the inexorable struggle against starvation. During the Middle Ages, most people lived off the land and relied on the cereal crop as the staple of their diet. [107] Agricultural productivity was impeded by primitive farming techniques, and even when peasants did accumulate a little surplus, agents of the seigniory usually appropriated it. Many different meteorological disasters could cause a crop to fail, bringing starvation, disease, or death to a family or indeed to an entire community. Insofar as the grain tale perpetuates the element of fantasy, it is significant that the fantasy relates to food. This theme is typical, for in many of the oldest folktales, particularly in France, wish fulfillment usually takes the form of food. [108] In this tale, the saint's miraculous intervention brings a plentiful harvest, yet the possibility of crop failure lurks underneath the story. The grain miracle legend thus reflects both the cruel social order that made sexual violence commonplace and the primitive agricultural conditions that made hunger endemic.

Chapter V

Folk Figures

As evidence for the veneration of the sowing goddess disappeared from the historical record during the centuries of conversion to Christianity, female saints associated with plowing and seeding began to emerge. Alongside these female saints, however, appeared numerous folk figures, the focus of rural invocations and ceremonies, figures whose roles in legend or pageant parallel that of the sowing goddess. Uncovering these agrarian protectors in the medieval context depends on finding texts that describe extra-ecclesiastical practices, a difficult task since almost all written sources from the epoch come from the pens of churchmen. Since rural lay people left practically no written record of any of their "suspect," paganlike activities, and since the objects that might have been fashioned in connection with their practices have rarely survived, we invariably must content ourselves with descriptions that come from the antagonistic perspective of the church, from the hostile eye that labeled the folk figures "daemons" and called the practices dedicated to them heinous. In spite of the ecclesiastical condemnations, the ceremonies were ongoing, for their continuance must have been of crucial importance to the ritual life of the community.

Daemon

A twelfth-century text, the "Chronicum Rudolfi," provides an ecclesiastic's account of a ceremony dedicated to an agrarian folk figure. It describes what obviously was an enduring festival devoted to a pagan deity.[1] From the point of view of the recording monk, it was not important to give the date the festival took place. Nor does he tell us the gender of the deity. But the activities described in the chronicle parallel in many ways those associated with the sowing goddess topos, for a "daemon" (what we would call a folk figure) was paraded through the countryside in a cart as the focus of a ceremonial attended by throngs of people. The celebration described by the monk occurred around the year 1133. I paraphrase from the Latin text:

In a forest near Inda (just west of Cologne) a shiplike "vehiculum" or vessel was built and wheels were affixed to it. Ropes were attached to the vessel and weavers drew it through the countryside accompanied by a great procession of women and men. The vessel was drawn first to Aachen, then to Maestricht, Tongres, Looz, and so on. The people drawing the vessel had the right to prevent others from coming too near the internal part of the ship. Everywhere crowds came out to greet it with great joyfulness and songs of triumph. This ceremony, which the chronicler calls a "ritus," was celebrated for more than twelve days, often well into the middle of the night.

By the twelfth century, the name of the figure to whom the procession was dedicated had been forgotten. There is no way of knowing whom the people thought they were honoring, for the monk recorded only vague suppositions as to which "malignant" pagan deity was corrupting the participants. He surmised that inside the vessel traveled some loathful spirit—Bacchus or Venus, Neptune or Mars. He may have imagined Bacchus or Venus, perhaps, because of the sexual license surrounding the activities, which were compared to a bacchanal; Neptune, because the vehicle seems to have been in the form of a ship, with mast and sail; Mars, because open warfare ensued when some towns refused to receive the procession.

Naturally, the monk was viewing the entire event from an antagonistic perspective. He called the vessel an image of the spirit of evil and the devil's mockery; its construction was an evil omen, executed by the zeal of heathens. The singing of foul and base songs as part of the "ludus" or pageant was particularly repugnant. For him, this was a vessel that should be burned, and a "ritus" that had to be crushed. He was particularly repelled by the role of women. Though both sexes participated in the proceedings, the cleric pointed most vehemently at the "shameless" activities of the females. He reported that they threw off their feminine modesty and eagerly rushed in to dance and sing around the vessel. Half-nude (says the chronicler), their hair strewn wildly around their heads, they formed a clamoring chorus around the ship. At dawn or dusk they slipped away to some secret place where they could engage in lusty celebrations. Though the monk's language reveals typical medieval misogyny, there is little reason to doubt his contention that the women celebrants engaged in special revelries.

Medieval texts tell us that women in particular held on to pagan forms of celebration—singing, dancing, and repeating suspect chants or litanies. A decree of the Council of Rome in 826 is typical of generations of ecclesiastical authorities who protested in vain these female proclivities: "There are certain people, chiefly women, who on festivals, holy days, and saints' days, are not delighted to attend because of desire for those things by which they ought to be delighted, but are concerned to come in order to dance, to sing shameful words, to perform choric dances, behaving just like pagans."[2] Numerous medieval documents show the church's attempt to prohibit crowds of women from singing "cantica diabolica, amatoria et turpia" (diabolical songs that are amorous and shameful) and dancing through the villages on religious festivals. Female choruses meeting and singing in or around churches were strictly forbidden; one fragmentary penitential indicates that dancing and singing songs of love were grounds for excommunication.[3]

Though all of these interdictions were not directed solely against women, the majority were, at least in the cases of singing and dancing. Taking the monk's words at face value, we have a picture of women's participation in this folk ritual: Their dancing and singing heightened the excitement of the celebrations; their semi-nudity (if in fact they were half-nude as he says) probably related to invocations for sexual fecundity; and perhaps their slipping away to lusty celebrations was part of a testing of their newly invoked fertility. Though written from the perspective of the church, the document still reveals how much support there was for the procession of the vessel. Town after town opened the gates for it; even the secular authorities in some places obviously supported the celebration. And the people apparently displayed great enthusiasm as they sang, danced, and acted like bacchanals for twelve days of raucous processions and fête.

The parallels with Tacitus's description of the Germanic festival in honor of Terra Mater are obvious.[4] In both instances, the symbol or statue of a deity, either female or of unspecified gender, was carried through the countryside from town to town. Though Tacitus does not tell us what kind of vessel was involved, the fact that the Terra Mater resided on an island in a lake suggests that her vessel may likewise have been shiplike. The earth mother in Tacitus was protected by a priest who limited popular access to her vessel, a role played by the weavers in the twelfth-century account. The ancient pagan procession, like the medieval one, was occasion for great rejoicing and merrymaking. Place after place honorably received the participants, and for a period of days great happiness reigned in the countryside. The main differences between the two processions were that in ancient days war was specifically proscribed during the rite, whereas the tensions ensuing from the medieval celebrations were apparently a source of conflict; and, because of Christianization, the sacrifice of slaves that ended the ceremony in Germania was not part of the medieval event.

Though the perspective of the recording monk allows only a glimpse of the attitude of the participants, some assumptions can be made: The joyful spirit probably reflects the hope and optimism that the cycle of vegetation will be prosperous; the allusion to sexual license, as well as women's importance in the ceremonial, points to the traditional connection in people's minds between the fertility potential of females and of the land. Though the monk attributed all sorts of nefarious influences to the celebration, popular enthusiasm ensured that it continued in one form or another for many generations.[5]

Bessey

In England and on the Continent the reverence for a vegetation protectress survived the conversion to Christianity. The concept of a mother earth, guardian of plowing and sowing, had been too potent to be cast aside. Not only had the earth mother been incorporated into an Anglo-Saxon, ostensibly Christian prayer charm;[6] popular imagination had transformed her into the female saint Milburga, patroness of those who plowed and sowed.[7]

In other areas of England, and outside the ecclesiastical context, a parallel but very different phenomenon occurred: The plowing and sowing goddess was superseded not by a female saint, but by a folk figure; she was transformed, during the Middle Ages, into the popular character Bessey of Plow Monday, a figure who was the focus of country-wide rural pageants and festivities in the month of February. Though the church was to assimilate some of the Plow Monday practices and attach them to Epiphany, the festival was to remain an essentially folkloric event.

Plow Monday took place in late January or early February.[8] Boys and girls, or sometimes just unmarried women, drew a brightly bedecked plow from place to place, generally from the outlying gates into the village center. The boys in the group, often dressed in white shirts, were known as plow bullocks. One of the participants masqueraded as an older woman, Old Bessey or Betsy, while another, designated the fool, dressed in animal skins and wore a long calf's tail. Bessey was the focal point of attention as the plow was drawn through field or village. As night fell a great feast was held: The villagers would bring the plow into the barn, Old Bessey would sit upon it, and the young men would perform a sword dance. In some regions, the celebrants would burn the plow or throw it into the water at the end of the festivities.[9]

In Germany the activities were associated with a Germanic Plow Monday. As in England, the procession was accompanied by dancing and merrymaking. A sixteenth-century observer gives the following account: "On the Rhine, Franconia and diverse other places, the young men do gather all the dance-maidens and put them in a plough, and draw their piper, who sitteth on the plough piping, into the water; in other parts they draw a fiery plough kindled with a fire very artificial made thereon, until it fall to wrack."[10] And in Corinthia (in southern Austria), the people dragged the plow around the borders of the field, a ceremony that may have incorporated the most primitive form of the custom.

The Plow Monday activities in all countries had the earmarks of very ancient practices. The circuit around the field with a plow and the veneration of a central female figure reflected pagan customs associated with the beneficent grain goddess. Over the centuries, the goddess had evolved into an inoffensive folk figure.[11] During this transformation no written records were made of how the preplowing veneration of the earth mother resulted in activities dedicated to figures like Bessey.[12]

The earliest document that alludes to the practice of drawing around the plow is an account book from the fourteenth and fifteenth centuries.[13] A monetary gift was made in 1378 at Durham to men who participated in a preplowing ceremony. In 1413 another gift is recorded, given to those who carried the plow on Old Elvett, a street in Durham. Another reference, from the year 1493, tells of "the ledingh of the ploughe aboute the fire as for gode beginning of the yere that they shulde fare the better all the yere followyng."[14] The importance of the customs of Plow Monday in England is indicated by frequent references to the plow and its accoutrements in the account book and by the "gatherings" or collections of money among the people who maintained the custom.[15]

The activities already traced resemble the mother goddess ritual revealed in the Anglo-Saxon plow charm, and replicate quite closely those associated with the Terra Mater topos described by Tacitus and others. These accounts also support the suspicion that the ancient mother goddess topos emerges in the figure of Old Bessey, who in the early spring sits atop the plow, symbolically bestowing fertility on the fields over which she moves.

Blaise

The ancient sowing ceremonies associated with the grain goddess attached themselves not only to folkloric figures and female saints; male saints also assumed some of the powers formerly attached to the grain goddess. One male saint who took over the grain protectress's role was Saint Blaise, whose name in French, Blaise, resembles blé, the word for wheat; his Flemish name Blas sounds like the word bloen, meaning flour.[16]

The historical Saint Blaise was a bishop in fourth-century Armenia.[17] There was no evidence for his cult before the eighth century, but in the 700s legends about his life began to emerge. It was said that as a young man he had healed wounded or sick beasts that came to receive his blessing; that he healed a boy with a fish bone caught in his throat; that he was tortured with iron combs that tore his flesh; and that after the torture he was beheaded. These legendary events were taken up in the hagiographic literature where he was known as the patron saint of wool combers, of sick beasts, and of all those who suffered from sore throats.

Still another tradition surrounded Blaise. In many areas of France, Germany, and Belgium, he became the patron saint of plowmen and was invoked at spring sowing time.[18] This particular role may have resulted from the coincidence that his name resembled the word for wheat and that his saint's day, February 3, fell right before the time when, in many areas, farmers commenced spring plowing and sowing. As Saint Blaise came to be associated with the sowing of wheat, peasants devised special blessings, observances, and even pageants dedicated to him. In some areas of Western Europe, Saint Blaise was empowered with the fertility functions formerly

connected with the grain goddess, and the preplowing and seeding ceremonies were transferred to him. [19]

The cult of Saint Blaise, the sowing saint, patron of plowmen and farmers,
manifested itself in two ritual activities. [20] One, within the church context,
consisted of the liturgical rite of the presowing benediction of the grain, the
"benedictio seminum granarum." In this ceremony, women carried little
pails of wheat seed to the church to be blessed by the priest. After the
blessing, each woman gathered her pail of grain, gave half of it to the clergy,
and reserved the other half to be mixed with her family's seed in order to
ensure its fruitful germination. Though the blessing of the grain seed was a
widespread custom, it was not included in any liturgical books. [21]

The second ritual of Saint Blaise's cult was a pageant. This pageant was a
very elaborate procession out into the countryside on Saint Blaise's Day,
February 3. The ceremony, documented in many villages of southeastern
France, occurred up until the first World War. [22] On Saint Blaise's Day, after
the priest said the rite of the benediction over the seed, he also blessed a train
of five wagons or carts that had assembled in the village square. Once the
blessing was given, the carts, surmounted by elaborately costumed participants, made their way out of the village and into the countryside.

On the first cart, drawn by the most beautiful horses of the region, sat a
man representing Saint Blaise, crowned with a miter and holding a cross. He
was dressed in the most sumptuous clothing of the parish. Moss, straw, hay,
and in some regions a plow were placed on the floor of his cart, and its
corners were decorated with young fir trees. [23] On the second cart was a
rustic kitchen, complete with an old woman spinning in a corner. In the
center of the kitchen, a young peasant woman worked on dough for *beignets*
(fried breads) that were to be consumed after the ceremony. (The custom of
eating grain products at sowing time is nearly universal.) Farmers holding
appropriate implements occupied the third cart; they acted out the various
agricultural labors of the season, such as hoeing, digging, and seeding. The
fourth cart, with a dirt floor, contained sticks placed upright like newly
planted vines; vintners with pruners and hoes acted out the trimming of the
vines. The last cart carried a pine tree with the remains of the previous
autumn's fruits suspended in its branches.

A celebratory crowd accompanied the carts. The girls and boys dressed up
in clothes signifying the four seasons: Spring and summer dressed in light-
colored clothes, ribbons, and decorated hats; autumn, accompanied by sheep
and goats, wore a sheep skin and held a crook; those representing winter
were dressed in heavy coats. As the procession advanced into the countryside
with song and merriment, the farmers of the third cart continually descended
and acted out their activities at the edges of the fields. [24] An evening of
feasting and drinking terminated this sowing festival.

Nothing in the official biography of Saint Blaise accounts for these links
with seeding, plows, or plowmen. Yet in the peasant imagination these

attributes were attached to him because of the sound of his name and the calendrical placement of his saint's day. At some point his figure came to be seen as an appropriate substitute for the formerly venerated grain goddess. Since Blaise was a male figure, a patron of seed, the village clergy could accept him more easily, and even assimilate him unofficially into the liturgical calendar.

Thus, Blaise became the central figure of the February preseeding ceremonial. Though the dedicatee was a male, this festival had all the allure of the rural practices associated with a manifestation of the sowing goddess. Saint Blaise was paraded in a cart, on a "throne," through the countryside so that his presence by the field would be felt at sowing time. The community, through prayer and ritual, invoked his protection of the seed; a seed offering was presented in his name to the clergy; on his "throne" in the cart at the head of the procession, he was honored while being drawn through the countryside. The community celebrated his protection with song and dance, and gave him thanks through their offering to the clergy.

The church hierarchy, however, felt uneasy with this assimilation, and did not include the Saint Blaise preseeding blessing in its liturgy. No mention was made of the plowing and seeding ceremonies in official prayer books. But where the ceremony had taken strong hold the church allowed it to continue, letting the practice pass as local variation. Though the sowing activities linked to Blaise were apparently too threatening to the church to become part of its official literature, the veneration of Blaise was acceptable enough to be part of church oral prayer services and church-sanctioned pageantry. Curiously, it is easier to find material linking Blaise to plowing and sowing than it is to uncover similar material regarding the female saints who took on a similar role. Though female saints played an important role in medieval life, the church was far more comfortable with a male saint presiding over the crucial acts of plowing and seeding. A female in this role, even semi-officially, may have connoted too strongly that powerful old connection between women's fertility and the fertility of the earth.

It is also of interest that, in many villages in France and Belgium, people considered Saint Blaise a patron of human fecundity.[25] For example, a folkloric document from the village of Torcieu near Savoy recounts that in many villages of the area it was common for young girls to have themselves *guignées* by the statue of Saint Blaise. *Guigner* signifies "to make a sign with the eye or with the head"[26] "When a young woman wants to marry quickly, she comes to make an ardent prayer at the feet of Saint Blaise, and if the saint winks his eye or lowers his head, the young woman will have her husband."[27] There is, however, a more pertinent etymology for the word *guigner*. *Guigner* is very closely related to the Latin word *gignere*, which means "to engender." Because of this linguistic relationship, a Saint Guignolé of Brittany was petitioned by women desiring children.[28] His chapel near Brest housed a Saint Guignolé statue that had an enormous erect wooden phallus.[29] When young women went to have themselves *guignées* by Saint Blaise, their desire was not only to secure a husband, but also to render themselves fertile. Therefore Blaise, along with his folkloric role as protector of grain seed, was also connected to human fertility, a connection that, in the pre-Christian period, had been characteristic of the grain goddess as well.

The Earth Mother at Maché and Bissey

In some areas a recognizable projection of the earth mother goddess—with her appropriate dress, attributes, and even distant echoes of her ceremony— survived intact in folklore and pageants. An example of this survival was found in the nineteenth century in Savoy, where a full-blown figure of the sowing goddess was part of the mid-February preplowing ceremonial, and was absorbed by semi-official ecclesiastical practices.[30]

This transformation from sowing goddess to folk figure took place in the villages of Maché and Bissey, where the following account from the mid-nineteenth century was recorded: "Since time immemorial the youth of Maché had the right to take part in the festival of Saint Valentine of Bissey. Under the tutelage of the abbey of Saint Valentine, the youth of the village were organized in groups (*bazoche*) especially for the occasion. With great pomp the young people journeyed to Bissey (a distance of about 3 kilometers). . . . The abbot and the monks, on foot or on horseback and armed with swords, very noisily conducted a cart on which sat a half-dressed woman. She had before her a horn filled with impure insects and a cage."[31]

When the procession arrived at Bissey, church officials put a live cock into the cage, and all those assembled drank wine together. Mass was said, dancing followed. Young, childless married people came carrying bouquets.[32] At nightfall the youths brought the cock in the cage back to Maché where the abbot fed him until the festival of Saint Peter (later in February), at which time it was pierced by a lance and killed. This remarkable Saint Valentine's Day festival of Maché and Bissey, practiced until the nineteenth century, had very little in common with Saint Valentine's Day as practiced in Europe from the later Middle Ages on, but in fact contained far more primitive elements.[33] This festivity constituted an example of a Christian saint, here a male, becoming the primary figure in a festival that originally had focused on the mother goddess.

A close reading of the description of this local event reveals that on Saint Valentine's Day at Maché, the young people of the village processed into the fields connecting the two villages just as they had done "since time immemorial." They conducted in a cart a symbol of the earth mother goddess—a half-dressed woman with a horn full of insects and a cage. The folklorist van Gennep believed this movement into the fields reflected a particular but unexplained relationship between Maché and Bissey;[34] but elsewhere he stated that the procession went through the arable land given over to cultivation on the outskirts of the villages.[35] This procession into the arable fields with the mother goddess figure in the cart is, as the recording folklorist suspected, a deeply rooted agrarian custom; yet he could not uncover those roots. What he did not understand was that this February procession into the arable fields reflects the ancient sowing goddess topos.

In Savoy the February procession was undertaken to protect the fields from harm, in particular from insects that would eat the seed, thereby destroying the possibility of a successful harvest. The festival was associated with dancing and singing, as well as with an animal sacrifice.[36] Though the mother goddess, as a folkloric persona, was part of the religious festival, the ceremony was performed in honor of Saint Valentine. But the female figure, and even her symbolic import, were retained. Seated on a chair, she held both the means for destruction of the crop (the insects) and the agent for its salvation (the cage for the cock, which could eat the insects). Though the chief officiants and titulary dedicatee of this festival were, respectively, the churchmen and Saint Valentine, a remnant, at least, of symbolic power still rested in the hands of the mother goddess figure. Her attributes demonstrate that symbolically she was still seen as the protectress of the fields and the nurturer of the crop. It was still she who could promote a good harvest and ensure the survival of the community for yet another year.

Thus, until the nineteenth century, the mid-February cavalcade between Maché and Bissey demonstrated the tenacious survival of a pre-Christian practice.[37] Though the male saint, Valentine, was the dedicatee of the festival, the sowing protectress played an important, albeit adjunct, symbolic role.

The Crazy Mother

Into the modern era numerous folk figures continued to populate the European countryside. Many, like Bessey were obvious substitutes for the sowing goddess. Others are more shadowy presences and are difficult to uncover, for the figures take on a negative cast and become "mother demons" or "crazy mothers." But sometimes behind such figures lurk the unsuspected form of the ancient mother goddess of sowing.

To explore one example of the crazy mother, let us return to Autun, where the mother goddess was honored with a great procession in the second century and where in the fourth century priests of Cybele accompanied the statue of the great goddess into the field for the protection of the crop. The area around Autun, like other sections of France, was slow to convert completely. Throughout the fourth and fifth centuries, Christian communities were just beginning to develop and church buildings were few.[38] By the late sixth century, however, church construction had begun: In 589 the Merovingian queen Brunehant ordered the erection of the double abbey of Saint Mary and Saint John. [39] The site chosen for the abbey had long been sacred to the people of Autun; it was the site of the ancient mother goddess Cybele's temple. Though no record of a substitution process exists, one suspects that a certain number of practices formerly associated with Cybele came to be associated with Saint Mary. [40]

The site of Cybele's temple and the Saint Mary/Saint John abbey may have been sacred even before the Roman penetration into the area in the first century B.C., for on the lands of the abbey was a hill called Mont Dru, a name that, for the people of the area, has Celtic or druidic associations. [41] The seventeenth-century history of Autun reports that since "time immemorial," the people of Autun had held a processional festival along the route to that site at the end of winter and on other significant days of the year. The dates of these processions to Mont Dru and to the ancient site of the temple of Cybele (in February, May, mid-August, and December) corresponded almost exactly to the divisions of the pre-Roman ancient Celtic year. This February procession to the site of Cybele's temple continued until the early modern period. [42]

During the Middle Ages, a sanitarium for lepers was built on the route to Mont Dru, and at the four yearly processions the faithful, passing from the abbey of Saint Mary/Saint John to nearby Mont Dru, offered alms for the sick in the leper hospital. The processions and sites that had formerly been associated with the cult of the Great Mother had been rededicated to the Virgin Mary and Saint John.

But that is not the only echo of the cult of the Great Mother in Autun. No historical document reveals what actually happened in the Autun area to the mother goddess procession that was recorded in the life of Symphorian and by Gregory of Tours (see Chapter II). We have surmised that in one form the procession was rededicated to the Virgin Mary. But the practices associated with the Great Mother may have splintered; and in another form she seems to have surfaced as a figure that is likewise paraded in a cart in February, but in a deprecating manner, as the crazy mother. Tucked away in the footnotes of the old history of Autun is this curious information: A certain number of initiations took place on the ancient site of the temple of Cybele, especially the initiation ceremonies for the association of clerks of the local judicial bureaucracy in charge of the state seals. [43] This association was the dominant one in the city, and its members, along with the members of the Society of Saint Valentine, participated in a startling activity: With great pomp, the members of the society would promenade through the streets of Autun on the mid-February celebration called "fête de la Mère Folle," festival of the crazy mother. This procession, also known since "time immemorial," had at its head "le char de la Mère Folle" ("the cart of the crazy mother"). The custom of parading around in mid-February with this cart survived until the mid-seventeenth century. Then, we are told, P. Eudes, a zealous missionary, "undertook with success the repression of this abuse," apparently meaning the bawdy behavior associated with the parade. "The young people of Autun gave in to his fervent exhortations."[44] They instituted in place of the procession of the crazy mother a service of devotion to the heart of the Virgin Mary.

Was the crazy mother a distant echo of the Great Mother drawn in the cart in the early spring processions of the pre-Christian past? Is this an instance where the goddess was supplanted by a folk figure who became, over the centuries, a focus of derision?[45] Direct answers to these questions are beyond our grasp, but the possibility of a survival and transformation should not be ruled out. Perhaps, in Autun, as in other places, she who had been the Great Mother became, over the course of generations, the crazy mother, and the rituals and beliefs linked to the goddess devolved into the raucous practices surrounding the crazy mother, a figure of ridicule, incorporating traits antithetical to those she had held in the ancient world.[46]

Chapter VI

Metamorphosis: From Goddess to Virgin Mary

The female saints who were substituted for the sowing goddess in the early Middle Ages all had festal days in February and were linked to grain by their iconography or in rituals. Except for Brigid, each saint was the protagonist in a legend that brought her by or around a field at sowing time, a passage that immediately caused a miraculous growth of grain. It is not known at what point these saints were first accepted and acknowledged as sowing protectresses. But one would tend to place the substitution process in the early Middle Ages. Their feasts were recorded in ninth- or tenth-century calendars as occurring during the sowing season and the earliest images of them included some element of grain iconography.

During the centuries of transition from paganism to Christianity, when the Virgin's Grain Miracle legends must have developed, the vast majority of people lived off the land. The few towns were tiny centers of population, each having only a couple hundred inhabitants, most of whom were connected with the life of the surrounding countryside. People depended primarily on their own vegetable produce. Any one of numerous meteorological disasters could destroy the crop and the community would face starvation.[1] In this precarious situation, those who planted would be reluctant to abandon any ceremonial protection of the harvest or any persona envisioned as a crop guardian. As we saw in Chapter IV, farmers would sometimes attempt to re-create, in a more acceptable Christianized form, their earth mother guardian and her ceremonial. This same adaptation process was likewise applied to the Virgin Mary. At some point in the early Middle Ages among certain rural peoples, Mary also took over the role of grain guardian. Peasants fashioned around her a variation of the tale associated with the other female saints, a tale taking place in a rural milieu, cast in a peasant vernacular, and reflecting peasant values and concerns.[2] By the twelfth century, in disparate areas of Europe, a variant of the Grain Miracle legend, featuring the Virgin and Christ child, began to appear in literature as well as in rustic stone sculpture and wall paintings.

The Virgin's Grain Miracle was envisioned as having occurred during the Flight into Egypt, when Herod's soldiers were pursuing the holy family. Because of the implied duration over a long time and the possible variety of spatial settings of the flight, popular imagination invented numerous episodes surrounding it. Apocryphal literature is replete with incidents elaborated around that journey. It is the perfect setting wherein to envision the Virgin passing along or around a grain field, causing a miraculous growth, and protecting human life and well-being by that act. It is impossible to determine when the Virgin was first connected with grain growth, but the wide dispersion of this grain legend when it first appeared in art and literature suggests that the tale had long been a part of popular culture.[3]

Three vernacular poems from the twelfth and thirteenth centuries record a form of the same legend we have already seen attached to the female sowing saints. During the Flight into Egypt, the Virgin, carrying the infant Jesus, passed by a field where a farmer had just begun to plow or sow his seed. The Virgin or child told the sower that if a crowd of soldiers should come seeking the holy family and should ask whether he had seen a mother and child go by, he should say that he saw them go past when he was plowing and sowing the field. The family then passed on by the field. Immediately a miracle occurred: The newly sown seed sprouted instantaneously, grew tall, and was ready to be harvested. Herod's soldiers appeared forthwith and asked the peasant if he had seen a mother and child go by. The peasant was able quite truthfully to say, "Yes, when I first began to sow the seed." Thinking that the peasant must have done his sowing long before, the soldiers abandoned their pursuit. The Virgin's passage produced the miraculous growth, protected the holy family from harm, foiled the forces of evil, and allowed the sower to tell the truth.[4] Though the name of the protectress is changed, the tale is the same as that attached to Radegund, Macrine, Walpurga, and Milburga. It is a disguised vessel intended to preserve traditions and beliefs associated with the topos of the ancient grain goddess.

The twelfth- and thirteenth-century texts and artworks that incorporate the Virgin's Grain Miracle testify to a transformation that had already taken place.[5] The steps of this transformation of the grain protectress into the Virgin are impossible to uncover. When the tale emerges in the twelfth century, however, it appears in several different places, cropping up in France, Ireland, Wales, and Sweden. The extent of this diffusion suggests that the tale had a long history in the oral tradition before these versions were recorded in art and literature.[6]

The legend does not occur in the Gospels, which are quite reticent about Mary. The Flight into Egypt, the episode to which the miracle is attached, is mentioned only tersely in Matthew 2:13, when an angel says to Joseph: "Arise, and take the child and his mother and flee into Egypt . . . for Herod will seek the young child to destroy him." One would expect to find the legend recorded in the New Testament Apocrypha, that compendium of extracanonical writings which embroiders a rich sequence of events around Mary. The Apocrypha recount miracles having to do with her birth, youth, and marriage, and with Christ's Nativity, events surrounding the Flight into Egypt, and details of Mary's mothering of Jesus. But the Virgin's Grain Miracle is absent from the Apocrypha.[7]

In the Middle Ages, however, popular imagination created many more tales revolving around Mary.[8] Many of these medieval tales had a long life before they were committed to writing. Some that were preserved orally went unrecorded until they were documented by folklorists in the eighteenth and nineteenth centuries. But the Virgin's Grain Miracle was recorded as early as the twelfth and thirteenth centuries.

The French Poem

Of the three twelfth- or thirteenth-century vernacular poems containing the Virgin's Grain Miracle, the longest version of the legend is found in a thirteenth-century Old French roman. The Grain Miracle is part of a long narrative poem composed of both canonical and legendary events in the lives of Christ and Mary, events united into one compilation with the Virgin and Christ as "heroine" and "hero."[9] The Grain Miracle is recounted in 178 lines of the poem, found in its earliest form in a manuscript in the Bibliothèque Nationale (MS. Fr. 1533).[10] The vocabulary, structure, and motifs of the poem show that this poeticized account of the Virgin's Grain Miracle is a Christianized version of the sowing goddess topos, and a repository for some of the ceremony formerly associated with the ancient grain protectress.

Though the roman is over five thousand lines long, a syntactically simple poem like this, with repeated formulas, was probably not at first composed as a literary work.[11] Over an unknown number of generations, the tales in the poem were strung together and disseminated orally. By the twelfth or thirteenth century, in the context of burgeoning minstrelsy, the tales were assembled in this "final" poeticized form by a jongleur or by various jongleurs and then set down in writing.[12] The jongleurs fashioned the tales into metrical and rhymed lines, linking the various sections with formulaic expressions.[13] Though individual singers may have determined the way in which the material would be told, they were essentially transmitters of old legends. Each successive raconteur took part in re-creating these works of popular culture.

Little information from the early medieval period remains to explain how the poet-storytellers learned to recast the mythic material they inherited.

They probably served long apprenticeships in the company of poets who had acquired wide repertoires of tales. One recorded instance of how a young poet learned to adapt legend or traditional themes into verse is found in the writings of the early medieval historian Bede, who tells the story of a late seventh-century farmhand, the unlettered singer Caedmon, who developed the art of orally composing narrative verse based on biblical themes. [14] The sacred narratives were read to him by monks; "'he was able to learn by ear [audiendo discere poterat] and, meditating on it as a clean beast chews its cud, he would turn [it] into the sweetest verse and, melodiously re-echoing this, made his teachers in turn his auditors.'" [15] Bede says that Caedmon composed poems based on stories he heard from ecclesiastical sources, but poets also took vernacular legends as sources for their compositions. In some such manner the Grain Miracle tale, as part of the oral vernacular tradition, found its way into medieval poetry or folksong, ultimately to be strung together with other tales into this poeticized thirteenth-century roman. From this perspective, the medieval manuscript recording the Virgin's Grain Miracle can be viewed as a witness to a long oral tradition that, in the case of the French poem, preserves syntactically a glimmer of the metamorphosis of a popular agrarian ceremony surrounding the grain protectress. Though the stages of oral transmission embodying the transformation process are lost, the written text can provide clues to the evolution of the protective goddess figure into the Virgin Mary. [16]

The poet (or poets) who strung together the traditional legends emphasized essential ideas by casting them into formulaic phrases or lines, words frequently repeated under the same metrical conditions. [17] As in so much other orally transmitted medieval poetry, the poem relating the grain legend contains several instances of similar phrases or words appearing under the same metrical conditions ("Vers i predome," "Et i predome," "Dist li predoms," "Quant li predoms," and so on). These "building blocks" or ready-made phrases are used at the beginnings of lines and fit the requirements of octosyllabic meter. Among those repeated phrases are specific references to the Virgin being led around the edge of a field. As the holy family journeys through the countryside, fleeing from Herod:

> Nostre dame s'en est tornée,
> Qui mult estoit espovantée,
> Et vers Egypte s'en aloit,
> Et saint Josep la conduisoit.
> Vers i predome sont venu,
> Qui semoit blé en i heru. [18]

> Our Lady turned around it,
> She who was very frightened,
> And toward Egypt went she,
> And Saint Joseph led her.

> They came toward a husbandman
> Who was sowing wheat in the furrow.

The phrase "Nostre dame s'en est tornée" ("Our Lady turned around it") is repeated twice within and once just before the recitation of the legend. The idea of the Virgin going around the field has become a leitmotif, one of those phrases given special emphasis in the poem both at the beginning of the tale and at the very high point of the miracle, when the growth of the grain protects the holy family from harm.[19] The repetition of the words "Our Lady turned around it" at these crucial places has nothing to do with the story, for the Virgin in this tale is at all times in flight, and as such would not be deviating from a straight course. The poet would have no reason to suggest circumambulation at any of these points. Could the repetition of the phrase "Nostre dame s'en est tornée" be the poet's unwitting preservation of the ancient ceremonial of the female deity going around the field to protect the land and energize the seed?

The structure of the poem provides insights into this question. Most of it is cast in dialogue form. A new speech never begins at the middle of a line, and is set off by an introductory line designating who is to speak. The parts in between the dialogues often read like stage directions and the actions attributed to the personae are simple and straightforward. In fact, the whole of this section of the roman would be easy to act out while the minstrel recited the verses.[20]

The church denounced miming and dramatic song-dance because they were known to harbor elements of pagan rites.[21] Nevertheless, the song-dances and the noncanonical legends persisted, and evolved into pageants and early theater. The passage from ritual to dramatization is a familiar evolutionary process in cultural history, and it is quite possible that the rituals surrounding the grain goddess evolved into dramatizations. From pagan magic to Christian miracle, the ritualized forms surrounding the grain goddess could have developed into mimetic elements accompanied by recitation.[22] Through these means, the early spring preplowing traditions associated with a protectress could be perpetuated.

The miming of the acts of plowing and sowing and of the passage of the protectress must have occurred first at a very early stage in the perpetuation of the topos (that is, during the early Middle Ages). And from the later Middle Ages, we have an account of a pantomime that includes the Virgin's Grain Miracle. The pantomime is described by Enguerran de Monstrelet in his chronicle.[23] Monstrelet, recording events of 1431, describes a wooden scaffolding at the little bridge at the Parisian Portal of Saint Denis. On the scaffolding three men and one woman acted out a combat for the king and his attendants. Along the street near the bridge were "characters who, without speaking, played out the Nativity of Our Lady, her marriage, the Annunciation, the Three Kings, the Innocents, and the good man who was sowing his wheat. And these characters were very well played."[24] This miming of the Grain Miracle legend can be clearly envisioned from the language of the earlier French roman as well. The particular combination of dialogue and simple stage directions in the French poem may reflect an earlier tradition of mimetic action that was attached to the legend and that continued into the fifteenth century.

There is no record of precisely how such mime performances evolved, but an account by the Welsh archdeacon and historian Giraldus Cambrensis (c. 1185) describes an elaborate ritual dance with mimesis. A procession around the cemetery along with song and prostration on the ground was followed by imitation of certain labors, such as plowing, spinning, and shoemaking. Clearly such a ceremony had pagan antecedents.[25] The Virgin's Grain Miracle legend no doubt has similar roots: The dramatic framework within which the legend is cast, the directions for mimetic actions so clearly indicated, the leitmotif of the Virgin being led around the field, the evidence that the legend belonged to the tradition of pantomime—all these facts point to the probability that the thirteenth-century poem reflects an earlier ritual drama, an enactment that supplanted the annual early spring procession of the grain goddess around the field at sowing time.[26]

Just as the goddess passed by or around the field to protect it and ensure a bounteous crop, the legendary passage of Mary by the field at plowing and sowing time not only incited the growth energy of the grain but also protected the plowman, the field, and the holy family from harm. This development from ritual to theater accords with what we know about the early development of drama, and with the mentality of conservative agrarian populations who were naturally reluctant to relinquish old habits.

This is just the type of legend and enactment that would have evolved in the rural ambience. A sower is the hero, or at least the costar, and is the one who has direct contact with the holy personages. The legend is not addressed to courtiers, wealthy landowners, or churchmen, but to the rural peasantry for whom grain cultivation was the major agrarian activity. The language used to recount the legend includes a whole series of words belonging specifically to the vocabulary of medieval grain cultivation: Besides the frequent references to sowing the grain ("semoit blé"), which will become wheat ("forment") we also see references to the plow, the edge of the field, and the numerous processes the wheat passes through before it is ready to be eaten: "meurez," "moisonez," "batuz," "vanez," "fornoiez," "cuis," and finally "mengiez." These terms demonstrate that the tale developed in an agrarian context.[27]

As long as people recalled the pagan antecedent to the Christian legend, it would have been difficult for the tale to become part of official church art or writing. Vestiges of obviously pagan ceremony were roundly denounced, but Christianized versions could survive and spread.[28]

Dreams may have played a major role in the transformation of pagan

deities into their Christian counterparts. There is much evidence from the
Middle Ages to show how dreams influenced daily thought.[29] For medieval
people, the modern analytical dichotomy between imagined perception and
actual event did not apply. History and imagination merged into each other
quite easily, and, furthermore, throughout much of the medieval period the
frontiers between the visible and invisible worlds were obscured. Chronicles
and other works record how phantoms, devils, angels, nameless horsemen,
and various manifestations of the deceased regularly "talked" to the living.[30]
The workings of dreams and imagination on the psyche are graphically
reflected in medieval art.[31]

It is possible that the substitution of Mary for the grain goddess was
influenced by dreams, such as those recorded reveries in which gospel
figures regularly became part of the peasants' environment, spoke their
language, and filled roles of protection and guardianship.[32] In the case of the
Grain Miracle legend, the product of the imagined perception or dream
attached itself to the Flight into Egypt, an authentic Gospel event, and thus
to a "true" story. Connected to such a story, the topos of the grain protectress in the form of the Virgin Mary could be perpetuated.[33] Once the
legend embodying the transformation emerged, it was kept alive orally until
minstrelsy began to embellish it in the twelfth and thirteenth centuries. At
some point the legend was fashioned into this particular versification
and strung together with the other apocryphal legends, all to be handed
down until the poem was committed to writing at the end of the thirteenth
century.

Some of the twelfth- and thirteenth-century embellishments of the Grain
Miracle are easily detectable in the French poem. For instance, the French
minstrel decided to elaborate on the character of the sower by conflating him
with Amadour, an Egyptian-born Gallic saint, whose "intact" body had
been "discovered" in 1166 in front of the chapel of the Virgin at Roc-
Amadour. The event was first recorded in 1183 in the chronicle of Robert of
Torigny.[34] After the discovery, the body was exposed to public view and,
Robert tells us, many miracles were accomplished at that site by the Virgin
Mary. The chronicler goes on to give the saint's very sparse history, which
includes only the statements that Amadour was Mary's servant as well as the
carrier and nurturer of Christ, and that after Mary's assumption Amadour
came to Gaul and lived the life of a hermit there.[35] The site Roc-Amadour
became a popular twelfth- and thirteenth-century pilgrimage spot. Even this
scant information about Amadour apparently attracted the attention of the
anonymous minstrel, and he conflated the persona of the sower with Saint
Amadour. He composed a transitional section in the poem in which the
sower, recognizing that a miracle had taken place when the grain grew
swiftly, left home and family to become the servant of Mary and Christ. The
poet recounts how, following in the steps of the donkey, the sower/Amadour
kissed its footprints. "All for the love of the maiden, / who nursed God at

her breast." He offers to be their servant, is taught the doctrine by Christ, and, for the love of the Virgin, he sings masses every day, a point the poet repeats several times.[36] The poet at last identifies the servant as Amadour and concludes, "There are many people who have seen / His arm and his rib completely nude"—an allusion to the body that had been exposed after its discovery "intact" in 1166.

Amadour's part in the poem's development illuminates how the minstrels worked. On the one hand they transformed legends to accord with their own time. They also took a legend, whether old or new, and preserved its important aspects by placing key elements at appropriate spots and repeating them for emphasis. Just as in the Grain Miracle verses, in the Amadour verses the poet transmitted words and repeated phrases that allow us to visualize the most important acts in the legend. By emphasizing the Virgin's act of turning around the field at the time of plowing and seeding, the singer has unknowingly preserved for us the ancient ceremonial of the grain goddess who for so many centuries had been honored as the protectress of the grain at sowing time and, by extension, as the protectress of life. Here she is placed in a new mythic construct, but her purpose and meaning live on.

Early Welsh Legend

The Welsh verses recounting the Grain Miracle are part of a poem recorded in the "Black Book of Carmarthen," a late twelfth-century manuscript that contains some of the oldest Welsh poetry.[37] Though poetry in the Welsh language was composed as early as the sixth century, none of the manuscripts that record it is older than the twelfth century.[38] Therefore, the poems in the "Black Book of Carmarthen" could have been composed at various times before the thirteenth century. Since scholars agree that early Welsh poetry had been transmitted orally before it was written down, the early Welsh version of the Grain Miracle, like the French poem, probably had a long life in the oral tradition.[39]

The poem incorporating the Grain Miracle in the "Black Book of Carmarthen" is an amalgam of panegyric and religious narrative. The first six lines belong to the ancient tradition of praising the kings and the nobility, a tradition that had long flourished in the early Celtic societies of Gaul and Ireland.[40] After the first six lines the poet addresses the blessed God to whom he sings this sacred song. Following this, there is an evocation of the Last Judgment, and then verses on penitence, praise of God, the submission of Job, and the story of Eve not respecting God's commandment concerning the apple tree. Forty-seven lines into the poem, the poet begins to recount what he calls the miracle of the instantaneous grain harvest. Either Mary or Christ is the protagonist of the first few lines (48–51); the text could be read either way and the translators give opposite readings.[41] She (he) wished to avoid being captured, and fled by a field where there was a plowman, plowing the ground. Then Mary, described as "faultless" and "wisely gifted," along with the "Trinity of Heaven"—again the text is unclear—said: "My good man, a crowd of men will come after us seeking our resting place and in haste will ask thee, 'Hast thou seen a woman with an infant son?' And do then tell them the manifest truth . . . that thou didst see us going past it, this field. . . ."[42] The tale is abbreviated; presumably the poet's audience knew it well. Though the poet does not say that the plowman was seeding, it seems that the grain grew immediately, for when the pursuing host asks, "'Hast thou, my fine fellow, seen people going past thee without stopping?'" the plowman says, "'Yes, when I burrowed this open meadow which you see being reaped.' And the children of Cain then turned back from the reaper, through the prayer of Mary Maria . . . for the Holy Ghost and the purity that was in her were her protection."[43]

The text is ambiguous. In the first part, one can accord the major role in accomplishing the miracle to either the Virgin or Christ. However, the last lines of the poem are unequivocal. It was the "purity" and "prayers" of the "faultless . . . wisely gifted" Mary Maria, through the Holy Spirit, that protected them.

To date, this Welsh version is the earliest preserved written account of the Grain Miracle. In a departure from the French Poem, Joseph is accorded no role in this legend and the plowman is plowing and harrowing, but not "seeding." The crop has grown instantaneously without the seed's having been sown, a miracle all the more stunning. But on a more profound level, the poet's omission of the seeding process may have a deeper meaning. Perhaps he is alluding symbolically to the immaculate conception, the fact that Christ too was engendered without "seed." If that is the intention of the poet, this is among the earliest texts to evoke that aspect of Mariological doctrine.

The Irish Poem and Celtic Connections

A version of the Grain Miracle recorded a little later than the twelfth-century Welsh text is found in a thirteenth-century Irish religious poem known by its first words, "Fuighell bennacht brú Mhuire" ("An outcome of blessings is Mary's womb").[44] Ascribed to Gilla Brighde Mac ConMidhe, the poem contains various canonical and apocryphal episodes from the life of the Virgin, including the Massacre of the Innocents, the Flight into Egypt, and the Miracle of the Palm Tree. The brief account of the Grain Miracle is given in verses 27 through 29:[45]

Being pursued, borne on Mary's back, the Son wrought a marvel,
    beside a great meadow (it was miraculous) sown with fine tender
    grains of wheat.

> A man tells that he had seen them through [word illegible]
>   while he was tilling it; that day, in the prints of their soles,
>   grows up by its ear and its haulm.
> Then there came through the ploughland the men of Herod of
>   heathen worship; though it was sudden, folk were reaping it
>   throughout the crop of the ploughland all at once. [46]

Even though the Irish version preserves the essence of the legend, there are several differences between this and the other versions. Unlike the French and Welsh versions that came out of minstrelsy or court poetry, this poem is decidedly religious. The ambivalence inherent in the early Welsh text as to who performed the miracle is not apparent in the Irish version. Though Jesus is a babe in arms, the miracle is attributed to him. The instances of this attribution reflect the early medieval church's reluctance to incorporate into Christian texts reflections of the powers attributed to female figures. [47] The church had ignored, or had tried to suppress, people's enduring attachment to a female component in divinity, or to female powers, especially those associated with vegetal growth and the land. And though in the majority of folkloric and other orally transmitted accounts the Virgin performs the miracle, when the legend was written down within the clerical context, as is the case with this Irish poem, Christ is sometimes substituted as the miracle worker.

These Irish verses are at variance with the French and Welsh versions in still other significant ways. Nowhere else, for instance, is Mary pictured as carrying the child on her back, though the text of the Gospels would not preclude this image. The image probably reflects the way an Irish peasant woman would transport her child over long distances. Moreover, in the Irish version the farmer is tilling and the field has been sown. Thus, the Virgin passes by a field that has already been planted. Two further contradictions are apparent within the text. The poet indicates that the grain grew up "in the prints of their soles," though only Mary's soles could have touched the ground. And, though the wheat grew up only in footprints, "folk were reaping it throughout the crop of the ploughland."

It is probable, therefore, that the poet took liberties with the legend as he knew it. He not only made it more solidly Christological; he also changed the story slightly to suit his poetic purposes. Yet in spite of the contradictions and deviations, the core of the legend remains intact. The mother and child pass by, or through, a wheat field, and a miraculous growth occurs. Thus, soon after the Welsh version, and probably contemporaneous with the French, this Irish text sketches the story of the fleeing mother and child, the pursuing forces of evil, the plowman's truthful words, and the Grain Miracle.

Since the three earliest extant literary renditions of the legend are in Welsh and Irish, that is, in Celtic tongues, and in thirteenth-century French (originating in an area where Celtic ceased to be spoken in rural sections only in the fifth and sixth centuries A.D.), one wonders if this "Celtic connection" points to anything significant about the early oral transmission of the legend. Could it have been formulated and transmitted among peoples of Celtic culture during the early Middle Ages, before the disparate national languages evolved? The disappearance of Celtic was a long-delayed process: Though not favored by the educated classes, it was kept alive in rural areas possibly as late as the sixth century.[48] Significantly, almost all of the Celtic words that survive in French pertain to rural life. As shown above, rural peoples who adhered to old ways are the most likely candidates to have fashioned the Grain Miracle legend. Could the tale have been formulated in a Celtic dialect, remained a part of the rural continental Celtic-speaking culture, and been transmitted during those centuries of cultural syncretism, when people of the originally Celtic cultures of France, Wales, and Ireland still spoke or understood each other's dialects?

Because a tantalizingly wide chronological gap exists between the textual account of the procession into the fields in honor of the grain goddess, recorded by Gregory of Tours, and the first textual or visual appearance of the legend in the twelfth and thirteenth centuries, these questions can probably never be firmly resolved. However, early contacts between Gaul, Wales, and Ireland are well attested; missionaries and merchants traveled back and forth during the fifth through the eighth centuries.[49] The work of the Gallic missionaries made a great impression on the Welsh countryside during the period of transition and syncretism.[50] Inscriptions on the earliest Christian memorial stones in Wales, dating from between 450 and 650, reveal that the Gallic immigrants into Wales were from the Lyon and Vienne areas of Gaul, the same region where the mother goddess was being combatted during the fourth and fifth centuries.[51] There was, in fact, a sustained evangelizing effort directed from Gaul to Wales.[52] Thus the Gallic merchants and "peregrini" (travelers) going to Wales and Ireland just after the time of Saint Martin could have brought with them tales and other elements of the newly syncretized culture.

Though such links are possible, they elude proof. In spite of the great lacunae in the surviving evidence, if one were permitted to suggest a theory of what might have happened, one would be tempted to propose the following: Within the Celtic (Gallic) peasant milieu described by Sulpicius Severus, Gregory of Tours, Eligius, and others, a legend arose in response to the church's suppression of the cult of the grain goddess. This legend told how the passage of the Virgin Mary (or a local female saint) at plowing and sowing time incited the growth energy of the grain, thereby protecting both human and divine life. In the still-Celtic-speaking rural milieu, the goddess on her circuit around the field was recast as a figure who was likewise envisioned going around the newly harrowed ground to protect the field and serve as the catalyst for the seed's growth. The tale, though formulated in an early Celtic dialect, eventually became part of that store of legendary material later tapped by the twelfth- and thirteenth-century poets of Wales, Ireland, and France.[53]

The Fourteenth-Century Play

The fourteenth century witnessed the burgeoning popularity and lively evolution of the Grain Miracle legend. In literature and art, new embellishments enriched the tale. Its wider appearance in materials such as embroidered textiles and costly ivory testifies to a growing acceptance of the story by the church and the aristocracy. The story continued to be popular among the masses as well, for in the fourteenth century we have the first documented evidence that it became part of popular vernacular theater.

The play that incorporates the miracle is entitled "Le Geu des Trois Roys" ("The Play of the Three Kings") and is dated to the early or mid-fourteenth century.[54] No doubt those who created this play were familiar with a version of the thirteenth-century French poem previously discussed; some of the language and incidents in the play are derived from that poem. But the play and the cycle in which it is found depend on another source: liturgical drama, specifically plays that relate the Nativity Cycle, and in particular a Latin play of the Three Kings. Thus, the legend that grew up in the popular agrarian milieu as a substitution for the grain goddess ritual was incorporated into a dramatization of the Gospel.

Peasant ritual practices, which evolved into folk festivals, legends, and vernacular dramatic dialogues, are known only through scant documentation. On the other hand ecclesiastical dramatized rituals, developing out of the service books and liturgy, have survived in textual form. The earliest church dramas grew out of the responses from the Vulgate or service book (as in the case of the passion play) or out of the antiphones and psalms sung in the Officium of Introit at the beginning of mass. The sung liturgical responses formed the earliest dialogues for the scenes. The words and music of these dialogues are known as tropes.[55] It is these chanted dialogues that eventually developed into church-sponsored liturgical drama.[56]

Sometimes these dramas became major ecclesiastical pageants.[57] One of the most important of these pageants cum dramas was a play about the Adoration of the Magi called "Tres Reges," "Magi," "Herodes," or "Stella." Existing in a large number of different but related forms, it was probably complete as a Latin liturgical play by the eleventh century.[58] The major episode, the Magi moving toward the star, would be acted out in the church, usually with monks or nuns playing the parts and the words of the Gospel or service books as dialogue. Though the core of the play involved just the kings, the star, and the adoration itself, other elements were gradually absorbed: the dramatizations of the interview with Herod, the Massacre of the Innocents, the plaint of Rachel, the Flight into Egypt, and the destruction of Herod.[59]

Religious Latin plays like "Tres Reges" set a model for vernacular dramatic composition. At about the time that the French roman incorporating the Grain Miracle was evolving into its "theatrical" form, religious plays in the French vernacular were also beginning to take shape. Some, like "Le Jeu d'Adam," exhibit a freedom of dialogue and a psychological subtlety that imply that they remained rather independent of the ecclesiastical tradition. Others stayed rigidly within the church context. One of the earliest surviving vernacular religious dramas, based on the Three Kings story, is a fragmentary play, "Reyes Magos," in Old Castilian.[60] We do not know whether it was actually staged, but the language exhibits a liveliness uncharacteristic of the Latin version.

The vernacular plays gained in popularity.[61] Some were performed outdoors, where the restrictions of the church building would not inhibit the staging, and where the plays might develop more freely and naturalistically;[62] audiences thus came to expect an enrichment of scope and content as well as more human-interest scenes. By the fourteenth century, the vernacular Gospel-based dramas were embellished with material from the Prophets and the Apocrypha, and, especially in France, with stories from long narrative poems. These additions were often made with an eye to pleasing the common people.

In this environment, sometime in the early fourteenth century, the grain legend was added to a vernacular dramatization of the Three Kings story which had evolved from ecclesiastical drama and had moved outside as it were, accommodating popular tastes and incorporating popular legends. Up to this time, neither the Latin dramas nor the surviving scenes of the Old Castilian "Reyes Magos" had contained the legend of the Grain Miracle. But by the fourteenth century, the Grain Miracle had become recognized and accepted in both church- and lay-sponsored art. Unlike in the contemporary pictorial tradition, the Virgin in the fourteenth-century dramatization did not have a leading role. New material was added to elaborate the character of the humble sower, who was most like members of the audience.

The main scenes in "Le Geu des Trois Roys" include the Adoration of the Magi, the Massacre of the Innocents, and the Flight into Egypt with the accompanying Grain Miracle. Scenes of the Grain Miracle are interspersed among others to heighten spectators' interest and create suspense. In successive short scenes the sower gets the ground ready and Herod angrily sends out his soldiers to find the Magi. Then the sower begins to plant his seed, and he appears to remain on stage sowing throughout much of the succeeding action until Joseph, leading a mule carrying Mary and the child, addresses him and asks the way to Egypt.[63]

Many of the words in the dialogue reveal that the playwright was familiar with some form of the thirteenth-century French roman. However, the legend as presented in the play differs in one important respect from the roman and from all other known versions as well. Joseph, who is the only member of the holy family to speak to the sower, asks him to lie. Joseph says, "If you see anyone pass by, could you tell him that you saw no one come by this way." The sower, in a neighborly fashion, obligingly agrees. When the miraculous growth takes place and the grain is ready to be harvested, the sower is able to tell the truth, and to tell the pursuing soldier that he has seen no one go by since he sowed his grain. It was the sower himself in this version, who, with the aid of the miracle, was able to figure out a way not to lie.

Though critics have seen Joseph's speech as a mistake of the playwright, this is the kind of "mistake" that illuminates the tenor of the times. Since vernacular plays such as this were no longer under the direction of churchmen, the playwrights, though they knew the traditional stories, were not necessarily well versed in doctrine or the Bible.[64] An egregious error such as a saint's asking a peasant to lie could pass uncorrected, especially if the peasant ultimately avoided lying. In view of the fact that the audience to be pleased was composed mostly of lay peasants, the playwright sought to expand the role and the value of the humble sower. He gave him a rather substantial part and had him voice topical maxims. In fact, the sower became the focus of a particular form of class consciousness. He makes his entrance as the three kings depart. A humble laborer, he serves as a contrast to the kings' profligacy and riches. Though sociable and helpful, he was interested not only in the holy family and Herod's soldiers, but also in feeding himself and his family, and his speech is speckled with proverbs to that effect: "He who wants to eat must work"; "One must do his duty"; "God helps those who help themselves." The speeches of the sower echo the spirit of a hardworking, dutiful farmer. In this fourteenth-century version of the legend, the sower is no longer Amadour, the famous Gallic saint, but an unpretentious figure who personifies the virtue of industriousness.[65]

The socioeconomic consciousness that informs the sentiments of the sower gives a new twist to the legend, for in this version a poor but diligent laborer is not only intimately connected to a great miracle, but also speaks directly to the holy family. No doubt this new slant increased the scene's appeal for the largely common audience. The character and actions of the sower, who was on stage so much of the time, were points of identification for a goodly portion of the viewers, and linked those who were continuously involved in similar kinds of everyday tasks to the dramatic action of the play.

This image of the humble but industrious farmer was very much in the air in the fourteenth century. Individual reformers within the church made an effort to reach out to peasants and "elevate" their spiritual status through education.[66] Treatises written in the vernacular were directed with an air of respect to farm laborers. The treatises contained precisely the language the sower uses: Love thy neighbor, do thy duty, God helps those who help themselves.[67] This respectful perspective on the peasant was to give impetus to the growing interest in peasant life. It is, perhaps, for this reason that the Grain Miracle grew in popularity in the visual arts and the role of the sower became so important that the humble laborer hardly ever left the stage.

In contrast to the emphasis on the Virgin in contemporary artwork depicting the Grain Miracle, Mary plays hardly any role in the theatrical version. We can surmise from one of Joseph's speeches that she is mounted on a donkey, and holding her child before her, but it is Joseph who speaks to the sower, and there is no sense of the Virgin's having a hand in accomplishing the miracle. The motif of the female presence encouraging the grain's growth has been completely obscured. No longer is there a refrain to emphasize her turning around. Her movements were relegated to stage directions.[68] It is through the sower (and probably also through some theatrical device) that we learn of the miracle.[69] It is the sower's truthful response to the soldiers that deters them from further pursuit. Though the Virgin has passed by, and a miracle has occurred, nothing in this play links the two events.

The Flemish Carol

One last textual bearer of the Grain Miracle tale which deserves some attention is an early Flemish carol known by its first line, "Alle enghelen van hemelrike," "All the angels of Heaven."[70] The folklorist who published it in the nineteenth century had uncovered this version in a manuscript dated not later than 1431; it falls into the last part of the Middle Ages. After one introductory verse and a refrain dedicated to Jesus, the account of the Grain Miracle in nine verses comprises the remainder of the song.

The story follows quite closely the scenes and the order of "Le Geu Des Trois Roys": Herod's decision to slay the innocents, the holy family's departure, their encounter with the sower, and so on. As in the play, the lines are arranged as stage directions and dialogue, and it is possible to envision the carol being acted out. The sower in the carol, however, is not instructed to lie as he was in the play. When Herod questions him about the Virgin's passage he can say quite truthfully that he saw a young woman go by when he was sowing what he is now harvesting.[71]

The carol devotes a good deal more attention to Mary than does the play. For instance, the discourse with the sower is not specifically attributed to Joseph; it could just as well have been spoken by Mary. It is specifically Mary that Herod is seeking, she alone that he asks for, and she that the sower affirms had long since passed. Though the refrain of the carol centers on Jesus, the stanzas of the song center on Mary.

Another Marian detail in the carol is worth pointing out, for it relates to Flemish visual iconography: When Herod asks about the Virgin's passage he designates her as the young woman wearing the white cloak. When the

sower responds to Herod he describes her in the same way: "joncfrou . . . mit witten habijt." In most late medieval pictorial representations
of the Virgin on the Flight into Egypt she wears her typical blue cloak. In
this carol, however, her cloak is specifically white. Could the unusual use of
the color white here be related to the theme of the Virgin's purity, which is
alluded to in other versions of the miracle?[72] Preplanting ceremonies nearly
always involved purifying the land, thereby preparing it to receive the new
seed.[73] Does the allusion to the Virgin's white cloak again evoke that age-old
link between the condition of women and the condition of the land? Though
rare, the idea of the Virgin of the Grain Miracle wearing a white cloak was
known in Flanders. There are a few unique pictorial renditions of the Grain
iracle from the late fifteenth and early sixteenth centuries wherein the painter
deviated from the normal use of the color blue for the Virgin's cloak and
painted her instead in white or white tinged with blue (figure 58).

Chapter VII

The Grain Miracle in Medieval Art

Many generations transpired between the centuries of conversion, when the Christianized adaptations of the Grain Miracle evolved, and the twelfth and thirteenth centuries, when those adaptations were first written down. Even before these texts appeared, Mary's Grain Miracle had also been depicted in works of art. The earliest known artistic renderings, executed in the first quarter of the twelfth century, are found on three baptismal fonts from the island of Gotland, in present-day Sweden (figures 39–43). That the earliest art-historical examples appeared in the newly Christianized north, while the first literary examples came from Wales, France, and Ireland, testifies to the wide dissemination of the legend and its extensive life in the oral tradition prior to being set down in tangible form.

The fonts are the work of a sculptor who signed his name, in runic letters, Hegwaldr.[1] The Grain Miracle, part of the elaborate sculpted decor on the fonts' tubs, is depicted emblematically as a sword-bearing soldier standing before a peasant reaping wheat (figure 41). It is included as part of the Nativity Cycle, appearing between the Massacre of the Innocents (represented by the beheaded child on the extreme right of figure 42) and the Flight into Egypt (Mary and Christ on the donkey, with Joseph leading, figure 42).

Master Hegwaldr was one of the earliest Christian sculptors in Scandinavia. Christianity had been brought there only a few decades earlier.[2] Both his sculptural style and the ways he interpreted the Christian scenes in his models demonstrate that he was a transitional artist. The dragons' forms that populated northern pre-Christian sculpture retain a prominent place in Hegwaldr's work (figures 39, 40). Monsters' heads—their hair twisted and interlaced or terminating in locks called *ringericke* lobes—grip quadrupeds

Figure 39. Baptismal font from När, sculpted by Hegwaldr. Soldier accosting a sower (not visible here) reaping his wheat (see figure 42). From left to right: An infant beheaded from the Massacre of the Innocents; Saint Stephen with the Roasted Cock; Herodias, Herod, and John the Baptist. Early twelfth century. From Når, Gotland.

in their gaping jaws. Hegwaldr's sculpted ornament is part of the metamorphic world of Nordic design in which animal hair twists into plaitwork (figure 40), and stone arches become dragon heads (figure 43).

Hegwaldr's handling of the human figure is likewise reminiscent of his pre-Christian forebears. Like the makers of the Viking Gotlandic picture stones, Hegwaldr was mainly concerned with telling the story.[3] His figures usually have large hands, feet, and heads, all of which are always shown frontally or in profile, never in three-quarter view. The figures gesticulate

Figures 40 and 41. Baptismal font sculpted by Hegwaldr. Flight into Egypt (extreme left) and detail of Herod's soldier before the sower, who cuts his wheat. From Ganthem, Gotland.

Figure 42. Drawing of scenes on baptismal font sculpted by Hegwaldr. När.

emphatically, and often one person's hand motions parallel those of another, thereby directing the viewer's attention to important visual points (figure 39). Hegwaldr had no interest in spatial depth and usually filled up most of the surface area. He showed no concern for anatomy, but unlike most of his pre-Christian Scandinavian predecessors he did include facial features.

Though the styles of the pagan north clearly informed his sculpture, Hegwaldr was working with a whole new iconography, an iconography that propounded a completely different message about the origins and meaning of the universe: The world was created by the God of Genesis, not by the various creation deities of Teutonic tradition, and God's son was born into this world for the eternal salvation of man's soul. The baptismal font was the means by which people could avail themselves of the promised salvation through Christ. The fiendish beasts of the pedestal represented the diabolical powers ready to overcome weak human souls, and the tub's biblical scenes (Genesis, the Nativity, and Christ's Passion) imbued the baptismal waters with the sacred powers of salvation.

Most of the scenes sculpted by Hegwaldr came directly from Scripture, and his figurative models were drawn from illustrated Gospels from monastic centers in northwest Germany. [4] However, among the many dozens of scenes executed on Hegwaldr's fonts, two do not occur in any known ecclesiastical source. One is the Grain Miracle (figures 40 – 42). Between the scenes of the Flight into Egypt and the Massacre of the Innocents, Herod's soldier stands before the sower, who has just cut or is about to cut some tall stalks of grain. In the baptismal font from Nar (figure 42), two temporal sequences are included in one scene; the soldier's raised sword serves both to threaten the sower and to cut off the head of the innocent to his right.

The other extracanonical, Nativity-related legend depicted on the fonts is Saint Stephen and the roasted cock (figures 39, 43). A discussion of the Stephen tale (which occurs two out of the three times that the Grain Miracle is depicted) illuminates the meaning of the Grain Miracle in Scandinavia and provides another example of how Christian figures and stories came to be substituted for old pagan paradigms. According to the Acts of the Apostles (chapters 6 and 7), Stephen was one of seven deacons appointed by the apostles to look after the distribution of alms to the faithful. Because it was alleged that he had made blasphemous statements, he was brought before the council. There he spoke of seeing in the sky the "Son of Man standing at the right hand of God," and he was subsequently stoned to death, with Saul (the later Paul) looking on as witness. From the fourth century on, his saint's day was commemorated in the West on December 26.

In the newly converted Scandinavian countries, the story of Stephen's life and death as told in Acts was greatly transformed. A new story was created, a story that, we shall see, must have incorporated elements formerly attached to pre-Christian Scandinavian figures venerated at the time of Saint Stephen's Day, that is to say, at the winter solstice. Though the local northern

Figure 43. The cock, Herodias, Herod, and Saint Stephen. Baptismal font at Stänge. Hegwaldr.

legend of Stephen was depicted in art during the early decades of conversion in Scandinavia, it did not surface in written form until it appeared in a fifteenth-century English manuscript.[5] The same motifs seen on Hegwaldr's font are present in the various versions of the ballad: It is December 25, the eve of Saint Stephen's Day, and Herod and Herodias are at a table feasting (figures 39, 43). Stephen, who is called in various versions a stable groom, coachman, and serving clerk of Herod, is either watering horses (in the ballad and Dädesjö painting discussed below), or bringing into the hall a boar's head for the Yuletide festivities of Herod and Herodias. Stephen sees the star of Bethlehem, casts down the boar's head, and tells Herod that a child "in Bedlem born / is better than we all." Herod does not believe his tale and says, "If these words be true, let this roasted cock spring up alive and crow." The roasted cock comes back to life and cries out, "Christus natus est." Herod calls upon his torturer to have Stephen stoned to death. Of all the events in this story, only the means of death accords with the account in Acts.

Why did the Scandinavian people change Saint Stephen from a deacon to a stable groom? This equestrian role is clear from both the language of the ballads and Stephen's depiction on the fonts, where he wears the belted tunic of the laborer rather than the dalmatic of the deacon or saint (figures 39, 43). The transformations in Stephen's persona reflect significant aspects of Nordic pre-Christian culture and suggest the possibility that Saint Stephen was amalgamated with a northern pre-Christian deity. His saint's day, December 26, coincided with the time of year when, in the pre-Christian era, there were horse races, dedicated to the deities Frey and Freya.[6] In Scandinavia and England Stephen became the patron saint of horses, and his day was celebrated throughout the northern countries; later, in England, it was a day when horses would be raced as fast as possible and then watered and bled. The tradition that links Stephen to horses was confined to Sweden, Denmark, and England.

It is also instructive that Stephen serves a boar's head to a feasting Herod and Herodias. From early on the boar was sacred to Frey and especially to Freya.[7] At the winter solstice feast Frey and Freya would be offered a boar's head. Stephen's association with horses, a boar's head, and a major banquet, and the fact that Saint Stephen's Day fell on a winter solstice festal day formerly dedicated to the Nordic divinities Frey and Freya, all make it probable that Saint Stephen was the successor to those Germanic deities.

Textual sources reveal that Frey and Freya were deities of peaceful relations, fecundity, and prosperity.[8] Intriguingly, they were conceived of as traveling in a cart drawn by oxen over the countryside to render the land, crops, and animals fertile and prosperous.[9] Though Freya in one saga is accompanied by her husband-brother Frey, scholars hypothesize that Frey is merely a later masculine substitute for an original mother goddess figure.[10]

The Nordic sagas contain few references to the cult of the goddess Freya. Whereas female deities were more prominent in earlier centuries, the cult of Freya was antiquated by the time our textual sources were being written; by then male Nordic deities had assumed primary importance. For instance, though Freya is one of the only goddesses mentioned in Old Norse texts, Tacitus, more than a millennium earlier, made several references to the worship of goddesses in Germania. One of the goddesses Tacitus mentions, Nerthus, is very much like Freya. Nerthus, Freya, and the other earth mother goddesses mentioned in this book, all journey across the land in order to render it more fertile. Though the time of Freya's journey over the lands was not specified, it probably took place at the beginning of winter, with the solstice banquet as its finale. The boar was the animal most closely associated with Freya.[11] As we saw in Chapter I, the boar or pig was also the animal most intimately connected with the worship of the mother goddess of fertility throughout the Mediterranean. This was the case in the north as well, where the boar was worn as a protective sign by tribes who venerated the mother goddess.[12]

Thus, Stephen's entrance with a boar's head at Herod's banquet can now be understood in all its complexity: In Scandinavia, Saint Stephen, whose saint's day was December 26, took on attributes associated with northern pre-Christian figures venerated at the winter solstice, a celebration that, in the eleventh and twelfth centuries, was syncretized with the festival of Christmas. The legend and font, both originating from the time when Scandinavian tribes were converting to Christianity, evoke the pre-Christian world of the solstice feast, the horse races, and the boar's head dedicated to

Figure 44. Ceiling painting, church at Dädesjö. The Massacre of the Innocents, the Flight into Egypt and the Grain Miracle (top register); Stephen as groom, Stephen at Herod's Feast and the Stoning of Saint Stephen (bottom register).

the mother goddess. And Stephen, because his saint's day was at the time of Freya's feast, was accorded the attributes of the horses and Freya's boar's head, and as such he became part of the Christmastime celebration, which perpetuated some of the old pagan forms in new Christian attire.

But what of the tale of the roasted cock that sprang up and crowed? A story of a revivified cock is known from many places on the Continent as early as the twelfth century. [13] The episode was a part of the apocryphal lives of Peter and James, as well as of Judas. [14] But only in Scandinavia and England is the revivified cock attached to the story of Saint Stephen, and here it is given a very special meaning. Since Herod tied Christ's birth to the resurrection of the cock, the roast bird's sudden resuscitation indicates that what the cock told Stephen is correct: "Christ is born." The miracle of the revivified cock shows that a savior was born whose birth promised human-kind a rebirth of the spirit and eternal life for the soul. As in the legend of the miraculous growth of grain, so in the resurrection of the roasted cock, miraculous revival of life—plant or animal—is the salient theme. [15] Both stories parallel the miracle of Christ's birth and the possible miracle that can occur for every person baptized with the waters of the font: He or she too can await the resurrection to eternal life.

The linkage of the Grain Miracle with the Saint Stephen legend continued in the visual repertoire of Scandinavia. A later Swedish example gives a more detailed depiction of both legends. The small church in Dädesjö has a wooden ceiling elaborately decorated with painted roundels containing scenes from the New Testament (figure 44). [16] Stylistically, the ceiling appears to have been painted in the mid-thirteenth century and was influenced by the fluid Gothic style current at that time in Paris. [17] In several of the roundels, there are graphic depictions of both the Grain Miracle and the Saint Stephen story. Though the initial reason for the linkage of the Grain Miracle with the Saint Stephen legend may no longer have been understood by the artist or the viewer, the two stories were still placed together. A folksong first transcribed six hundred years later was to perpetuate this linkage. [18]

Both extracanonical parts of the Stephen story—his position as groom and his appearance before Herod's table—are illustrated on the Dädesjö ceiling (bottom register, figure 44). In one roundel Stephen is watering two horses at a stream; one horse drinks while the other looks up at the star of Bethlehem. In the next roundel Stephen stands before the table of Herod, who points to a cock on a dish. In the final scene Stephen is being stoned by three men.

The Grain Miracle (top register, figure 44) is depicted in a row of roundels contiguous to that relating to Stephen's story. In the first roundel Mary and Joseph approach the sower, who, with seed bag slung over his left shoulder, has just sown a handful of seeds. In the next roundel two soldiers on horseback approach the sower. He now has a sickle in one hand and wheat stalks in the other. A woman, harvesting with him, continues working with her sickle, her back to the soldiers. This inclusion of the harvesting woman is unique in medieval renderings of the scene.

Though the iconography of the Dädesjö ceiling is specifically northern, the style is very much influenced by the painting of thirteenth-century France, the area from which most of the Grain Miracle depictions survive. The tale, however, did not surface in the French visual repertoire until the late twelfth and early thirteenth centuries. This is because during the Romanesque era the visual arts were dominated by iconographic themes derived from the Old Testament and the Apocalypse. But during the late twelfth and early thirteenth centuries, a new iconography began to develop. Marian themes in particular came to play an ever larger role. Most of the Marian artworks centered around her early life and the infancy of Christ.

During the twelfth century, artists treated the Virgin Mary with awesome respect. By the early thirteenth century, she was interpreted less majestically and with more gentleness. Whereas the typical Romanesque Virgin had been depicted as a queen, seated and rigid, holding the Christ child frontally before her, in the Gothic period, Mary's form and features embodied motherly tenderness. [19] Both of these interpretations of the Virgin are present in the cycle of illustrations that contains the first known appearance of the Grain Miracle in pictorial art in France, the Infancy Cycle in the village church of Asnières-sur-Vègre. [20]

During the late Romanesque period, the brilliant art of stained glass grew dominant while mural painting became less important and decreased in

Figure 45. Mural painting, north wall of church at Asnières-sur-Vègre, France. Presentation of Christ in the Temple, Grain Miracle, Flight into Egypt.

Figure 46. Mural painting, church at Asnières-sur-Vègre, France. Adoration of the Magi.

quality. The great artists of the period worked in the large urban centers designing cartoons for windows or painting the glass itself. Many a small village church, however, still received a painted decor, and that decor, though rustic, was often influenced by the stylistic attributes of stained glass. Such was the case with the chapel at Asnières-sur-Vègre, where all of the walls, including those of the choir, were covered with episodes from the lives of Christ and the Virgin.

The Infancy Cycle, wherein the Grain Miracle is found, decorates the north wall of the church (figures 45–48). The cycle originally began with

Figure 47. Mural painting, church at Asnières-sur-Vègre, France. Purification of the Virgin, Presentation of Christ in the Temple.

Figure 48. Mural painting, church at Asnières-sur-Vègre, France. Grain Miracle and Flight into Egypt.

scenes from the life of the Virgin, such as the Annunciation and the Nativity. But the paintings on the westernmost part of the north wall have been destroyed, so the cycle begins with the Adoration of the Magi (figure 46). A haloed "Madonna in majesty" faces us. She wears the same crown as the kings, and beneath the crown is a veil. She sits on a monumental throne and is clothed in an ermine-lined cape. She holds the Christ child, who is turned to the left to receive the approaching Magi. Except for the profile view of the child, the scene has more of a Romanesque than a Gothic presence. The Virgin has that stately appearance more typical of earlier works, but the static quality that derives from the dark lines surrounding figures and features recalls thirteenth-century stained-glass work, in which malleable lead ribbons surround each different color in the windows.

Immediately to the right of the Adoration is a scene that conflates the Purification of the Virgin with the Presentation of the Christ child in the Temple (figure 47). The old man Simeon stands at the far right next to the altar. He receives the infant from the hands of his mother. The Virgin is followed by two companions, one holding three candles and a circular object, the other holding the offering of doves in a basket. Thirty-three days after the birth of Jesus, Mary had to undergo ritual purification in accordance with Old Testament law (Lev. 12:4, Num. 18:15, Luke 2:22). From the sixth century on, this event was celebrated on February 2 in the Western church. [21] In medieval iconography the Purification scene is conflated with another event, the buying back of Christ who, according to Old Testament law, as a first-born male belonged to God during the first thirty days of his life (Exod. 13:2, Num. 8:16–17). Accordingly, a family would bring an offering of two turtledoves to the temple in symbolic exchange for the baby. This event is recorded in Luke 2:23–35. In Luke's account Simeon, an old man in Jerusalem, saw the Christ child and recognized him as "a light to the revelation of the Gentiles, and the Glory of thy people Israel." The candles associated with the Presentation and depicted in the Asnières version of this scene allude to Simeon's metaphorical comment about light. But the roots of this candle ceremony go back even farther, to pre-Christian practices. [22] As indicated above, the buying back of Christ was conflated with the episode of Mary's purification and, in the Eastern church, Mary's purification feast was assimilated with pre-Christian customs that took place in February. In pre-Christian Greece, women would run through the fields with torches, simulating Demeter's search for her daughter Persephone, whose capture by Pluto brought about the death of vegetation. The pre-Christian procession with torches became assimilated with the Eastern Purification/Presentation feast, and was brought to the West in the sixth century.

It is pertinent to point out that the notion of purification implicit in Eastern and Western pagan and Christian practices was also reflected in agrarian custom. Throughout the Middle Ages and into modern times February was considered a month of purification. It was the time of the ceremonial purification of the fields before the seed could be placed in the ground. And it was also the time for the purification of women who had given birth during the preceding year. Until the last century women would come to the church on February 2 for a postchildbirth blessing and would take home with them their blessed candles. [23] Since the pagan torch or candle procession had been assimilated into Christian ritual, an originally pagan seasonal practice was to endure, transformed, until the twentieth century. These February customs and associations also mirrored the ancient biblical mentality. Before a woman could receive a new "seed," she had to be cleansed of the impurities of the old birth. Mary, though forever pure, likewise submitted herself to this purification process.

Directly following the Purification scene is the depiction of the Grain Miracle and the Flight into Egypt (figure 48). Three of Herod's soldiers address the sower. They carry swords and lances and are dressed in coats of mail and knee-high greaves. Their faces are painted a bright and fearsome red. The sower confronts them and gestures toward the wheat that has grown since the Virgin's passage. He is dressed in the short tunic of the simple laborer. This sower, however, wears a pointed cap instead of a head-dress tied under the chin, more typical in depictions of medieval work-ingmen. This pointed cap, sometimes pictured on Joseph, reflects the distinc-tive head-covering worn by the Jews in late medieval Europe.[24] In his right hand the sower grasps his sickle, ready for reaping; on his left side he seems to be concealing from the soldiers the seeds he had so recently been sowing. With both sickle and seeds in hand, and with the grown grain behind him, the sower becomes, for those who are familiar with the story, an emblem of the entire miracle.

The depiction of the Flight into Egypt is very damaged, but its general outlines provide some important iconographic indications. The Virgin on the donkey is flanked by two fruit-bearing trees, not fully visible in this photograph. Though the flat, spreading leaves of the tree to her left are very cursorily executed, the tree seems to be a palm. One of the well-known recorded apocryphal legends associated with the Flight into Egypt is that a palm tree "bent down" to offer the Virgin its fruit.[25] The artist has depicted the branches of both trees as bending in toward the Virgin. This kind of detail, which lends specificity to the whole rendering, cannot have been included merely as a decorative motif.

The trees in this context can perhaps be seen as having still further import. Both of them are fruit bearing, and as such surround her with a kind of throne of vegetal life. The Grain Miracle is complemented by the miraculous fruit tree that bends to her service. With the added emphasis on Mary's nursing breast, we have the image of a figure who nourishes and energizes both human and plant life. The child prospers from her milk, the palm bends to her service, the grain springs up at her bidding. These powers are used to protect the holy family, but, by implication, this figure, crowned like a queen, would likewise extend herself to help those simple villagers who looked up at this scene. She would help sustain the nursing child and protect the farming families in their efforts to realize an adequate grain harvest.

At the beginning of the thirteenth century, as soon as simple scenes of everyday human life begin to dominate iconography, the Grain Miracle becomes widely illustrated. As soon as the Virgin's life was depicted in detail, this very old motif of her relationship to plant life appears. This link will be affirmed as the Grain Miracle scene becomes even more fre-quently depicted in art in the fourteenth and fifteenth centuries.

Another, even more rustic village church, Saint-Maurice-sur-Loire, pro-

Figure 49. Mural painting, church at Saint-Maurice-sur-Loire, France. Annunciation, Visitation, Nativity (top register); Flight into Egypt, Grain Miracle (bottom register).

vides a second example of a thirteenth-century wall painting depicting the miraculous growth of grain (figure 49).[26] The cycle in which it is included adorns a low vault. Two scenes depicting the creation of Adam and Eve begin the narrative cycle. The decor continues with the Infancy Cycle and terminates with the Massacre of the Innocents.[27]

The artist executing this work has organized the scenes in such a way that the sower's role has become unclear. According to the chronological ordering of the episodes in the other registers, the scenes should be read from left to right. Thus, Joseph, Mary, and the child have passed by the field on their way to Egypt, and to their right is the sower standing in a field of nearly knee-high wheat. Yet, as Herod's henchman approaches, the sower is pointing in the direction of the holy family. Perhaps the artist has understood the sower as showing the henchman where the mother and child had passed when he was sowing his wheat. But given the way the two scenes are juxtaposed, the viewer cannot help seeing the sower as an accomplice of Herod's henchman. In no other version is the sower's gesture so pointedly contrary to the meaning of the story.

During the thirteenth century the Grain Miracle was to appear in other media as well—sculpture, stained glass, and manuscript illuminations. In what was an abbey church in the present-day village of Rougemont in northern Burgundy, an Infancy Cycle adorns the two lower registers of the

Figure 50. Detail from sculpted tympanum of central portal, west facade, church at Rougemont, France. Grain Miracle and Flight into Egypt.

tympanum over the west-central portal (figure 50). Two horsemen carrying weapons and riding through knee-high wheat approach a peasant who carries a farming implement, perhaps a hoe, over his left shoulder. Though the bottom part of the peasant's figure has broken off, it is apparent that when whole he would have been an imposing figure. His placement parallels that of Herod enthroned on the left. Like the shepherds below him, but still more important than they, he stands as a heroic figure for the peasants living in the area of this simple village church.

To the right of the sower, the Virgin is flanked again by trees. Though the Virgin is depicted frontally and respectably enthroned on the donkey, the position of her hands and the tilt of her head endow her with a great tenderness. The warmth and humanism so typical of thirteenth-century Marian iconography and so evident in the Asnières-sur-Vègre Flight into Egypt scene are present here as well.

Another thirteenth-century representation of the Grain Miracle—this one in stained glass (figure 51)—is located in the church of Saint-Julien-du-Sault, southeast of Paris, near Sens.[28] The three scenes that depict the legend are part of a window in the choir. The compositions and the tonalities of the colors are traditional for mid-thirteenth-century glass work. The gestures and costumes reveal a touch of the delicate mannered art of Parisian ateliers manifest in the windows of Sainte-Chapelle. The three framed compartments that illustrate the legend are organized so that the central compartment is given over to the sower. He stands in hip-high wheat and his seed sack, slung over his left shoulder, is clearly articulated. He raises his right hand in a typical medieval speaking gesture as he turns toward the soldiers to his

Figure 51. Stained-glass window. Herod's soldiers, sower, and Flight into Egypt. Church of Saint-Julien-du-Sault, France.

right. The soldiers carry swords and are dressed in coats of mail, greaves, and helmets. One of them has his hand raised, speaking back to the sower. The holy family moves off to the right.

The window in which this scene appears is one of ten, all dating from the middle of the thirteenth century. At that time Saint-Julien-du-Sault was only a village church; it acquired its costly decor because the church was under the protection of the powerful archbishops of Sens who were the seigneurs and barons of the region. Their support provided the village with the architecturally elegant structure containing what originally were magnificent windows.[29] We can perhaps understand the inclusion of the sower motif in this context: To appeal to the majority of the village people, who were agriculturalists, those planning the decor found a place for this peasant hero, the simple farmer who played such an important role in saving the savior.

By the end of the thirteenth century, the Grain Miracle legend had become a part of the urban aristocratic repertoire. Beginning in about 1275 the legend appeared in numerous northern French and Flemish books of hours, which only very wealthy people could afford.[30] The earliest known example is in the "Book of Hours of Yolanda, Vicontess of Soissons" (figures 52–53).[31] Executed in the long, flowing drapery lines characteristic of the late thirteenth-century Parisian school of illumination, the episode of the Grain Miracle is illustrated on two facing pages. The harsh-featured soldiers and mild-mannered sower exchange glances, as one horseman points to the proplike grown wheat. The scene takes place on a kind of stage set with cathedral gables, trefoils, and lancet windows adorning the upper border. The fleeing holy family is depicted in half-size within the letter *D* on the facing page. As can be seen by the statue falling off the column, the family has already gone on to the site of the next miracle, the destruction of the statues of the gods of Aphrodisias as recorded in the Apocrypha. But it is clearly the Grain Miracle that has received most attention. It is accorded a whole page and the sower's figure is set clearly against the plain background.

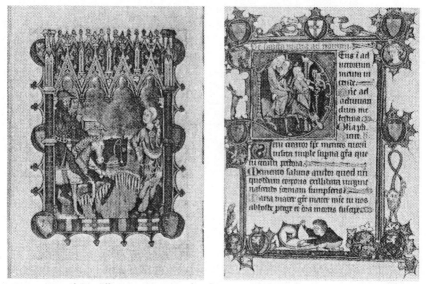

Figures 52 and 53. Illumination, Book of Hours of Yolanda, Vicontess of Soissons. Grain Miracle and Flight into Egypt.

The prominence of this agrarian scene in an aristocratic book of hours is evidence that by this time the inclusion of the tale in oral courtly literature had exposed an aristocratic audience to the legend and endeared them to it.

By the fourteenth century, the Grain Miracle legend had infiltrated the luxurious medium of ivory, as on an ivory box decorated with scenes from the Infancy Cycle (figure 54).[32] Whether the peasant is shown alone, pointing out the miracle, or harvesting and confronting the soldier, by the fourteenth century the artist had an ample repository of models of the scene to inspire him. And costly works such as this testify to the popularity of the scene within the upper echelons of the church and the laity.

In England, as in France and Scandinavia, artists incorporated the Grain Miracle scene into the Infancy Cycle. The Holkham Bible, a remarkable fourteenth-century Anglo-Norman Old and New Testament, contains, on one page, a version of the text of the Grain Miracle as well as accompanying illustrations (figure 55).[33] Though the first folio of the manuscript tells us that a Dominican preaching friar commissioned the book, such individuals had no personal funds so the actual patron was someone else.[34] But it was no doubt produced under the direction of the Dominican, who would have had a hand in choosing the texts and who instructed a professional lay artist in the content, design, and execution of the scenes. The Bible, directed at the educated, upper-class laity, was written totally in the vernacular, the language used by the Dominicans when they preached.

Figure 54. Ivory box. Grain Miracle, Flight into Egypt (top register); Nativity, Presentation of Christ in the Temple (bottom register).
Figure 55. Holkham Bible Picture Book. Flight into Egypt, Grain Miracle.

The fact that no heraldry appears in the Holkham Bible indicates that the patron was not an aristocrat. The great profusion and detailed renderings of tools suggests that he might have been a wealthy carpenter or builder; in this Bible, such trades receive much attention.[35] Accordingly, the status of Joseph is greatly elevated. There is an example of this in the Grain Miracle scene. Joseph is placed in the center, followed by Mary and the child. He has his axe slung over his shoulder, and extra clothing hung over its handle. He is wealthy, for both he and his wife are dressed in garments with richly embroidered bands, contrasting sharply with the simpler garb of the sower. He has his accumulated capital, in the form of cattle, following behind. In the Holkham Bible it is Joseph who speaks to the sower, and we know from the text that it is specifically Christ who performs the miracle.

The illustrations as well as the text of the Holkham Bible were very much influenced by medieval theater. As we have seen, the Grain Miracle had become part of medieval French theater by the early fourteenth century. There is little doubt that a similar Nativity Cycle play was performed in the Anglo-Norman milieu of London during this time as well. The illustrations and text of the Holkham Bible reflect the impact of these theatrical performances. The stories are often told in dialogue form, and the actions and gestures of the figures are portrayed in a studied, theatrical manner. One example of the influence of theatrical gestures is found in the confrontation between the sower and the soldiers. The sower's open arms suggest honesty itself and underscore the truth of his response.[36] Though the text is not the

Figure 56. Drawing of detail from silk embroidered pluvial (cloak).
Grain Miracle.

same as in "Le Geu des Trois Roys," the play cited in Chapter VI, the Grain
Miracle's inclusion in the Holkham Bible suggests that a similar play must
have been performed in London in the early fourteenth century.

Another interesting element in the Holkham Bible illustration is the use
of a harrow by the sower and his assistant. Before the fourteenth century the
Grain Miracle depictions included very simple agricultural implements, such
as a sickle and a seed bag. From the fourteenth century on, however, various
renditions of the scene show the use of other implements. Though harrowing
was not mentioned in farm accounts or other agrarian documents at this
early period, the Holkham Bible illustration proves that the harrow was in
use. The depiction of harnessing and tethering is likewise of interest to those
who study agricultural technology.

The Grain Miracle is depicted in an English (or possibly French) work in
still another medium—a magnificent silk cloak from the late thirteenth or
early fourteenth century, embroidered with threads of gold (figure 56).[37]
Though the history of this particular garment is not known, such long
cloaks were worn by ecclesiastics on important ceremonial occasions. One
half of the cloak is adorned with scenes from the Passion, the other half with
scenes from the early life of Christ. The center scenes emphasize the Death
of the Virgin, the Ascension, and the crowning of Mary. The Grain Miracle
roundel is surrounded by depictions of Herod and the Magi, the Massacre of

Figure 57. Hours of the Rohan Master. Flight into Egypt, Grain Miracle.

the Innocents, the Flight into Egypt, and Christ among the doctors. The sower with his seed bag stands between his fully grown wheat and the two soldiers. Beneath his feet is the as yet unsown land. It is curious that the sower is given more individual space than are many of the figures in the other roundels.

124 THE GODDESS OBSCURED

Though many of the preceding examples of the Grain Miracle have emphasized Joseph or the sower, another work, from the very late Middle Ages, aggrandizes the Virgin and appears to elevate her role. This Grain Miracle illustration is part of a recognized masterpiece, the "Grandes Heures de Rohan," a book of hours illustrated and executed under the direction of an anonymous French artist, called the Rohan Master, who lived during the first quarter of the fifteenth century (figure 57).[38] While most French artists of that period were seeking a more naturalistic means of expression by developing linear and atmospheric perspective, and by exploring the nuances of texture and color, the Rohan Master avoided these modes in favor of an art of insistent, strong color and swirling line. He rejected the anatomical study of the human body and created figures that exceeded the bounds of rational three-dimensional space. He opted for an art of intense feeling, and in doing so created what art historians call the expressionism of the fifteenth century. The Grain Miracle appears as one of the illustrations accompanying the text of the "Hours of the Virgin."[39] In the bottom half of the illumination an emaciated peasant flanked by a sleeping companion bends before the soldiers who ride prancing decorous horses.[40] In looking at this peasant, we are confronted with a major expressive device of the Rohan Master—enormous differences in scale. Though the dozing peasant is in the immediate foreground, he is the most diminutive figure of all.

Behind the distant mountains, yet looming largest in the whole scene, is the holy family, led by an angel disguised as a laborer.[41] Their enormous scale and elevated position speak eloquently of their great importance. The Rohan Master here uses the archaic device of making the most important figures highest on the page, and though most distant, largest in scale. Such exaggeration of scale is associated, in earlier artworks, with the varying religious significance of the figures. It was used by artists working in non-naturalistic modes to indicate the hierarchical status of saintly or regal persons. The device here takes on a decidedly expressive value. The Rohan Master's rejection of naturalistic and rational canons enables him to create these compelling compositions, wherein certain events, though terrestrial, are placed in a celestial-like milieu. This otherwordly, non-naturalistic atmosphere makes the Virgin a divinelike figure. The intense emotionalism that permeates the scene becomes focused on this lofty personage.

At the end of the Middle Ages, in the troubled years of the 1420s in France, the Rohan Master reinterpreted the Grain Miracle. He Marianized the legend once again. Looking away from the natural world that was so attractive to other artists of his time, he set about to explore another realm. In so doing, he unconsciously tapped into one of the ancient topoi of the human subconscious. He centralized Mary, elevated her, and surrounded her with heavenly rays. She has once more become the dominating queen whose potent presence caused the miraculous growth of grain. The artist could not have known or intended this, but he has placed the Virgin's form between two swelling hills. For the archeologist, land formations such as these have a particular import. A study of ancient sites suggests that to our prehistoric ancestors, twin hills such as these symbolized breasts, which in turn were envisioned as belonging to a reclining mother goddess of the earth.[42] Such twin mountains, in different places of the world, are often given appellations equivalent to "paps" or "breasts."[43] Archeology has shown that prehistoric temples were frequently placed in alignment with such breastlike land formations. Thus, the Rohan Master has preserved a vestige of the ancient belief in the connection between the female and the earth, the archaic assumption that the female possessed the power to make the land fertile. To the twentieth-century viewer, this analogy is suggested by the enormous scale and heightened religious significance of the Virgin in this Grain Miracle scene. For the modern viewer who understands the deep roots of the paradigm, the Rohan Master's interpretation, elevating and enlarging the Virgin and engulfing her in heavenly light, is a haunting evocation of the Great Mother of vegetation, awesome antecedent of this Christian grain protectress.

My purpose has not been to catalog the numerous representations of the Grain Miracle. Scholars over the last six decades have noted more than 125 examples of the scene in a variety of media, and more examples remain to be uncovered, particularly in fifteenth- and sixteenth-century books of hours.[44] This review of some of the appearances of the Grain Miracle in visual arts is meant to complement the information gained from the literary sources and to point out that in art, as in literature, as soon as conditions were ripe the tale incorporating the motif of the grain protectress came to the fore and was widely represented. The meaning and import of the scene was in constant flux, and not all examples can be said to emphasize purposefully the Virgin's role in the miracle. And further, without a doubt, the notion of the Virgin as successor to a pre-Christian grain protectress was completely absent from the conscious minds of all the medieval artists, literary and visual, who worked with the legend. Yet, fortunately, the earliest examples of the artistic depiction of the Grain Miracle demonstrated the importance of the pagan past in both the choice of this theme and its visual execution.

The fact that this legend, previously unknown in any ecclesiastical text, was, in the Middle Ages, so widely recorded textually and artistically, demonstrates the tenacity of the notion of a grain protectress and reveals what a grip that idea had on popular imagination. That it spread so profusely reflects its profound appeal. The literary and artistic image was so potent precisely because the Virgin grain protectress perpetuated a very ancient image, an image that haunted human imagination from the time when our ancestors first began to depend on the earth to quicken the seed and bring forth plant life. In the medieval world, the Virgin as grain protectress succeeded those pre-Christian female personae who were sovereigns over vegetal life and who, as such, were ultimately responsible for sustaining and nourishing humankind.

Chapter VIII

The Grain Miracle in Folklore

We have examined the recurrence of the Grain Miracle in poetry, drama, and the visual arts through the end of the Middle Ages. In fifteenth- and sixteenth-century Flemish art the legend became particularly important (figure 58) and then rapidly diminished in popularity. After the Reformation, at least in Protestant countries, the theme had little opportunity to spread, and in Catholic countries it seems to have slipped out of the official repertoire altogether. The tale continued to live, however, in folklore and folksong.[1] Right through to the twentieth century, various versions of the Grain Miracle were still being recorded.

Since the theme had been part of late medieval theater and mime, and was represented on church façades and in wall paintings, we can assume that the wide knowledge of the legend was due to written sources and public artworks. However, the tale has been recorded in more than sixty regional variants, in many different languages and dialects, and in such diverse places as Sweden, Italy, Portugal, and the Middle East. Such a wide and diversified dissemination usually implies that the tale had a lively existence in the oral tradition, a tradition that was not necessarily dependent on written or art-historical sources.[2] Oral tradition alone is known to have kept alive tales for millennia, so the visual representations and textual recordings of various versions of the Grain Miracle in the thirteenth through sixteenth centuries may not have influenced the tale as formulated, say, in Aramaic, in Wendish, or in dialects of semi-isolated rural areas. Such versions could have been dependent on a parallel oral tradition of their own, independent of written literature or artistic representations. Folklorists warn that we cannot assume

Figure 58. Painting by Patinir. Virgin and Child resting in *Flight into Egypt*. Grain Miracle in right middle ground, Massacre of the Innocents in right background.

that the oldest presently available written forms of a tale are the forms from which all other variants originate.[3]

Folkloric scholarship can help us determine why only certain tales, such as the Grain Miracle, are transmitted and diffused.[4] First of all, like many other long-preserved tales, the Grain Miracle is connected to a traditional task, undertaken at a specific time of the year; and the work methods mentioned in the tale, whether plowing, hoeing, or seeding, did not change much through the centuries. Whether with hoe or plow, farmers loosened the soil and planted seed in similar ways up until recent decades. It is probable that quite often the Grain Miracle tale was transmitted when these traditional tasks were undertaken in the early spring. Second, the acts of plowing and seeding are everywhere fraught with fears and expectations. A legend such as the Grain Miracle alludes to those fears and expectations as well as to the promised protection and recompense that every farmer desired: that some guardian figure was present and capable of influencing indifferent nature.

In almost all of the folkloric versions of the tale, it is Mary (or a female saint), not Jesus, whose presence is associated with the Grain Miracle. Therefore, the wide dissemination and enormous popularity of the tale suggest a continuing propensity on the part of peasants and farmers to imagine the fertility of their fields and the growth of their crops as remaining under the guardianship of a protectress. Furthermore, farmers were unlikely to discard a tale in which their own status is so elevated. Not only does the story point to an alliance between the plowman and the world of nature, but also to a close relationship between the peasant and saintly figures. This tale, intimately connected with farming work and the agrarian mentality, was an excellent candidate for a long transmission, especially since peasant farmers are the most active bearers of traditional lore.

There are, however, other reasons that various versions of this tale have been transmitted for so many generations. It is possible to demonstrate that, as with many folktales, this story contains some material that goes deeper than the Christian roots; that in some versions it incorporates pre-Christian allusions, however oblique.

Many of the transmitted versions are in the form of songs. It is now rarely challenged that some folksongs contain ancient pagan lore.[5] Though the metrical structure or rhyme scheme of a ballad may reflect linguistic developments that could not have evolved before the late Middle Ages, the theme and combination of motifs can have a far more ancient history. The orally transmitted versions of some folksongs provide information and contain allusions that the corresponding medieval texts did not preserve, and there are incidences in folklore of the oral tradition retaining a more accurate account of an event or ritual than any written reports have.[6]

Thus a folksong incorporating the Grain Miracle, though among the youngest Grain Miracle documents, can potentially retain more primitive pagan elements than any other version, especially since this theme in particular expresses unchanging aspects of the agrarian mentality. Despite changes of religion, the evolution of language, and vast cultural upheavals, the agricultural way of life consistently favored practices and acts designed to maintain the soil's fertility and to protect the crop at various stages. Soliciting protection from the earth via propitiation or sacrifice was a natural part of life and lore. A particularly striking example of the retention of these very ancient attitudes emerges in the English version of the folksong in which the Grain Miracle was transmitted, a song entitled "The Carnal and the Crane."[7]

"The Carnal and the Crane," one of the ballads collected by Francis Child in the second half of the nineteenth century, relates the legend through a discussion between a carnal, or crow, and a crane. It had first appeared in written form on a broadsheet in 1750. But the earlier history of this or any ballad is a problem. The dating of folk literature is nearly impossible; unlike written literature, folk literature does not usually respond to the conventional approaches of literary scholarship.[8] Each generation passes down the lore to the next, adapting themes or changing words, sometimes in inscrutable ways. We know that poetry and melody combined as dance-song existed in antiquity and survived into the Middle Ages, and further, we have actual songs from the later Middle Ages. But a precise chronology for this or any other orally transmitted folksong will probably always remain elusive.[9] Yet, a study of the imagery in "The Carnal and the Crane" will indicate that even though its dialect is postmedieval, the pre-Christian themes and rituals that stand behind the Grain Miracle are there to be uncovered. Beneath the seemingly simple literal meaning of the words is a rich symbolic language, evoking the fears and expectations of the agrarian people from whom this ballad sprang.[10]

1   As I passd by a river side,
     And there as I did reign,
     In argument I chanced to hear
     A Carnal and a Crane.

2   The Carnal said unto the Crane,
     "If all the world should turn,
     Before we had the Father,
     But now we have the Son!

3   From whence does the Son come,
     From where and from what place?"
     He said, In a manger,
     Between an ox and ass.

4   "I pray thee," said the Carnal,
     "Tell me before thou go,
     Was not the mother of Jesus
     Conceivd by the Holy Ghost?"

5   She was the purest virgin,
     And the cleanest from sin;
     She was the handmaid of our Lord
     And mother of our king.

6   "Where is the golden cradle
     That Christ was rocked in?
     Where are the silken sheets
     That Jesus was wrapt in?"

7   A manger was the cradle
     That Christ was rocked in:
     The provender the asses left
     So sweetly he slept on.

8   There was a star in the east land,
     So bright it did appear,
     Into King Herod's chamber,
     And where King Herod were.

9   The Wise Men soon espied it,
     And told the king on high
     A princely babe was born that night
     No king could eer destroy.

10 "If this be true," King Herod said,
   "As thou tellest unto me,
   This roasted cock that lies in the dish
   Shall crow full fences three."

11 The cock soon freshly featherd was,
   By the work of God's own hand,
   And then three fences crowed he,
   In the dish where he did stand.

12 "Rise up, rise up, you merry men all,
   see that you ready be;
   All children under two years old
   Now slain they all shall be."

13 Then Jesus, ah, and Joseph,
   And Mary, that was so pure,
   They travelld into Egypt,
   As you shall find it sure.

14 And when they came to Egypt's land,
   Amongst those fierce wild beasts,
   Mary, she being weary,
   Must needs sit down to rest.

15 "Come sit thee down," says Jesus,
   "Come sit thee down by me,
   And thou shalt see how these wild beasts
   Do come and worship me."

16 First came the lovely lion,
   Which Jesus's grace did bring,
   And of the wild beasts in the field
   The lion shall be king.

17 We'll choose our virtuous princes
   Of birth and high degree,
   In every sundry nation,
   Whereer we come and see.

18 Then Jesus, ah, and Joseph,
   And Mary, that was unknown,
   They travelled by a husbandman,
   Just while his seed was sown.

19 "God speed thee, man," said Jesus,
   "Go fetch thy ox and wain,
   And carry home thy corn again
   which thou this day hast sown."

20 The husbandman fell on his knees,
   Even upon his face:
   "Long time hast thou been looked for,
   But now thou art come at last.

21 And I myself do now believe
    Thy name is Jesus called;
    Redeemer of mankind thou art,
    Though undeserving all."

22 "The truth, man, thou hast spoken,
    Of it thou mayst be sure,
    For I must lose my precious blood
    For thee and thousands more.

23 If any one should come this way,
    And enquire for me alone,
    Tell them that Jesus passed by
    As thou thy seed did sow."

24 After that there came King Herod,
    With his train so furiously,
    Enquiring of the husbandman
    Whether Jesus passed by.

25 "Why, the truth it must be spoke,
    And the truth it must be known;
    For Jesus passed by this way
    When my seed was sown.

26 But now I have it reapen,
    And some laid on my wain,
    Ready to fetch and carry
    Into my barn again."

27 "Turn back," says the captain,
    "Your labor and mine 's in vain;
    It's full three quarters of a year
    Since he his seed has sown."

28 So Herod was deceived,
    By the work of God's own hand,
    And further he proceeded
    Into the Holy Land.

29 There's thousands of children young
    Which for his sake did die;
    Do not forbid those little ones,
    And do not them deny.

30 The truth now I have spoken,
    And the truth now I have shown;
    Even the Blessed Virgin
    She's now brought forth a son.

The song is cast as a tale within a tale. The narrator's opening words (verse 1) indicate that the scene is a riverside, a geographical demarcation in medieval England that usually separated one property from another, and that was often regarded as having been the site of a sacred happening.[11] The narrator "passed by" the riverside, thereby engaging in an action that would be repeated three times in the ballad (verses 23–25), at the moments immediately surrounding the occurrence of the miracle. Thus, the ballad straightaway introduces the idea that an event of some moment occurs when there is a passing by at the boundary.

When the narrator stopped, he heard an "argument" or conversation between a carnal and a crane. As we will see from the succeeding verses (2–7), this argument takes the form of a series of questions and answers. The technique of questions and answers focuses attention on the matters at hand and invites, if only silently, a kind of audience participation. The queries of the carnal, and the crane's familiar responses, create the echo of a liturgical pattern, the catechumen being instructed by the docent. Such questions and answers are, in fact, commonly found in liturgical use, where they often appear in chants addressing the basic questions of life and death. The similarity of these questions and answers to liturgical chants suggests that the song may have grown out of agrarian ritual, a ritual taking place at a sacred boundary and incorporating questions and responses.[12]

What of the roles of the carnal and the crane within the pattern of the song? Does their dialogue in fact relate to ritual? The first words spoken by the carnal, though containing Christian referents, point distinctly to a specific pagan idea, the cyclical notion of time, the turning cycle of the agrarian year of growth, decay, and rebirth. "The Carnal said unto the Crane, / If all the world should turn [sure all the world will turn], / Before [but once] we had the [a] Father, / But now we have the [a] Son!"[13] Within the inevitable cycle of the turning world, there was the "breaking in" of the Son.

But "'from whence does the Son come,'" continues the questioning carnal, "'from where and from what place?'" The crane gives the standard liturgical response, "In a manger, / Between an ox and ass." But the carnal has a more basic question in mind, a more probing question about the origin of the godhead. He asks about the mother of Jesus; was she not "'conceivd by [sprung from] the Holy Ghost?'"[14] The language of this question is ambiguous. On the one hand the words "conceived by" could mean "become impregnated by" the Holy Ghost. This accords with the Gospel account that relates that Mary was with child by the Holy Spirit (Matt. 1:18). But the words "conceived by" can also be understood as meaning that Mary herself was "conceived by" the Holy Ghost.[15] The variant, which uses "sprung" in place of "conceived by," supports the interpretation that Mary herself was created by Divine Spirit, for combined with the preposition "from," it can be read only in the intransitive sense, that is, that Mary "issued forth from" or "originated by birth from" the Holy Spirit. This kind of question then, when taken to mean that Mary herself "sprang from" the Holy Ghost, is blatantly not part of the official litany. According to Catholic doctrine as expressed in the liturgy of the mass, Mary was considered (after the Council of Ephesus in 431) the Mother of God, but was not herself divine; she was not "sprung from" or "conceived by" the Holy Ghost.

This question would be considered blasphemous in the orthodox Catholic context. Yet, in this version of the ballad, the question is not only asked but asked in a form that anticipates an affirmative answer. And a Gypsy version of the ballad is constructed so that the implied answer is definitely yes.[16] Though no response is given in Child's version, the next four lines (verse 5) characterize Mary as the purest, cleanest "handmaid of our Lord / And mother of our king." This stanza, combined with the preceding unanswered question about the Virgin's divinity, elevates Mary well above her traditional status. It at least suggests that the place whence the son came was a divine mother. Nothing in the "argument" belies this conclusion, and we shall see that there are elements in the rest of the ballad that support it. In any case, the whole of this section, structured as query and response and dealing with fundamental issues of belief, is certainly couched in a liturgical mode.

Before moving to the exposition of the major theme of the song, let us examine the nature of the speakers, the carnal and the crane. It has been suggested that the instructing crane may be a Christological symbol; the Gypsy version of the folksong specifically names the one who answers the questions as the "blessed Savior."[17] Even if the crane is not a Christological symbol, the bird definitely acts in the role of docent.[18] The word *carnal* is obsolete. The *Oxford English Dictionary* indicates that it probably came from the French *corneille*, meaning "crow," but suggests there may be some association with the adjective *carnal*, meaning temporal, bodily, worldly, unspiritual.

The language of the dialogue in stanzas 2 through 7 does reveal that the carnal is the more secular, uninstructed party, and that the crane is the more spiritually knowledgeable of the two. In view of this dichotomy, two other connotations possibly implicit in the obsolete word *carnal* present themselves. The Middle English word *carl* designates a husbandman or rustic, certainly the role played by the carnal in this song. This is indeed a catechumenal dialogue between an uninstructed country rustic and an erudite instructor. But probing still further, we find that the crow (carnal, *corneille* in French) was one of the symbols or perhaps totems of one of the old Celtic gods.[19] The questions and answers of these anthropomorphized birds may harbor a many-layered dialogue between the voice of a *rusticus qua deus* of the ancient Celtic world and a *doctus qua dominus* of the Christian. It is the rustic whose sphere of experience is the agrarian cycle of the turning world; who asks for an explanation of the origin of the two separate deities, the Father and then the Son; who elevates Mary by asking if the Mother of the Son was not conceived by the Holy Ghost; who accepts the Son as the new king and asks where his golden cradle and silken sheets are (verse 6). The rest of the ballad (verses 7–30) is cast as the response of the knowing, learned crane.

Three extracanonical legends are couched in the crane's response: the legend of Herod and the cock, which is depicted on the twelfth-century Gotlandic baptismal fonts (figures 39, 44); the legend of the wild beasts worshiping Christ; and the Grain Miracle. The legend of Herod and the cock (verses 8–12) had become very widely known.[20] In the English version it is the Wise Men and the star that alert Herod to the birth of the new king, the princely babe who could not be destroyed. Thus, verses 8 and 9 set up the struggle, at the celestially appointed time, between the old king Herod and the new "princely babe." Herod asks for a sign of the truth of the Wise Men's words; in essence, he asks for the roasted cock's resuscitation (verse 10). The cock, whose three cries in the Gospel foretell Peter's denial of Christ, not only comes to life resurrected but crows three times.[21] The placing of these two verses here not only heightens the conflict between Herod and Christ, but also introduces the theme of resurrection and foreshadows its importance in the rest of the ballad. The standing cock becomes the signal for Herod and his men to go out to slay all children under two years of age in an effort to destroy the "princely babe."

The next section of the ballad contains the apocryphal tale of the wild beasts worshiping Christ (verses 13–17). As the holy family traveled into Egypt, Mary became weary. "'Come sit thee down,' says Jesus, / 'Come sit thee down by me, / And thou shalt see how these wild beasts / Do come and worship me.'" Jesus, the new king, sits down on the ground by his mother and is worshiped by the beasts, the lion first. Jesus designates the lion as king of the beasts, and says that he, Christ, will go about "in every sundry nation" and "choose . . . virtuous princes." His words foretell a new reign replacing the old order that had been symbolized by the child-slayer Herod, for whose sake "thousands of children young / . . . did die" (verse 29).

The Grain Miracle (verses 18–30) is both the core and the culmination of the ballad. Jesus, Joseph, and Mary "travelled by a husbandman, / Just while his seed was sown." The three-folk repetition of the words "passed by" (verses 23–25) obliquely mirrors the ancient ritual wherein the mother goddess figure "passed by" or through the fields, thereby activating the seed. Though in other folkloric versions of the tale Mary accomplishes the miracle, in this account Christ assumes her powers. Jesus tells the husbandman that the corn he has just sown will be ready to carry home "this day." Like the lion, the husbandman falls down in worship and recognizes Christ as the new king who, with his ability to make the grain sprout and grow immediately into mature wheat, has demonstrated his power to bring miraculous fertility to the field (verses 18–21). The husbandman calls him the 'Redeemer of undeserving' mankind. This designation connects the miraculous growth of the grain with redemption through sacrifice — not the human or animal sacrifice of the old Herodic order, but the symbolic sacrifice of Christ's blood. Christ's words corroborate and clarify the husbandman's belief:

> "The truth, man, thou hast spoken,
> Of it thou mayst be sure,
> For I must lose my precious blood
> For thee and thousands more."

Christ is presented here as the victim, a willing, knowing, sacrificial victim whose "precious blood" will be shed "for thee and thousands more."

The juxtaposition of the Grain Miracle with the blood sacrifice alludes to elements of pre-Christian belief. In this ballad Christ is the new king who, in imitation of the vegetation cycle, must die in order that new life may be born. This theme in Western religion and mythology may be traced back to ritual practice. [22] The pattern is one of life-death-resurrection and is found in religious thinking from the earliest stages of worship. The origins of the sacrificial rite were based on empirical observations of the vegetation cycle: With the changing of the seasons, plants that are born out of the earth, die and return back into the earth, and then, in a transformation process, are born once again. Christ's loss of "precious blood" is intimately linked in this ballad with the growth of grain, like the sacred mythic king who was killed at a certain time of the year in order that crops would grow. The blood of Christ is now the sowing sacrifice that, in the Anglo-Saxon plowing charm, included oil, honey, milk, and holy water, and that prehistorically may have been a human being. With Christ's sacrifice and with the ensuing growth of grain, people will be saved from want and starvation.

One of the variants of the ballad gives this precise reason for Christ's sacrifice. In the version gathered from Gypsies, it is Jesus who concludes the ballad with these words to the husbandman:

> ". . . And carry home your ripened corn,
> That you've been sowing this day.
> For to keep your wife and family
> From sorrow, grief, and pain,
> And keep Christ in your remembrance
> Till the time comes round again."[23]

This ballad then alludes to the early ritual practices surrounding the sacred king. Though ceremonies and rituals varied greatly at different times and in different places, the ancient pattern included the ritual destruction of a young god-king whose death assured the rebirth of foliage the following year. The cycle of birth, death, and rebirth was unending, all controlled by the divine earth mother who brought forth the new king, with the foliage, in the spring. [24]

Clearly, the resurrecting powers of the earth mother were completely subsumed by the Father in the context of Christianity. But knowing what we do about the origin of the Grain Miracle encourages a closer look at the

accumulation of imagery surrounding Mary in "The Carnal and the Crane."
The unanswered question of Mary's divinity punctuates the opening liturgical dialogue. Mary is characterized in quite orthodox fashion as "purest" and
"cleanest" (verse 5). On the Flight into Egypt, Mary is described as sitting
down to rest, presumably on the ground. One of the most ancient preseeding
rituals was the purification of the land. [25] The land-purifying ceremonies in
primitive societies and in the ancient world were held in February before
implantation of the spring seed. Manuscript illustrations as well as folk
customs reveal a concern with the purity of the fields and vineyards in the
month of February. [26] The Welsh and Flemish medieval texts discussed in
Chapter VI allude to Mary's purity. Is the emphasis on Mary's purity symbolic as well as literal here? Does this ballad retain an allusion to the female's
imparting purity to the land through her bodily contact with it? As the
"pure" Mary sits beside Christ while he is worshiped by the beasts, is she
symbolically preparing the land for new implantation? It is she, after all,
who has miraculously brought forth the god-king-son to be sacrificed for
the land's fertility.

The song begins and ends with direct reference to the Mother. "'From
whence does the Son come?'" is the first question; and the final answer:
"Even the [thus the] Blessed Virgin / She's now brought forth a son
[Brought forth our Lord the Son]." Beneath the surface of Christian theol-
ogy, the ancient theme still pulsates: It is the Mother's "bringing forth" of
the victim that enables the sacrifice to take place, the cycle to continue, and
the grain to grow. The images in this song reveal that it is really about
sacrifice, resurrection, and new life; about the ritual death of the Son
brought forth by the Mother, a death that assures new growth and redeems
people from hunger and starvation. [27] Though the female life power has lost
her primacy on the literal level, the symbolic imagery and the structure of
the song still allude to that power which ultimately has as its domain all life
and death.

How much store can be put in the symbolic imagery and structure that
allude to early ritual and mythical themes? Are these truly relics of a pre-
Christian mentality? The insights of the anthropologist and the folklorist
have shown that folk memory acts as an unconscious store of power images,
and ballads such as this can be fully understood only if the remnants of pagan
belief are considered. [28] In this version of the Grain Miracle, the Christian
imagery has almost completely obscured the pagan material, yet the ballad
does allude to pre-Christian elements. We have seen that with the growing
dominance of Christianity in the early Middle Ages, ritual sometimes
devolved into folklore, which in most cases lost its original meaning. But
occasionally the images of pagan worship were preserved, sometimes con-
sciously, more often unconsciously. If these essential symbols and images
had not been retained, the ballad might never have been transmitted.

As if to corroborate these instincts of the modern scholar, this ballad emphasizes a particular refrain, a leitmotif that occurs at crucial moments in the song, and that, though contained partially in numerous versions of the tale, is here even more forcefully emphasized. When Herod was told that an indestructible princely babe had been born, he says, If that is *true*, this roasted cock will crow. The miracle occurred, by "God's own hand," and Herod learned the *truth;* when the husbandman recognized Jesus and called him the redeemer, Christ responded: "'The *truth*, man, thou hast spoken, / Of it thou mayst be sure. . . .'" (emphasis mine). Of course, the Grain Miracle itself occurs so that the husbandman can both save the holy family *and* tell the *truth:* "'Why, the truth it must be spoke, / And the truth it must be known; / For Jesus passed by this way / When my seed was sown.'" "So Herod was deceived, / By the work of God's own hand. . . ." And again, we find an emphasis on truth in the last stanza, at the end of the litany, presumably uttered by the crane: "The truth now I have spoken, / And the truth now I have shown; / Even the Blessed Virgin / She's now brought forth a son."

At all the crucial points in the ballad, the truth is emphasized: the truth of the birth of the new king, the truth of his being both victim and redeemer, the truth of Christ's bringing about the instantaneous growth of grain, and likewise the final truth of the Virgin's miraculously bringing forth the Son. The "doctrine" of this song is clearly to be *believed*, because, we are told, it is the truth.

Ancient lore survives in this and other folksongs because the agrarian way of life common to peasants for centuries perpetuated an unchanging outlook, an outlook common to both pagans and Christians. The assimilation of pagan imagery to later Christian concepts is to be expected when we realize that both grew out of the human experience of the agricultural cycle. Death preceding new life is a natural part of the cycle of the seasons. These were the processes by which the rural community lived, so a song like this, commemorating these processes, would continue to enjoy a life in memory and performance.

Though other Grain Miracle folksongs likewise appear to be rich in pagan imagery, my linguistic limitations prevent a close analysis of them here.[29] However, even a superficial knowledge of the languages in which a folktale was transmitted permits an analysis of the ways in which the tale was adapted to the varied cultural and geographical milieux. As we saw in Chapter VI, the earliest written versions of the tale, in French, Welsh, and Irish, already exhibited different motifs. Each of the three sociolinguistic groups had adapted the story in its own way. The tale was not "controlled" or "fixed" by an official church version.

When a tale forms special types through adaptation to certain cultural districts or through isolation, those special forms are called ecotypes.[30] If a tale is spread only through its written form, it usually remains more or less stable. But with oral transmission, new ecotypes develop as details are

modified for new circles of listeners or as local landmarks, flora, or fauna
are included to make the tale more immediate and familiar. If the folktale
seems too strange or foreign, or if it agrees too little with the temper and
traditions of a people, it dies. [31]

When different motifs are added to a tale, they often provide an insight
into such things as the agrarian economy, the technology, or the ethno-
psychology of a region. [32] For instance, though the farmer is usually
described as employing a plow, in some areas the tale was adapted so that the
farmer was using a hoe, a less complicated instrument that would not imply
the need for costly draft animals. Sometimes it is one man alone working the
fields; at other times several are working together; very frequently the whole
family or household is said to participate in the cutting of the sheaves and the
binding of the stalks. Each of these variants gives a slightly different picture
of the working habits or economy of the area in which the tale was adapted.

Perhaps the most obvious difference in ecotypes relates to the kind of crop
that the farmer sows. In some of the French, Catalán, and Flemish versions
the crop is specifically designated as wheat, and on occasion the twelve-week
spring wheat is specifically mentioned. In some, the tale was adapted to
reflect the growing of barley (in Sorbian) or oats (Wendish). In the Aramaic
versions, the crop is chickpeas or fruit. And in one Maltese version, Mary
and the child pass by the house of a vintner planting grapevine cuttings. By
the time the soldier arrives a few hours later, the ripened clusters have been
harvested and pressed, and the vintner is able slyly to offer the pursuers a
drink of wine, thereby fully deceiving them by his remark that the fugitives
had passed when the vine shoots were being planted. In the Portuguese tale,
the Virgin comes by a group of peasants who are sowing stones. "Stones you
will harvest," she says. In three days, rocks covered the field. The Virgin
then passes by a group of peasants sowing wheat. The wheat sprouts and the
Virgin and child are saved. The "rock" crop appears to be a local variant that
reflects grimly on the nature of the soil and the dire expectations for harvest
in some particularly barren areas of Portugal.

In several of the versions (Catalán, Provençal, and in dialects of southwestern France), the Virgin hides in the laborer's cloak or in the newly grown
crop, either among the harvested sheaves or in the high stalks. The Virgin
hiding underneath or within the grain stalks is a suggestive motif indeed, for
it seems linked to the widespread European practice of fashioning a "grain
mother" of straw. [33] In some cultures the last-reaped stalks are twisted into
special shapes (crosses, figures) and preserved, for their presence is purported to ensure a plentiful crop in the following year. Such shaped grain
sheaves have been used as protective symbols and play a role in agrarian and
harvesting rituals to this day (figures 38, 59).

One version of the tale, again from Catalunya, specifically refers not only
to the Virgin covered by the stalks of grain but also to a "straw Christ":
When Mary hears Herod going about the town seeking to kill the innocent

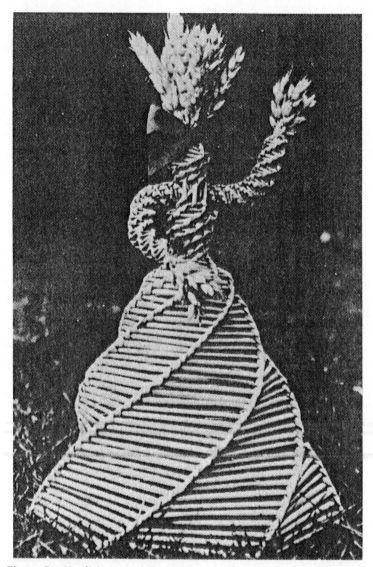

Figure 59. English corn dolly. This type of straw harvest figure is braided from wheat of one harvest and returned to field the following spring to act as guardian over the next year's crop. The type is known as Mother Earth.

children, she declares, "He will not kill mine"; "I will hide him well." At the door of her house, as she begins her flight, she comes upon Herod. "What are you carrying here, Mary; What are you carrying so well hidden?" "I am carrying a little bit of wheat [*xiquet de trigol*, which can also mean "child of wheat"], wheat that has been hulled." "Will you sell me the wheat or give it to me on deposit?" "No, I will not sell it or give it to you on deposit, for this little bit of wheat [child of wheat] will be the salvation of the world."[34] The word *xiquet*, rich with possible implications, might designate a straw image such as those discussed above. Highly perishable, the straw-fashioned figures usually do not survive; but they are an art form that reflects popular tradition and provides us with clues about the artifacts that may have been a part of the ceremonies that accompanied the first spring plowing and seeding in rural communities.

In Italian, Provençal, Catalán, and dialects of southwestern France, the Grain Miracle tale was fused with local flora and fauna lore and an ecotype developed in which a treacherous plant or bird betrays the Virgin, or a benevolent plant or bird saves her.[35] While Mary hides in the sheaves or stalks and Herod's soldiers make ready to leave, a mint plant (or sometimes a partridge, quail, or jaybird) calls out, "sota la gabera [garbereta, gaberta]" ("underneath the sheaves"), thereby betraying her hiding place. The mint was incorporated in this way because its name in the Romance languages (*menta, menthe*) sounds like the word for liar (*menteur*). And, predictably, the curse flung at the mint for betraying the Virgin is "Tu ets menta y mentirás, / florirás y no granarás"[36] ("You are mint and you lie, / you will flower but not come to seed"). The jay is likewise cursed: "As much as you eat you will not fatten."[37] In the case of the cursed bird, whether jay, quail, or partridge, the tale reveals an acculturation to farming concerns: The jay, partridge, and quail are all birds that live near arable land and feed on seeds (as well as on insects). They would have been particular pests at the time when the seed was being scattered. As annoyances to the farmers, they became betrayers of the Virgin as well.

In other folkloric versions of the Grain Miracle, plants and birds help the holy family. In the Italian version the juniper tree, whose branches were often hung in houses, hides the family in its boughs. In a version from Roussillon basil or sage covers Mary's cloak, and ever since basil has been the favorite plant of young girls, who make it part of their corsages.[38] And in Limousin the swallow, harbinger of spring and friendly to mankind, is the Virgin's protector. It chirps out that those who reveal her presence lie.[39] Thus, the flora and fauna adaptations are quite consistent with agrarian life. These additions make the tale not only a little more suspenseful, but also more acceptable to the people of the area.

In the Scottish highlands and in Ireland, an ecotype developed involving a treacherous beetle. In this variant, the traitor is the *darbh daol*, the devil's coach-horse beetle. It sang out to the pursuer that the holy family had passed by yesterday, and in retribution its color was transformed from a bright red to a dingy black, or it lost its wings. In memory of the beetle's evil deed, country people forever after have been permitted to crush it whenever they come upon it. This variant demonstrates how the Grain Miracle fused with a local tale that purported to explain why the devil's coach-horse beetle is black and is constantly subjected to death by crushing.

In the Wendish version of the tale, Mary carries a falcon.[40] Falconry was a principal sport among the European aristocracy, so a falcon would appear to give Mary an aristocratic allure. However, in the context of this tale the falcon could be seen as a necessary protection against evil. Falcons frequently chased partridges, quails, and jays, those birds that, as seed-eating enemies at sowing times, were cast as the enemies of the Virgin, the ones who reported her hiding place, in the Franco-Catalán versions of the Grain Miracle. Thus, the falcon, as predator of the enemies of both Mary and the peasant, is an understandable attribute for the Virgin in the Wendish tale.

One of the other noticeable variants is found in the nomenclature used to identify the pursuers. Most frequently they are called Herod or simply Herod's men, in agreement with the text of Matthew, which is the only Gospel to relate the story of King Herod's pursuit of the family and the slaughter of the innocents. In the Gypsy version, Herod is conflated with Pharaoh ("Pharim"), perhaps because the Gypsies connected themselves with the ancient Egyptians and, adapting the flight to their culture, they, like others, linked the Pharaoh who ordered the slaughter of the Hebrew children in Moses' time with the wicked Herod.[41] They may also have been assimilating Christ's escape with that of Moses. In any case, they would not have been bound by the Gospel version of the flight and massacre.

In the Aramaic version the pursuers are called "bani isra'il," the children of Israel, a phrase frequently used for the twelve tribes in the Old Testament.[42] In the Portuguese, Provençal, Sorbian, and several of the French versions, the pursuers are specifically referred to as the Jews. These explicit references to Jews instead of to Herod or Herod's soldiers are a reflection of the deep-rooted anti-Semitism that held the Jews collectively responsible for the Passion and death of Christ. Though the Gospel of Matthew identifies the pursuers as Herod's soldiers, the popular mind, responding to centuries of anti-Semitism, eventually defined them simply as Jews. In fact, the historical King Herod, who would accord with the king mentioned in Matthew's Gospel, was the son of an adventurer who had made himself "king" of a sizable part of Judea with Roman help and protection. Though his family had been converted to Judaism three generations previous, he was hated by the Jews as a foreign usurper and Rome's puppet ruler.[43] Though the historicity of the Massacre of the Innocents is in doubt, the story that Matthew records derives in part from the very strong Jewish hostility to Herod.[44]

A few versions deserve special mention. In one Irish variant men were sowing late in the season, that is, around Easter time, and the adult Christ passed by, fleeing those seeking to put him to death.[45] The devil's coach-horse beetle betrays him to the pursuers by crying out that he had just passed "yesterday." So Christ was easily taken and put to death. Though nearly every peasant must have been acquainted with the Gospel story of Judas's betrayal, this beetle, who played the treacherous role of informant in the Irish Grain Miracle folktale, supplants Judas's role as betrayer.

In a Wendish version it is Luther who is in flight from threatening forces.[46] He has "rescued" the Bible from its "slavery" to the Catholic Church, and he hurries over a newly plowed field in his attempt to escape the threatening men pursuing him. The Grain Miracle enables him to get away safely. And in an Aramaic version of the tale the protagonist is a young bride fleeing from an unwanted marriage. She is able to promote the instantaneous growth of fruit, thereby fooling her pursuers into thinking she had passed by long before, and thus foils the plans of her heathen relatives who wanted to marry her to an undesired suitor.[47]

Thus, as the Grain Miracle was disseminated it was transformed and adapted to various historical situations and cultural contexts. It developed into a story that emphasized how the force of good, with the compliance of the natural, could overcome the forces of evil. As it spread, it came to be known in areas throughout Western Europe, and is recounted in villages to this day.

Conclusion

The evidence for the worship of a mother goddess of vegetation is multi-faceted, and veneration of her through history is complex. Perpetuated in agrarian contexts, the figure remained part of humankind's religious history for millennia. Agriculturalists, seeking to understand the relationship between the tangible world and another, transcendent reality, devised a figure who could protect family and community from crop calamity and resulting starvation. The basic human fear of uncontrollable, malevolent forces assured that each successive culture would incorporate a form of this protectress into its religious life.

This book has explored one strand of mother goddess veneration—as protectress of sowing—in an essentially Western European cultural context. Anthropologists are currently engaged in research on cultures in Western Europe and elsewhere in an attempt to uncover remnants of goddess worship in a variety of present-day contexts.[1] Some scholars are finding evidence of transformations similar to those undergone by the grain and sowing figure, transformations that have not totally dimmed all traces of the age-old female divinities. Maternal goddess figures have been shown to insinuate themselves into local or national rites, some religious and some secular. But the specific cross-cultural study of the phenomenon of a sowing protectress has yet to be undertaken.

The study of the beliefs of agrarian peoples who could not write and who left no textual record has its pitfalls.[2] The sparse documents that do provide clues to their beliefs emanate from the pens of the literate, who were themselves outside the agrarian culture. A study of those extrinsic documents, combined with an analysis of extant archeological and art-historical data, provided the initial impetus for this book. But as research progressed, the limitations of the traditional methodology of medieval-art-historical research became apparent. Fortunately, new, broader approaches to medieval history and art history are currently possible. The art historian can now make use of the oral tradition as it has been cataloged by folklorists. This material is often cast in a vernacular idiom and reveals the fears, hopes, and tensions that preoccupied rural people. These newly accessible sources, viewed with the insights of the anthropologist and psychologist as well as the archeologist and art historian, allow for a fuller interpretation of rural culture and permit us to unravel themes and patterns that were previously indistinct. This broader approach is of particular importance for medievalists studying the people living during the period called, by some, the Dark Ages.

The current interchanges among historians, anthropologists, folklorists, psychologists, and church historians open the possibility of examining a new set of concerns. All fields will benefit from this dialogue. We can offer each other not only information but also new methods for analyzing our respective sources. Uncovering the meaning of the sowing protectress as she migrated from culture to culture was possible only by adopting some of the methodologies and insights of these diverse disciplines.

In each era, people interpret anew the original revelatory paradigms of their faiths. They make selections from the patterns of received traditions, selections that make sense in their lives. At the present time, a vigorous exploration is afoot, an exploration of ancient prepatriarchal values.[3] Some of those involved in the quest are seeking access to new forms of spirituality. This is, for some, a personal quest, deriving from a feeling of alienation from the Judeo-Christian conceptions of the divine as masculine. It takes the form of a search for ways to envision divinity as genderless. The unraveling of the history of the transformed grain protectress can point out ways to reinterpret age-old symbols that may have been obscured over time. Those intrigued by uncovering and documenting the survival of any of the feminine dimensions of the divine can explore not only the way goddess imagery was suppressed, but also the instances in which goddess figures were transformed and given a new content.

As we have seen, the protectress figure, radically changed, continued to be present in peoples' imaginations in the form of various female saints. In certain milieux she became a folkloric figure. In a related phenomenon in some areas, pagan goddesses such as she were recast as demons, crazy mothers, or wood spirits. Her traces may be dim, but in many cultures during various historical periods the footsteps of the great goddess are not totally obliterated.

Notes

Introduction

1. Marija Gimbutas, *The Goddesses and Gods of Old Europe* (Berkeley, 1982), pp. 152–214.

2. Jane Ellen Harrison, *Prolegomena to the Study of Greek Religion* (Cambridge, 1908), pp. 271–273; Gimbutas, *Goddesses and Gods*, p. 238.

3. Jacques Le Goff, "Les paysans et le monde rural dans la littérature du haut moyen âge (Ve–VIe siècles)," "Culture clericale et traditions folklorique dans la civilisation merovingienne," and "Culture ecclesiastique et culture folklorique au moyen âge: Saint Marcel de Paris et le Dragon," and other essays in *Pour un autre moyen âge* (Paris, 1977); Raoul Manselli, *La religion populaire au moyen âge. Problèmes de méthode et d'histoire* (Montreal, 1975); Pierre Boglioni et al., *La culture populaire au moyen âge* (Montreal, 1979).

4. Boglioni, "La culture populaire au moyen âge: Thèmes et problèmes," in Boglioni et al., *Culture populaire* (Montreal, 1979), pp. 13–37, esp. pp. 26ff.

5. The term *topos* as used in this book means an image or figurative idea handed down from antiquity to the Latin Middle Ages, and sometimes uncovered in the literature and art of the modern world. See Ernst Robert Curtiers's discussion of *topoi* in *European Literature and the Latin Middle Ages* (New York, 1953, English-language ed.), pp. 79–105.

6. On the transformation of tales, see C. W. v. Sydow, "Geography and Folk-tale Oicotypes," in his *Selected Papers on Folklore* (Helsinki, 1948), pp. 44–59.

7. Ernest Jones, *Nightmares, Witches and Devils* (New York, 1932), pp. 58ff., for the influence of dream imagery on the formation of waking thoughts and beliefs in the Middle Ages, and Jacques Le Goff, "Les rêves dans l'Occident medieval," in *Pour un moyen âge*, pp. 299–306.

I: The Goddess in the Ancient World

1. The Neolithic and early Chalcolithic periods in Anatolia extend from 7500 to 5650 B.C. The statuettes discussed in this part are from about 5650 B.C., that is, the early Chalcolithic, literally the "copper-stone" phase. See James Mellaart, *Excavations at Hacilar* (Edinburgh, 1970), vol. 1, p. 10. These dates have been arrived at by the use of radio carbon techniques, as well as dendrochronology (the recording of time in the annual growth rings of trees). James Mellaart, *The Archaeology of Ancient Turkey* (London, 1978), p. 13.

2. Mellaart, *Excavations at Hacilar*, vol. 1, pp. 166–175, vol. 2, plates 125,158.

3. Alexander Marshack, "The Art and Symbols of Ice Age Man," *Human Nature* 1, no. 9 (Sept. 1978), pp. 32–41.

4. Mellaart, *Excavations at Hacilar*, vol. 1, p. 170; and James Mellaart, *Çatal Hüyük* (New York, 1967), pp. 201–202.

5. Mellaart, *Excavations at Hacilar*, vol. 1, p. 168. See also Mellaart, *Ancient Turkey*, p. 24; and Mellaart, *Çatal Hüyük*, p. 181.

6. Mellaart, *Çatal Hüyük*, p. 183.

7. Mellaart, *Çatal Hüyük*, p. 202; and Mellaart, *Excavations at Hacilar*, vol. 1, p. 170. See also James G. Frazer, *The New Golden Bough*, ed. and with notes and foreword by Theodor H. Gaster (New York, 1959), pp. 366ff. According to this view, when men took over the main role in agriculture, the plow acquired a phallic significance, being the implement used to break into the ground and enhance its fertility. See E. O. James, *The Cult of the Mother Goddess* (New York, 1959), p. 230.

8. Gimbutas, *The Goddesses and Gods*. Gimbutas examines archeological data from the seventh, sixth, and fifth millennia B.C. The area defined in her study extends from the Aegean

and Adriatic including the islands, to Czechoslovakia, southern Poland, and the western Ukraine. To this area and time period Gimbutas gives the name Old Europe. According to Gimbutas, between 4500 and 2800 B.C., these civilizations were overrun by waves of patriarchal, horse-riding steppe pastoralists whose culture contrasted sharply with the sedentary, matrifocal, peaceful peoples of Old Europe, who possessed a matriarchal, earth- and water-bound pantheon of goddesses. See also Marija Gimbutas, "The Transformation of European and Anatolian Culture 4500–2500 B.C. and Its Legacy," *The Journal of Indo-European Studies* 8, no. 1 (1980), p. 1.

9. Gimbutas, *Goddesses and Gods*, pp. 201–211.

10. Gimbutas, *Goddesses and Gods*, pp. 201–205.

11. Gimbutas, *Goddesses and Gods*, pp. 201–205.

12. Gimbutas, "Women and Culture in Goddess-Oriented Old Europe," in *The Politics of Women's Spirituality*, ed. C. Spretnak (New York, 1982), pp. 24, 29. In some instances the evidence of impressed grain is found on small statues of pigs. Since Neolithic times, pigs have been sacred to the goddess of vegetation, and some early vegetation goddesses have been discovered wearing pig masks. Folklore reveals a continuous connection between the pig and the grain spirit. See Chapter I, "Greece," and Chapter VII, pp. 000–000.

13. Gimbutas, *Goddesses and Gods*, p. 236.

14. Archeological and linguistic evidence from southeastern Europe point to a number of potent goddesses from the prehistoric period: a snake-bird goddess; a "mistress of animals" goddess; the Great Mother goddess. Some scholars see this pre-Indo-European, Neolithic/Chalcolithic pantheon as being assimilated with those goddesses represented in the later Indo-European pantheon. See Miriam Robbins, "The Assimilation of Pre-Indo-European Goddesses into Indo-European Society," *The Journal of Indo-European Studies* 8, no. 1 (1980), pp. 19–29.

15. See note 8.

16. Samuel Noah Kramer, *History Begins at Sumer* (Philadelphia, 1981).

17. From Kramer, *History Begins at Sumer*, pp. 303–304; see also pp. 314, 320.

18. Kramer, *History Begins at Sumer*, p. 315. See also Diane Wolkstein and Samuel Noah Kramer, *Inanna, Queen of Heaven and Earth* (New York, 1983), pp. 107–110.

19. Kramer, *History Begins at Sumer*, p. 305. In historical times the role of the goddess would have been played by an Inanna devotee.

20. James B. Pritchard, *Palestinian Figurines in Relation to Certain Goddesses Known Through Literature*, American Oriental Series, vol. 24 (New Haven, 1943); W. F. Albright, *The Archaeology of Palestine* (London, 1954), pp. 104–105, fig. 27; and W. F. Albright, *The Excavations of Tell Beit Mirsim*, The Annual of the American Schools of Oriental Research, vols. 21–22, 1941–1943, plate 55, nos. 1–3.

21. James B. Pritchard, *The Ancient Near East in Pictures* (Princeton, 1954), pp. 303–304, and plates 469–480, esp. plate 469; Pritchard, *Palestinian Figurines*, p. 42; and André Lemaire, "Who or What Was Yahweh's Asherah?" *Biblical Archaeology Review* 10, no. 6 (1984), pp. 42–51.

22. Pritchard, *Palestinian Figurines*, pp. 21–23, 55ff.

23. Pritchard, *Palestinian Figurines*, pp. 10–13, 23–27.

24. Pritchard, *Palestinian Figurines*, pp. 6–8.

25. Pritchard, *Palestinian Figurines*, pp. 68–70.

26. Pritchard, *Palestinian Figurines*, pp. 76–82.

27. Pritchard, *Palestinian Figurines*, pp. 62–65.

28. Tikva S. Frymer, "Asherah," *Encyclopaedia Judaica* (Jerusalem, 1972), vol. 3, cols. 703–705. Another of her names, Qudsu (QDS, holiness), is frequently inscribed on plaques of nude female figurines. See Pritchard, *Ancient Near East*, plates 471, 473, 474.

29. Frymer, "Asherah," vol. 3, cols. 703–705.

30. Judg. 3:7, 1 Kings 16:32–33, 2 Kings 17:9–10, 2 Kings 17:16, 2 Kings 21, 2 Kings 23:4–16, Isa. 17:7.

31. Pritchard, *Palestinian Figurines*, p. 62.

32. Millar Burrows, *What Mean These Stones* (New Haven, 1941), p. 211. For a contrary view, see Lemaire, "Yahweh's Asherah," who proposes that *asherah* means sacred tree.

33. Exod. 34:12–14.

34. 1 Kings 15:13, 2 Chron. 15:16.

35. 1 Kings 18:19.

36. 2 Kings 21:7.

37. 2 Kings 17:9–10, Jer. 17:2.

38. 2 Kings 23:7.

39. Lemaire, "Yahweh's Asherah," p. 50.

40. Pritchard, *Palestinian Figurines*, p. 63.

41. Pritchard, *Palestinian Figurines*, p. 63.

42. O. R. Gurney, *Some Aspects of Hittite Religion* (Oxford, 1977), pp. 4–5.

43. O. R. Gurney, *The Hittites* (reprint London, 1981), pp. 138, 144.

44. Gurney, *Hittites*, pp. 141, 154.

45. Françoise Dunand, *Le culte d'Isis dans le bassin orientale de la Méditerranée* (Leiden, 1973), p. 9.

46. R. E. Witt, *Isis in the Graeco-Roman World* (Ithaca, 1971), pp. 14–15.

47. Witt, *Isis*, pp. 16–17.

48. Dunand, *Culte d'Isis*, p. 23.

49. As quoted in Friedrich Solmsen, *Isis Among the Greeks and Romans* (Cambridge, Mass., 1979), pp. 3–4.

50. R. F. Willetts, *The Civilization of Ancient Crete* (London, 1977), p. 116. For Arthur Evans's interpretation of the Minoan goddess's sacred tree, see *The Palace of Minos at Knossos* (New York, 1965, a reprint of volumes published in the 1920s), vol. 1, pp. 432, 635; vol. 2, p. 250; vol. 3, pp. 137, 138, 142; vol. 4, pp. 346, 393, 951.

51. Willetts, *Ancient Crete*, p. 120.

52. *Odyssey* 5.125–128.

53. Pausanias 8.4.1.

54. On the Thesmophoria, see Allaire Chandor Brumfield, *The Attic Festivals of Demeter and Their Relation to the Agricultural Year* (New York, 1981), pp. 70–103; Jane Ellen Harrison, *Prolegomena to the Study of Greek Religion* (Cambridge, 1922), pp. 120–131; and Frazer, *New Golden Bough*, pp. 450–454.

55. Brumfield, *Festivals of Demeter*, pp. 70–73, for a summary of the arguments.

56. The scholium is attributed to Arethas of Caesarea, a tenth-century bishop, probably relying on the work of Didymas, a grammarian of the first century B.C. The text is confused, but the material is generally regarded as reliable. For a translation from the Greek see Brumfield, *Festivals of Demeter*, pp. 73–74. The original Greek is in H. Rabe, *Scholia in Lucianum* (Leipzig, 1906), pp. 275–276.

57. Frazer, *New Golden Bough*, p. 450.

58. Ovid, *Fasti* 4.465–466.

59. Pausanias 1.14.3.

60. Brumfield, *Festivals of Demeter*, pp. 236ff.

61. Brumfield, *Festivals of Demeter*, p. 237.

62. Eric Neumann, *The Great Mother* (Princeton, 1970), p. 308, where the pomegranate is interpreted as a sexual symbol.

63. The ancients defined the fructification of vegetation as "conception" and the maturation of vegetation as the "birthing" of the plant. The gestation of vegetation is compared to that of a fetus in Varro, *Rerum Rusticarum* 1.44.4, and Pliny, *Natural History* 18.56. See also Henri Le Bonniec, *Le culte de Cérès à Rome* (Paris, 1958), p. 128.

64. For the complex relationship between Tellus and Ceres see Le Bonniec, *Culte de Cérès*, pp. 48–107.

65. Le Bonniec, *Culte de Cérès*, pp. 128–129.

66. Though by 153 B.C. the beginning of the year had been moved to January 1, the year's old beginning, March 1, held its meaning for a long time in folk memory and belief, even into the tenth century. This was because it coincided with seeding and the awakening of vegetable life. See Dieter Harmening, *Superstitio, Uberlieferungs- und theoriegeschichtliche Untersuchungen zur kirchlich-theologischen Abergeaubensliteratur des Mittelalters* (Berlin, 1979), p. 146. And Le Bonniec, *Culte de Cérès*, p. 138, n. 2.

During the Roman period and into the Middle Ages, the most favored of all wheats was the *triticum vulgarum*, the 'three-month' wheat sown in the spring and ready to harvest in May or June. In the southern Mediterranean, grain was also sown in the fall to take advantage of the winter rains. See Palladius, *De Re Rustica* 3, 4; and Virgil, *Georgics* 1.44.64: "In the early spring, when the chill slush melts upon the hoary hills, and the crumbling clod is thawed by the west wind, even then let my steer begin to groan over the deep-driven plough, and my plough share, worn by the furrow to glisten." Trans. A. W. Young and W. F. Mason, *Virgil: Georgics* (London, n.d.), p. 4. See also Geoffrey Rickman, *The Corn Supply of Ancient Rome* (Oxford, 1980), pp. 4, 6–7.

67. Ovid, *Fasti* 1.655–704 illustrates the special days of the year and anniversaries of historical events. Ovid reports that he used old annuals as sources (1.7, 4.11), and that he spoke with farmers and occasionally participated in the rituals he describes (4.727ff.). This English translation is from *Ovid's Fasti*, trans. James George Frazer, Loeb Classical Library (Cambridge, Mass., 1959), pp. 51–53.

68. J. Bayet, "Les 'Feriae Sementivae,'" in *Croyances et rites dans la Rome antique* (n.p., 1971), pp. 177–205 (first appeared in *Revue d'histoire des religions* 137 (1950), pp. 172–206); Le Bonniec, *Culte de Cérès*, p. 58; L. Delatte, "Recherches sur quelques fêtes mobiles du calendrier romain," *L'antiquité classique* 5 (1936), pp. 381–391.

69. Ovid's poetical description leaves the precise order of the day somewhat obscure: Did the sacrifices and prayers occur just after the seeding or just before? In the Latin, see lines 667ff., 703–705.

70. From the earliest periods of Roman history, when the city, army, crops, or herds seemed endangered, a *lustratio* was performed, a procession that went around the objects to be purified or protected. The victims that were subsequently to be slaughtered were led around the area. Macrobius, *Saturnalia* 3.5, 7: "lustrare significat circumire"; Cicero, *Tusculan Disputations* 5, 27, 79. See also Virgil, *Georgics* 1.338–350.

71. Though named as two separate deities, Ceres and Tellus are very closely joined. See V. Basanoff, *Les dieux des Romains* (Paris, 1942), pp. 67–68.

72. Joannes Laurentius Lydus, *Liber de Mensibus,* ed. R. Wuensch (Leipzig, 1898), 3.9 (p. 42).

73. Lydus, *Liber de Mensibus* 3, lines 16ff. (Wuensch, p. 42).

74. Other authors providing brief notices but not more information about Sementiva are Varro, *De Lingua Latina* 5.26, 6.25; Varro, *Rerum Rusticarum* 1.2.1.

75. See Kirby Flower Smith, *The Elegies of Albius Tibullus* (Darmstadt, 1971), pp. 134–137 and notes, pp. 391ff.; and *The Poems of Tibullus*, trans. Constance Carrier (Bloomington, Ind., 1968), pp. 64–67.

76. Virgil, *Georgics* 1.337–350. The English translation is from Theodore C. Williams, *The Georgics and Eclogues of Virgil* (Cambridge, Mass., 1915), p. 38.

77. Le Bonniec, *Culte de Cérès*, pp. 134ff., 142–144; G. Wissowa, "Das Proemium von Virgils Georgica," *Hermes* 52 (1917), p. 99. Wissowa recognizes three *ambarvalia* (circuits around the field): one at the end of winter, one in summer, and one before the harvest.

78. Le Bonniec, *Culte de Cérès*, pp. 139–148. See also Macrobius, *Saturnalia* 3.5, 7.

79. Le Bonniec, *Culte de Cérès*, pp. 143–144.

80. April 25 is the saint's day of Mark the Evangelist. But the Rogations have nothing to do with that figure, whose saint's day was not even liturgically recognized until later in the Middle Ages. *Butler's Lives of the Saints,* ed. H. Thurston, S.J. (New York, 1956), vol. 2, pp. 161–162, vol. 1, p. 234.

81. For example, on Floralia, see Arnobius, *Adversus Nationes* 7.33; Saint Augustine, *De Civitate Dei* 2.27. See also Harmening, *Superstitio*, pp. 145–155.

II: The Goddess in the North

1. *Germania* 40.

2. *Germania* 40.2.

3. *Germania* 40.3.

4. *Germania* 40.5.

5. Henri Graillot, *Le culte de Cybèle, Mère des Dieux* (Paris, 1912); Maarten J. Vermaseren, *Cybele and Attis* (London, 1977), pp. 38–41.

6. Graillot, *Culte de Cybèle*, p. 136; Vermaseren, *Cybele and Attis*, pp. 113, 119–122.

7. Frazer, *New Golden Bough*, pp. 47–48.

8. H. M. Chadwick, *The Origin of the English Nation* (Cambridge, 1924), pp. 25ff., 231–240. The name of the goddess is connected with the Celtic word *nerto-* (Welsh *nerth*), "power."

9. See J. G. C. Andersen, ed., *Cornelii Taciti De Origine et Situ Germanorum* (Oxford, 1938), pp. 187–188; Chapter VII of this book; and also H. R. Ellis Davidson, *Scandinavian Mythology* (London, 1969), p. 91.

10. See Chapter V, "Daemon."

11. J. De Vries, *La religion des celtes* (Paris, 1963), pp. 125–126; Barry Cunliffe, *The Celtic World* (New York, 1979), p. 7.

12. De Vries, *Religion des Celtes*, pp. 125–132.

13. E. Esperandieu, *Recueil général des bas-reliefs, statues et bustes de la Gaule romaine* (Paris, 1910). Supplementary volumes 1–16 are by Raymond Lantier. For just a few instances of the many examples of mutilation, see nos. 1272, 1309, 1317, 1826, 1827, 1840, 1848, 2064, 2157. See also E. Esperandieu, *Recueil général des bas-reliefs, statues et bustes de la Germanie romaine* (Paris and Brussels, 1931), no. 198.

14. Richard E. Sullivan, "The Carolingian Missionary and the Pagan," *Speculum* 18 (1953), p. 720.

15. Garrett S. Olmsted, *The Gundestrup Cauldron*, Collection Latomus (Brussels, 1979), p. 129.

16. J. V. S. Megaw, *Art of the European Iron Age* (Bath, 1970), p. 59.

17. Olmsted, *Gundestrup Cauldron*, pp. 129–132.

18. Olmsted, *Gundestrup Cauldron*, pp. 129–130.

19. Olmsted, *Gundestrup Cauldron*, p. 131.

20. Olmsted, *Gundestrup Cauldron*, p. 131; and Megaw, *Iron Age*, p. 129.

21. Illustrated in Esperandieu, *Gaule romaine*, no. 2325, and Simone Deyts, *Sculptures gallo-romaines mythologiques et religieuses*, Dijon, Musée Archéologique (Paris, 1976), no. 134. Esperandieu indicates that a similar group in terra-cotta was housed at the Museum of Autun, but a letter from the curator informs me that no such group is presently housed there.

22. See Esperandieu, *Gaule romaine*, nos. 1817, 1819, 2064, 2081, and dozens of other examples in the indices.

23. Few texts defending the ancient religious practices survive. But some pagans did show the ability to defend their old religion. See Sullivan, "Carolingian Missionary," pp. 734–735.

24. Gordon W. Herves, "Cultural Continuity from the Paleolithic Onward," *Comparative Civilizations Bulletin* 10, no. 2 (Summer 1981), pp. 5–9.

25. Gregory of Tours, *Liber in Gloria Confessorum*, chap. 77, in Joannes Zwicker, *Fontes Historiae Religionis Celticae* (Berlin, 1934), p. 180.

26. Lewis Thorpe, *Introduction to Gregory of Tours, The History of the Franks* (London, 1974), pp. 33–34.

27. Berecynthia is a poetic name for Cybele, the Great Mother goddess of the East. Imported into Rome from Asia Minor in 204 B.C., Cybele's cult spread to the provinces as well. (There is now evidence that the cult had practitioners in Marseille as early as the sixth century B.C. See Vermaseren, *Cybele and Attis*, p. 132. The Cybele cult as practiced in Rome included the ceremony of *lavatio*: Once a year the statue of the goddess was carried through the streets as part of her early spring festival. She was then bathed in the river Almo and returned to her temple on the Palatine. (This washing of the statue does not, however, seem to have been part of the mother goddess rite as practiced in Gaul.) See Vermaseren, *Cybele and Attis*, pp. 113, 119–122. On the fusion of the cult of Cybele with that of the indigenous Celtic "Matres," see Graillot, *Culte de Cybèle*, pp. 445–465.

28. Thorpe, *Gregory of Tours*, pp. 33–34.

29. Certain musical instruments used in these processions were long prohibited by the church, especially the cithara and the *tibia*, frequently employed in the rituals of pagan cults. See A. Gastone, *L'église et sa musique* (Paris, 1936), p. 111.

30. E. K. Chambers, *The Mediaeval Stage* (Oxford, 1903), vol. 1, p. 161, n. 3; p. 169. Also Harmening, *Superstitio*, p. 143.

31. By contrast, Tacitus, in writing about Nerthus, made very clear that he stood outside the belief system of the tribes about whom he was reporting.

32. On the acceptance of the miraculous among both clergy and the general population in the Middle Ages, see Manselli, *Religion populaire*, pp. 21–22, 44–51, 55.

33. Manselli, *Religion populaire*, pp. 22–26.

34. Joannes Zwicker, ed., *Fontes Historiae Religionis Celticae* (Bonn, 1935), vol. 2, pp. 163–164; and *Passio S. Symphoriani* 6, in *Acta Martyrum Sincera et Selecta*, ed. Ruinart, sec. 1713, p. 82. The story of the martyrdom of Symphorian for refusing to worship Berecynthia/Cybele was well known to Gregory in the sixth century. See Gregory of Tours, *Liber in Gloria Confessorum*.

35. Vermaseren, *Cybele and Attis*, pp. 131–138.

36. Sulpicius Severus, *Vita S. Martini* 12.1–2, in *Sulpice Sévère, Vie de Saint Martin*, ed. J. Fontaine (Paris, 1967), vol. 1, p. 279. Sulpicius's life of Saint Martin was substantially written before Martin died in 397.

37. Sulpicius's use ot the term *sacrificium* here refers to the animals that would have been sacrificed after the procession.

III: The Mother Goddess in Art from Antiquity to the Middle Ages

1. A study of the "Déesse Mère" figures indexed in Esperandieu, *Gaule romaine*, will reveal the nature of this destruction. See Chapter II, note 13, on mutilated statues. For missionaries destroying pagan objects of worship see Sullivan, "Carolingian Missionary," p. 720.

2. Harmening, *Superstitio*, pp. 43–48.

3. Mathias Delcor, *Les Vièrges romanes de Cordagne et Conflent* (Barcelona, 1970), pp. 23–25. See also J. Adhémar, *Influences antiques dans l'art du moyen âge français* (London, 1939).

4. Eugenie Strong, "Terra Mater or Italia?" *Journal of Roman Studies* 27 (1937), pp. 114–126.

5. Strong, "Terra Mater," p. 115.

6. C. T. Seltman, ed., *Cambridge Ancient History, Plates* (Cambridge, 1934), vol. 4, p. 184.

7. On classical gods and personifications used in the art of late antiquity, see Richard Brilliant, "The Classical Realm," in the Metropolitan Museum of Art catalog *Age of Spirituality*, ed. Kurt Weitzmann (New York, 1979), pp. 126–181.

8. J. Schwartz, "Quelques sources antiques d'ivoires carolingiens," *Cahiers archéologiques* 11 (1960), pp. 145–162.

9. Strong, "Terra Mater," p. 118; E. Strong, *Roman Sculpture* (n.p., 1907), plate 36. The nursing mother goddess image is popular in the art of Neolithic/Chalcolithic southeastern Europe, the ancient Near East, and in Egyptian art until the Ptolemaic period. See Gimbutas, *Goddesses and Gods*, p. 194; Pritchard, *Ancient Near East*, fig. 469, bottom center; and Françoise Dunand, *Religion populaire en Egypte romaine* (London, 1979), plates 1–7.

10. K. A. Wirth, "Erde," *Reallexicon zur Deutschen Kunstgeschichte*, vol. 5, cols. 1056–1059.

11. Jacqueline Leclercq, "Sirènes-poissons romans," *Revue belge d'archéologie et d'histoire de l'art* 40 (1971), pp. 17–18.

12. G. Bachelard, *L'eau et des rêves* (Paris, 1947), p. 99; cited by Leclercq, "Sirènes-poissons," p. 3.

13. Leclercq, "Sirènes-poissons," pp. 5–7.

14. Maximus of Turin, *Homilies* 49, in J. P. Migne, *Patrologiae Cursus Completus*, series Latin (Paris, 1857–1866), vol. 58, cols. 339, 342; cited by Leclercq, "Sirènes-poissons," p. 12.

15. Though called Honorius of Autun, he was probably active mainly in Regensburg. *Speculum Ecclesiae*, in Migne, *P.L.*, vol. 172, cols. 885–886; cited by Leclercq, "Sirènes-poissons," p. 13.

16. Jacqueline Leclercq-Kadaner, "De la Terre-Mère à la Luxure," *Cahiers de civilisation médiévale* 17, no. 1 (1975), pp. 37–43, esp. p. 40.

17. Leclercq cites other examples on a capital at Perrecy-les-Forges (Saône-et-Loire) and at the church at La Jarne (Charente-Maritime); Leclercq, "Sirènes-poissons," p. 17.

18. Leclercq-Kadaner, "Terre-Mère," pp. 37–43.

19. Cited in the French by Y. Labande-Mailfert, *Poitou Roman* (La Pierre-qui-Vire, 1957), p.

180. This punishment as imaged in the figure of Luxuria was not reserved for adulteresses alone; unmarried mothers were likewise destined for this fate.
20. Wirth, "Erde," cols. 1064ff.
21. Leclercq-Kadaner, "Terre-Mère," pp. 39–40; and Adhémar, *Influences antiques*, p. 197, n. 4, fig. 49.
22. Wirth, "Erde," p. 4, cols. 1009–1011.
23. Esperandieu, *Gaule romaine*, nos. 1326, 1333, 1334. N. Mueller-Dietrich, *Die romanische Skulptur in Lothringer* (Munich, 1968), pp. 106–7, nn. 395, 398, fig. 62, interprets a destroyed capital from the church at Lorry-les-Metz as revealing an intermediate iconography; a young woman offered her breast to animals and to a human being at the same time. Mueller-Dietrich interpreted this image as evidence for the Christianization of the pagan symbol of Terra Mater into the figure of Mary.

IV: Metamorphosis: From Goddess to Saint

1. Elaine Pagels, "What Became of God the Mother? Conflicting Images of God in Early Christianity," *Signs* 2, no. 2 (1976), p. 298. The texts that included feminine symbolism for the divine usually contained other unorthodox perspectives as well.
2. For a recent attempt to uncover those few similes or metaphors that escaped this expurgation, see Carolyn Bynum, *Jesus as Mother: Studies in the Spirituality of the High Middle Ages* (Berkeley, 1982).
3. On the survival of pagan elements into the Middle Ages see Le Goff, "Culture cléricale," pp. 223–235; Boglioni, "Culture populaire," pp. 13–37; and Sullivan, "Carolingian Missionary," pp. 705–740, esp. p. 716.
4. Venerable Bede, *Historia Ecclesiastica Gentis Anglorum*, trans. Sherley-Price, Penguin Classics (Harmondsworth, 1955), 1.30 (pp. 86–87).
5. These mild instructions were followed only in certain places. Other methods were used by some missionaries to persuade pagans to abandon their old religion and convert to Christianity. For a description of missionary activities in the Carolingian empire see Sullivan, "Carolingian Missionary," pp. 705–740, esp. p. 720.
6. For ancient cultic practice evident in early records of rural drama, see Charles Read Baskervill, "Dramatic Aspects of Medieval Folk Festivals in England," *Studies in Philology* 17 (1920), pp. 61ff.
7. Sullivan, "Carolingian Missionary," p. 712.
8. Bede, *Historia Ecclesiastica* 2.15 (Sherley-Price, p. 128).
9. Lives of saints, penitentials and sermons are particularly rich sources for this kind of information. See Harmening, *Superstitio*; Manselli, *Religion populaire*, pp. 20ff., 35ff.; and Abbot E. Vacandard, "L'idolatrie en Gaule au VIe et au VIIe siècles," *Revue des questions historiques* 65 (1899), pp. 443–445.
10. *Vita Eligii* 2.15, in Migne, *P.L.*, vol. 87, cols. 528–529. The catalog in this sermon reflects the doctrine expounded by contemporary church councils (for example, the Council of Nantes) and reproduces almost the same ideas as the Homilies of Saint Caesarius: 53, 58, 64, 66, 74ff., etc. See Harmening, *Superstitio*, pp. 34, 43–45, 69–71, 79, 329.
11. "Nullus praesumat lustrationes facere nec herbas incantare . . . ," Migne, *P.L.*, vol. 82, col. 528C.
12. Manselli, *Religion populaire*, p. 20.
13. For example, between 1236 and 1244 Robert Grosseteste forbid his clergy to appear in "luda quos vocant Inductionem Maii, sive Autumni," "plays (or games) that they called the bringing forth of May or of autumn." He also disapproved of "Ludus de Rege et Regina," "King and Queen play." These *ludi* incorporated traditional pagan spring and harvest customs. See William Tydeman, *The Theatre in the Middle Ages* (Cambridge, 1978), p. 19; and Chambers, *Mediaeval Stage*, vol. 1, p. 91.

14. E. M. R. Ditmas, "The Way Legends Grow," *Folklore* 85 (1974), pp. 244ff. For examples of folk theater relating to long-enduring agrarian practices, see Leopold Schmidt, *Le théâtre populaire européen* (Paris, 1965), esp. pp. 23ff., 43ff. We have few medieval records of the assimilation of pagan deities with folkloric figures, because extra-ecclesiastical rural ceremonial was rarely referred to let alone described in the Latin clerical texts of the Middle Ages; and if it was mentioned, that was because the writer was either criticizing the activity for its pagan content or unwittingly revealing pagan elements in seemingly Christianized rites. Folklore gathered since the early modern period, however, provides at least some record of traditions that otherwise would have gone unreported by the literate classes. With evidence from these sources at hand, it is possible to show that though they were denounced by religious officials, important figures of the pre-Christian belief systems could often survive innocuously as characters in rural pageants and ceremonies.

15. Celtic festivals were syncretized with the following Roman celebrations: Brumalia (November 24), the Saturnalia (December 17–19), the Mithraic feast of Sol Invictus (December 25), and the Kalends (January 1). Summer rites came to coincide with the Roman Floralia (May 28–June 3).

16. H. Grisar, S.J., *Rome and the Popes in the Middle Ages* (London, 1912), vol. 3, pp. 282–283.

17. The Nativity feast coincided with the December 25 celebration of Sol Invictus, and the Circumcision with the January 1 celebration of the Kalends. The Purification rites of the Virgin would likewise pick up strands of ancient pagan February festivals of purification. See Chapter VII.

18. Migne, *P.L.*, vol. 87, col. 528B.

19. Manselli, *Religion populaire*, pp. 28ff.

20. Manselli, *Religion populaire*, p. 40; Ditmas, "The Way Legends Grow," p. 244.

21. For an excellent recent study of this substitution process, see Jean-Claude Schmitt, *Le saint lévrier: Guinefort, guérisseur d'enfants depuis le XIIIe siècle* (Paris, 1979).

22. Manselli, *Religion populaire*, pp. 22–25.

23. For examples and further bibliography, see Marie Durand-Lefebvre, *Art gallo-romain et sculpture romane* (Paris, 1937), pp. 173–250.

24. C. Lecouteux, "Paganisme, Christianisme et merveilleux," *Annales* 37, no. 4 (1984), pp. 700–716; and J. A. Maccullock, "Folk-Memory in Folk-Tales," *Folklore* 60 (1949), pp. 307–315.

25. On the difficulties that beset a researcher in the area of popular religion of the early Middle Ages, see Boglioni, "Culture populaire," pp. 13–37; and Lecouteux, "Paganisme, Christianisme." The illiterate were known by various terms: *indocti, idiotae,* and, most significantly, *rustici.* See Brian Stock, *The Implications of Illiteracy* (Lawrenceville, N.J., 1983), esp. pp. 8, 27. The role of technological development during certain centuries has been neglected by historians, because technology was chiefly the concern of groups who wrote little; see Lynn White, *Medieval Technology and Social Change* (Oxford, 1962), p. vii.

26. On the structure of folktales, see Vladimir Propp, *Morphologie du conte,* trans. from the Russian (Paris, 1970).

27. For a review of the literature concerning dreams from the Old Testament through the medieval period, see Jacques Le Goff, "Les rêves dans l'Occident médiéval," in Le Goff, *Pour un autre moyen âge* (Paris, 1977), pp. 299–306. See also E. Ettlinger, "Precognitive Dreams in Celtic Legend and Folklore," in *Transactions of the Folk-Lore Society,* LIX, 43, 1948.

28. See Le Goff, "Rêves," p. 306, n. 32.

29. The two accounts are by Saint Fortunatus, the chaplain of her community, and by the nun Baudonivia. Gregory of Tours contributes additional information. Hildebertus (1057–1134), bishop of Mans, also wrote a life of the saint. See René Aigrain, *Sainte Radegonde* (Paris, 1924); Benedictines of Paris, *Vies des saints et des bienheureux* (Paris, 1949), vol. 8, pp. 227–234; *Acta Sanctorum,* Aug. 13, vol. 3, pp. 74–83.

30. Paris, Bibliothèque Nationale, MS. Fr. 1784. The account published in modernized French is in Aigrain, *Sainte Radegonde*, pp. 63–64; in Old French in Xavier Barbier de Montault, *Oeuvres complètes* (Poitiers, 1889–1901), vol. 9, p. 201.

31. My translation of Bibliothèque Nationale, MS. Fr. 1784, as published by Aigrain and Montault.

32. *Vita Radegundis,* bk. 2, chap. 2, in *Scriptores Rerum Merovingicarum,* ed. B. Krusch and W. Levinson (Hannover, 1937–1951), vol. 2, p. 380.

33. Baudonivia wrote shortly after 600. See Vacandard, "Idolatrie en Gaule," pp. 431–432.

34. On early idol-like statuary, see Ilene Forsythe, *The Throne of Wisdom* (Princeton, 1972), pp. 62ff.

35. Calendar entries show that a February festival associated with Saint Radegund was celebrated in the tenth century. The "Leofric Missal" (c. 970), Oxford, Bodleian Library, MS. 579 fol. 39v, has the entry "Pictavis [Poitiers] sanctae Radegundis virginis" for February 11. Other early calendars that mark February 11 as Saint Radegund's Day are Bodleian Library, Hatton MS. 113 (latter half of eleventh century); and Cambridge, Corpus Christi College, MS. 391 (latter half of eleventh century). See Francis Wormald, *English Kalendars before A.D. 1100* (London, 1934), pp. 45, 199, 213. This February date corresponds roughly to "Sainte Radegonde les Avoines," Saint Radegund of the Oats, a Radegund/grain festival not accepted formally by the church until the seventeenth century, but no doubt celebrated among farmers since many centuries earlier.

36. Folio 66v of Poitiers 253 begins the account of a series of miracles attributed to Saint Radegund. The last two, dating from 1303 and 1306, contain within them allusion to but not accounts of the miracle of oats. See Largeault and Bodenstaff in *Analecta Bollandiana*, 1904, pp. 434–437; and Montault, *Oeuvres complètes*, vol. 9, p. 201.

37. Jean Filleau, *Les preuves historiques des litanies de la Grande Reyne de France Sainte Radegonde* (Poitiers, 1643), p. 44.

38. Aigrain, *Sainte Radegonde*, p. 64.

39. See *Analecta Bollandiana*, 1904, p. 446 and notes.

40. Roman custom marked spring arriving at the midpoint between the winter solstice and the vernal equinox. For Mediterranean people, the onset of the western wind (Favonius, Zephyrus) signaled spring and planting time; Ovid, *Fasti* 2.149–150; Pliny, *Natural History* 2.47; Varro, *De Re Rustica* 1.28. And modern agricultural historians note that though grain was sown in the fall in the Roman and medieval periods, the preferred grain was spring wheat, called the three-month wheat, which both Roman and medieval farmers planted. See Rickman, *Corn Supply of Ancient Rome*, pp. 6–7.

41. Jack B. Oruch, "St. Valentine, Chaucer, and Spring in February," *Speculum*, 1981, pp. 549–551.

42. Wormald, *English Kalendars*, pp. 45, 199, 213. See also note 35, preceding. Radegund's name is contained in the original or Lotharingian portion of the "Leofric Missal" (c. 970) as well as in its calendar (on February 11). Her name also appears in the "Missal of Robert of Jumièges" (c. 1008–1025). See H. A. Wilson, *The Missal of Robert of Jumièges* (London, 1896), pp. xxiv, xxxi, 10. F. Brittain asserts that the earliest known mention of the name of Saint Radegund in England is in a calendar written by a priest of Winchester, probably around 850. See F. Brittain, ed., *The Life of Saint Radegunde* (Cambridge, 1926), p. x.

43. Cambridge, Corpus Christi College, MS. 422, c. 1061. See Wormald, *English Kalendars*, p. 185.

44. Filleau, *Preuves historiques*, p. 44.

45. Baskervill, "Dramatic Aspects," pp. 64–65.

46. *Macrée* in French means "spring tide at the mouth of rivers." In the sixth century, the estuary of the Sèvre River formed a bay 19 miles wide; one arm of the bay extended up to Niort. The area was much more fluvial than it is today. Francis Ambrière, ed., *Pourtou, Guyenne*, Guides Bleu (Paris, 1958), pp. 142–144.

Saint Macrine is sometimes called Saint Magrine, or Maigrine, as well as Saint Matrine (*matrice* in French means uterus or womb) and Saint Materne (which at the root is *mater*, mother). See Mgr. Paul Guérin, *Les petits bollandistes*, vol. 8 of *Vies des saints* (Paris, 1878), pp. 101–102. See also *Analecta Bollandiana* 12 (1898), p. 364.

47. Guérin, *Petits bollandistes*, pp. 101–102. Barbier de Montault cites Alfred Largeault, *Hagiographie poitevine* (Melle, 1896), referring to a "martyrologe Hieronymian," which is supposed to mention Macrine. Largeault neglected to cite the text and neither Barbier de Montault nor I have been able to uncover this source. See Montault, *Oeuvres complètes*, vol. 13, pp. 542–543.

48. Montault, *Oeuvres complètes*, vol. 13, pp. 542–543.

49. Leo Desaivre, *Recherches sur Gargantua en Poitou avant Rabelais* (Niort, 1869), p. 2; Paul Sébillot, *Gargantua dans les traditions populaire* (Paris, 1883), pp. 173–174.

50. My translation and paraphrase from Sébillot, *Gargantua*.

51. Sébillot, *Gargantua*, pp. 174–175.

52. No representation of her has been noted in iconographic catalogs of Wolfgang Braunfels, *Lexikon der Christlichen Ikonographie* (Rome, 1976), or in Louis Réau, *Iconographie de l'art chrétien* (Paris, 1959).

53. Guérin, *Petits bollandistes*, p. 102, quoting from M. Ch. de Chagé.

54. Hermann Holzbauer, *Mittel-alterliche Heiligen-verehrung, Heilige Walpurgis* (Kevelaer, 1972), pp. 51–55. She is also honored in France under the names of Waubourg, Gauburge, and Falbourg, and in Germany and the Netherlands as Wilburger, Warpurg, and Walpurgis. See *Butler's Lives of the Saints*, vol. 1, p. 415. For the missionary activities of her brothers see Sullivan, "Carolingian Missionary," pp. 705–711.

55. Holzbauer, *Heilige Walpurgis*, pp. 57–58.

56. Butler mentions the iconographic tradition in which Walpurga is represented holding three ears of corn, and suggests "Some of her *cultus* with which she was formerly honoured—including her attribute of corn—may possibly have been transferred to her from the old heathen goddess Walborg or Mother Earth." (*Butler's Lives of the Saints*, p. 415.)

57. *Butler's Lives of the Saints*, pp. 415–416.

58. Walpurgisnacht, May 1, the night of one of her festivals, is in popular culture supposed to be the night when witches hold their revels at Blocksberg in the Hartz. *Butler's Lives of the Saints*, pp. 415–416.

59. L. Réau, *L'iconographie des saints* (Paris, 1955–1959), vol. 3, p. 1338.

60. E. L. Rochholz, *Drei Gaugöttinnen* (Leipzig, 1870), p. 27: "Korn wird Gesäit auf Mariae Geburt und schosset um Waldpurgi." "Wenn der Roggen vor Walburgis schosset und vor Pfingsten blüht, so wird en vor Jacobi nicht reif."

61. L. Schütz, "Walpurga," *Lexikon der Christlichen Iconographie* (Rome, Fribourg, 1976), vol. 8, pp. 544–545.

62. Version taken from J. v. Grohmann, *Sagen aus Boehmen* (Prague, 1863), pp. 45–46; and T. Vernaleken, *Alpensagen* (Vienna, 1858), p. 110.

63. V. Grohmann, *Sagen aus Boehmen*, p. 45.

64. T. G. E. Powell, *The Celts* (London, 1958), pp. 153–154.

65. Frazer, *New Golden Bough*, pp. 401–405. See also Mircea Eliade, *Traité d'histoire des religions* (Paris, 1964), pp. 286–289.

66. Translated and published by Thomas Oswald Cockayne, in *Leechdoms, Wortcunning, and Starcraft of Early England* (London, 1864), vol. 1, pp. 498–504. The Anglo-Saxon text is from British Museum, MS. Cott. Calig. A.vii, fol. 172b–173a. More recent translations of selected parts are found in S. A. Brooke, *The History of Early English Literature* (London, 1892), pp. 219–221; and R. K. Gordon, *Anglo-Saxon Poetry* (London, n.d.), pp. 99–100.

67. "Crescite et multiplicamini et replete terram."

68. Translation by Gordon, *Anglo-Saxon Poetry*, pp. 99–100.

69. Translation by Brooke, *Early English Literature*, pp. 219ff.

70. Brooke, *Early English Literature*, pp. 219ff.

71. R. Koegel, *Geschichte der Deutschen Litteratur* (Straussburg, 1894), vol. 1, pp. 40–44.

72. Baskervill points to how ceremonies attached to the earth mother were appropriated by the church and worked into the ecclesiastical calendar. In relation to England, Baskervill mentions in particular the assimilation of the earth mother goddess ceremony with the practices surrounding Epiphany, Candlemas, and Lent. Baskervill, "Dramatic Aspects," pp. 28, 37–38, 79.

73. Sources for Milburga's life are found in William of Malmesbury (twelfth century), *Gesta Pontificum Anglorum*, ed. N. E. S. A. Hamilton (Kraus Reprint, 1964), p. 306; William of Malmesbury, *De Regibus* or *History of the Kings*, bk. 2, chap. 13, in Bohn's Antiquarian Library, pp. 243–244; John of Tynemouth, "Sanctilogium Angliae" (MS. Cot. Tib. El., from Saint Albans, between 1325 and 1350), published in Carl Horstman, *Nova Legenda Anglie* (Oxford, 1901), vol. 2, pp. 188–192; see also vol. 1, pp. x–xii. Other documents related to Milburga are in Lansdowne MS. 436, a collection of lives of saints that belonged to the nunnery of Romsey and that was mentioned by A. J. M. Edwards, "An Early Twelfth Century Account of the Translation of Saint Milburga," *Transactions of the Shropshire Archaeological Society*, 1962, pp. 134–151; and Odo of Ostia, "Miracula Inventionis Beate Mylburge Virginis," in Edwards, "Translation of Saint Milburga," pp. 143–151.

74. Edwards, "Translation of Saint Milburga," p. 135.

75. See note 73 on sources.

76. William of Malmesbury, *De Regibus*, p. 244.

77. Another twelfth-century manuscript by Odo of Ostia goes into great detail about the healing miracles. See Edwards, "Translation of Saint Milburga," pp. 143–151.

78. Edwards, "Translation of Saint Milburga," p. 135.

79. John of Tynemouth, "De Sancta Milburga," in Horstman, *Nova Legenda*, vol. 2, pp. 188–192.

80. Horstman, *Nova Legenda*, vol. 1, pp. x–xi.

81. John of Tynemouth, "De Sancta Milburga," p. 191.

82. Lines 6–7: ". . . eam per violentiam rapere et in coniugium sibi copulare affectabat."

83. John of Tynemouth, "De Sancta Milburga," lines 16–25.

84. Charlotte Sophia Burne, *Shropshire Folk-lore* (London, 1883), pp. 416–419.

85. Quoted from Burne, *Shropshire Folk-lore*, p. 418.

86. Burne, *Shropshire Folk-lore*, p. 419. See also Horstman, *Nova Legenda*, vol. 1, p. xiii. In some areas, both the February and the May dates are celebrated. These two celebrations coincide with the seeding and the harvesting of the spring grain, which is called the twelve-week grain. See Rickman, *The Corn Supply of Ancient Rome*, pp. 6–7.

87. Caoimhin O Danachair, "The Quarter Days in Irish Tradition," *Arv (Journal of Scandinavian Folklore)* 15 (1959), pp. 47–55.

88. Imbolc is also known by the name *Oimelc*, which has been called a secondary deformation by one Celticist. See De Vries, *Religion des celtes*, p. 234.

89. O Danachair, "Quarter Days," p. 47.

90. O Danachair, "Quarter Days," p. 47.

91. K. Meyer, ed., *Hibernica Minora* (Oxford, 1894), p. 49: "Fromad cach bid iar n-urd, / issed dlegair i n-Imbulc, / diunnach laime is coissi is cinn, / is amlaid sin atberim," found in Harley, MS. 5280, fol. 35b, 2.

92. See the discussion of Sementiva, Chapter I, "Rome."

93. J. Vendryes, "Imbolc," *Revue celtique* 41 (1924), pp. 241–244.

94. Vendryes, "Imbolc," p. 243.

95. E. Bachellery and P. Y. Lambert, *Lexique étymologique de l'Irlandais ancien de J. Vendryes* (Dublin and Paris, 1981), p. B–66–67; Kuno Meyer, *Contributions to Irish Lexicography* (Halle, 1906), vol. 1, pt. 1, p. 236. The word existed in Gaulish, Gothic, and Old English, where it likewise meant "belly."

96. Nora Chadwick, *The Celts* (Harmondsworth, 1974), p. 181: Chadwick states that "St. Brigid herself . . . appears to have taken over the functions of a Celtic goddess of the same name and comparable attributes." See also Donal O Cathasaigh, "The Cult of Brigid: A Study of Pagan-Christian Syncretism in Ireland," in *Mother Worship*, ed. J. J. Preston (Chapel Hill, 1982), pp. 75–94, esp. pp. 81, 89.

97. O Cathasaigh, "Cult of Brigid," pp. 81–82.

98. The goddess Anu was connected with the hills called Paps Anu (literally Breasts of Anu); Boann with lakes and the River Boyne.

99. O Danachair, "Quarter Days," p. 49; O Cathasaigh, "Cult of Brigid," pp. 87–89.

100. The preparation and consumption of grain products at sowing time is frequently observed by anthropologists and folklorists, who see in this practice an expression of the wish to have the copious eating of grain reflect the desired plentiful harvest.

101. Significantly, the modern festival is marked by a procession of young people carrying an effigy of Saint Brigid through the countryside around the fields from farm to farm. See O Danachair, "Quarter Days," p. 48.

102. Powell, *Celts*, p. 118.

103. For another example of a Celtic goddess metamorphosed into a Christian saint, see the study of Caillech Bherri, a titulary deity associated with the Kerry peninsula who was transformed from an ancient divinity into an aged nun. O Cathasaigh, "Cult of Brigid," p. 82.

104. O Cathasaigh, "Cult of Brigid," pp. 90–91

105. O Cathasaigh, "Cult of Brigid," pp. 90–91.

106. O Cathasaigh, "Cult of Brigid," pp. 90–91.

107. George Duby, *Rural Economy and Country Life in the Medieval West*, trans. C. Poston (Columbia, S.C., 1968), pp. 3–5; English ed. of *L'économie rurale* (Paris, 1962).

108. For the reflection of hunger in folktales, see Robert Darnton, *The Great Cat Massacre* (New York, 1984), pp. 23–34.

V: Folk Figures

1. *Rodulfi Chronicon Abbatiae S. Trudonis,* bk. 11. The Latin account is printed in Jacob Grimm, *Teutonic Mythology,* trans. J. S. Stallybrass (London, 1880), vol. 1, pp. 259–262. See Migne, *P.L.,* vol. 173, pp. 11–434, for the complete chronicle. The first seven books of the chronicles were by Rodulfus, elected abbot of Saint-Trond in 1108.

2. Quoted in translation by Tydeman, *Theatre in the Middle Ages,* p. 16; and Chambers, *Mediaeval Stage,* vol. 1, pp. 161–162, n. 3: "sunt quidam, et maxime mulieres, qui festis ac sacris diebus atque sanctorum natalitiis non pro eorum quibus defent delectantur desideriis advenire, sed ballando, verba turpia decantando choros tenendo ac ducendo similitudem paganorum peragendo, advenire procurant."

3. Chambers, *Mediaeval Stage,* p. 162n.

4. See Chapter II, "Germania."

5. We have no other twelfth-century accounts of such processions, but descriptions of like practices are found in records from the early modern world. In Swabia, which had become the seat of the Suevi mentioned by Tacitus, several traces of processions with shiplike carts are known. See Grimm, *Teutonic Mythology,* vol. 1, p. 263, vol. 4, p. 1366. See also Julius Zacker, "Handschriften im Haag," *Zeitschrift für Deutsches Altertums* 1 (1841), pp. 266–267; Chadwick, *Origin of the English Nation,* p. 223; and O. von Reinsberg-Dueringsfeld, *Das Festliche Jahr* (Leipzig, 1863), p. 27.

6. See Chapter IV, "Milburga."

7. See Chapter IV, "Milburga."

8. Chadwick, *Origin of the English Nation,* pp. 223–224; Baskervill, "Dramatic Aspects," pp. 37–38.

9. Chadwick, *Origin of the English Nation,* p. 224.

10. Quoted in J. Grimm, *Teutonic Mythology,* vol. 1, p. 264.

11. Chadwick, *Origin of the English Nation,* pp. 223–225.

12. Venerable Bede alludes to a spring goddess Eoster. See Bede, *De Temp Ratione* C 15, in *Opera,* ed. Giles, vol. 4, p. 179: "Eoster-monath qui nunc paschalis menses, interpretatur, quondam, a dea illorum quae Eostre vocabatur, et cui in illo festa celibrabant, nomen habuit; a cuius nomine nuve paschale tempus cognominant, consueto antiquae observationis vocabulo gaudia novae solemnitatis vocantes."

13. Baskervill, "Dramatic Aspects," pp. 37–38.

14. John Brand, *Observations on the Popular Antiquities of Great Britain* (London, 1849), vol. 1, p. 506.

15. Baskervill, "Dramatic Aspects."

16. Arnold van Gennep, *Manuel de folklore français* (Paris, 1943–1958), vol. 1, pt. 6, p. 2759; and A. van Gennep, "Le culte populaire de Saint Clair et de Saint Blaise en Savoie," *Revue d'ethnographie* 18 (1924), pp. 141–147.

17. *Butler's Lives of the Saints,* vol. I, p. 239.

18. Van Gennep, *Manuel de folklore français,* vol. 1, pt. 6, p. 2759.

19. The areas where there is evidence of Blaise's role as sowing saint include France, Macedonia, Romania, the Slavic countries, and Italy (Santo Biagio). See van Gennep, *Le folklore du Dauphiné, Isère* (Paris, 1932), vol. 1, pp. 230–236.

20. Van Gennep, *Manuel de folklore français,* vol. 1, pt. 5, pp. 2465–2749; and van Gennep, *Folklore du Dauphiné,* vol. 1, pp. 231–232.

21. A blessing for the grain, though not the specific "benedictio seminum granarum," is recorded in the "Missal of Elne." See van Gennep, *Manuel de folklore français,* vol. 1, pt. 5, p. 2466. For the other prayers addressed to Saint Blaise in liturgical books, see A. Franz, *Die Kirchlichen Benediktionen im Mittelalter* (Berlin, 1909), vol. 1, pp. 202–206.

22. Van Gennep, *Folklore du Dauphiné,* pp. 233–235. The description van Gennep published was sent to him by one M. Molméret. The event was last celebrated on February 3, 1914.

23. Van Gennep, *Manuel de folklore français,* vol. 1, pt. 6, p. 2760.

24. This kind of mimesis is very ancient. In the twelfth century Giraldus Cambrensis described a dance of peasants in which the ordinary operations of village life like plowing and spinning were mimetically represented. Such dances seem to survive in dramatic games and even nursery rhymes, such as "Oats, peas, beans, and barley grow," a rhyme game that may have originated as a mimicry of plowing and sowing. See Baskervill, "Dramatic Aspects," pp. 28, 79; and C. R. Baskervill, "Mummers' Wooing Plays in England," *Modern Philology* 21, no. 3 (1923–1924), p. 236.

25. Van Gennep, "Culte populaire," pp. 147–148.

26. Van Gennep, "Culte populaire," p. 148, quoting from Vingtrinier, *Bresse et Bugey*, p. 189.

27. Van Gennep, "Culte populaire," quoting Vingtrinier.

28. J.-A. Dulaure, *Des divinités generatrice* (Paris, 1905), p. 211.

29. Dulaure, *Des divinités generatrice*, p. 211.

30. For other examples of folk figures supplanting pagan deities in seasonal ceremonies, see Chambers, *Mediaeval Stage*, vol. 1, pp. 184ff.

31. My translation of part of an extensive description in A. Perrin, *L'abbaye de Saint Valentin de Maché* (1869), quoted by A. van Gennep in "La chandeleur et la Saint-Valentin en Savoie," *Revue d'ethnographie* 19 (1924), p. 33.

32. Van Gennep suggests that the bouquets called valentines are symbols of the fecundity promised by the mother goddess. See van Gennep, "La chandeleur," p. 236.

33. Jack B. Oruch, "St. Valentine, Chaucer and Spring in February," *Speculum*, 1981, pp. 534–565. The Saint Valentine's Day lottery and the custom of choosing a sweetheart have been known in Europe only since the later Middle Ages (c. 1400).

34. Van Gennep, "La chandeleur," pp. 235–236.

35. Van Gennep, "La chandeleur," pp. 236–237.

36. Van Gennep remarks that this sacrifice is equivalent to the *taurobolium*, a sacrifice rendered to both Cybele and Mithra. Be that as it may, it is curious that the cock *(gallus)* sacrificed here came to be a symbol in the medieval encyclopedic tradition for the Galli, the ancient priests of Cybele. See Wirth, "Erde," vol. 5, col. 1009.

37. Perrin records that the Savoy senate officially suppressed the custom. See van Gennep, "La chandeleur," p. 234.

38. Emile Mâle, *La fin du paganisme en Gaule* (Paris, 1950), p. 33.

39. Mâle, *Fin du paganisme*, p. 36.

40. Records of processions to the Cybele sanctuary have survived in the nineteenth-century footnotes to a seventeenth-century text on the history of Autun: Edme Thomas (1591–1660), *Histoire de l'antique cité d'Autun*, Société éduenne publication (Autun and Paris, 1846). Thomas was a canon of the cathedral of Autun. The author of the notes is not identified.

41. See Vermaseren, *Cybele and Attis*, p. 92.

42. Thomas, *Histoire d'Autun*, p. 159. For the divisions of the pre-Roman Celtic year see Chapter IV, p. 000.

43. Thomas, *Histoire d'Autun*, pp. 170–171.

44. Thomas, *Histoire d'Autun*, p. 171.

45. For the transformation of pagan gods and goddesses into foolish figures or into one form or another of the devil, see Franz Joseph Dölger, "'Teufels Grossmütter'? Magna Mater Deum und Magna Mater Daemonum. Die Umwertung der Heidengötter im Christlichen Daemonenglauben," *Antike und Christentum* 3, pt. 3 (1932), pp. 153–176; C. Pascal, *Dei e diàvoli. Saggi sul paganésimo morènte* (Florence, 1904); in art, Marie Durand-Lefebvre, *Art gallo-romain et sculpture romane* (Paris, 1937), pp. 199–201, and Jean Adhémar, *Influences antiques dans l'art du moyen âge français* (London, 1939).

46. A similar custom is recorded to have occurred in the sixteenth and seventeenth centuries in England at Shrovetide, or Shrove Tuesday, a mid-February pre-Lenten festival: A woman of ill fame was placed by the peace officer in a cart and led around the city; sometimes the woman was a prostitute, sometimes a procurer. For some, particularly "mad-brain'd" apprentices, it was an event of great revelry; yet there was a harsher side. It appears that some sort of flagellation ceremony was involved. A play from the 1630s describes this aspect of the event: "The whips we use let forth their wanton blood, / Making them calme, and more to calme their pride, / Instead of coaches they in carts do ride." See John Brand, *Observations on the Popular Antiquities of Great Britain* (1873), pp. 89, 90, 93–94.

VI: Metamorphosis: From Goddess to Virgin Mary

1. For an overview of the unending toil and inexorable conditions that made medieval farming life so difficult see Duby, *Rural Economy,* pp. 3–5.

2. Derek Brewer, "The Gospels and Laws of Folktales," *The Journal of the Folklore Society* 90 (1979), p. 39; E. M. R. Ditmas, "The Way Legends Grow," *Folklore* 85 (1974), pp. 244–253.

3. See the forthcoming book by Caroline Bynum on female saints in relation to food motifs in the Middle Ages and her "Holy Feast and Holy Fast," lecture given at Bunting Institute, Radcliffe College, Cambridge, Mass., Feb. 14, 1984.

4. This summary is based on the texts to be treated below.

5. For a discussion of the ways in which folk memory persists in legends, and how some folktales reveal early, even prehistoric phases of society, see J. A. Maccullock, "Folk-Memory in Folk-Tales," *Folklore* 60 (1949), pp. 307–315.

6. C. W. v. Sydow, "Geography and Folk-tale Oicotypes," and "On the Spread of Tradition," both in *Selected Papers on Folklore* (Copenhagen, 1948), pp. 11–43, 44–59.

7. See C. Tischendorf, *Evangelia Apocrypha* (Leipzig, 1876); and B. H. Cowper, *The Apocryphal Gospels* (London, 1881). The apocryphal gospels do mention Christ as a boy planting one grain that produced a hundred *choros* (rows). But this is not at all the Grain Miracle legend being discussed here. See *Evangelary of Thomas* 12; *Treaty of the Infancy of Jesus According to Thomas* 10; *Histoire de la Nativité de Marie* 34; *Miracles de l'enfance,* Paris, Bibliothèque Nationale, MS. 4313, xxxiv; Tischendorf, *Evangelia Apocrypha;* and D. Arbaud, *Chants populaire de la Provence* (Aix, 1864), vol. 1, p. 38.

8. See, for example, the many Mary legends recorded in Frederic C. Tubach, *Index Exemplorum, A Handbook of Medieval Religious Tales* (Helsinki, 1969), as well as those recorded among the British Museum Romances and the Miracle Plays of the Virgin. The grain legend occurs in none of these sources.

9. More than twenty somewhat different manuscripts of the long poem are known. See Ruth Whittredge, *La Nativité et Le Geu des Trois Roys, Two Plays from Manuscript 1131 of the Bibliothèque Sainte Geneviève* (Bryn Mawr, Pa., 1944), p. 46. The poem has no name, but is sometimes called *L'histoire de Marie et de Jesus* or *Le roman de l'Annonciation Notre-Dame.* See E. Roy, *Le Mystère de la Passion* (Dijon, 1902–1904; reprint Geneva, 1974), p. 26. Versions of the long poem appear in Paris, Bibliothèque Nationale, MS. Fr. 1768, fol. 101–134, from the fourteenth century; Bibliothèque d'Arras, no. 139; and Berne 634. See Jean Bonnard, *Les traductions de la Bible en vers français au moyen âge* (Paris, 1884), p. 227. For the complexity of the manuscript tradition, see P. Meyer, "Notice du Ms. de l'Arsenal 5201," *Romania* 16 (1887), pp. 44–45.

10. Some of the approximately five thousand octosyllabic lines of that version are published by Robert Reinsch, *Die Pseudo-Evangelien von Jesu und Maria's Kindheit* (Halle, 1879), pp. 42–74, and by Bonnard, *Les traductions de la Bible,* pp. 227–231. Paris, Bibliothèque Nationale, MS. Fr. 1533, fol. 10b–36, is the oldest text, c. 1275; Jean d'Outremeuse copied a prose version, based directly on the poem, into his *Myreur des Histors,* see his *Chroniques Belges* (Brussels, 1864), vol. 1, pp. 356–357.

The lines dealing with the Grain Miracle are the only part of that version of the poem which does not derive from a known apocryphal text. See Reinsch, *Die Pseudo-Evangelien,* p. 60. As with so many legends, at least one variant exists: this variant, in which the infant Christ sows the grain, is inserted into *La Vie de Nostre Benoit Sauveur Ihesuscrist,* a late fourteenth-century free translation and expansion of Pseudo-Bonaventura, *Meditationes Vitae Christi* (the grain legend does not occur in the *Meditationes*); see Millard Meiss and Elizabeth H. Beatson, *La Vie de Nostre Benoit Sauveur Ihesuscrist & La Saincte Vie de Nostre Dame* (New York, 1977). See also note 7, preceding.

11. Alfred B. Lord, *The Singer of Tales* (Cambridge, Mass., 1960; reprint New York, 1965). For a discussion of the abuses of the oral-formulaic theory, see Ruth Finnegan, *Oral Poetry* (Cambridge, 1977), pp. 69–72.

12. The names *jongleur* and *minstrel* seem to be terms used interchangeably for the professional medieval storyteller. The distinction is sometimes made between the minstrel, attached to the court of a nobleman, and the jongleur, who moved about and recited his tales to any audience he could assemble. A trouvère is sometimes distinguished as the composer. See Ruth Crosby, "Oral Delivery in the Middle Ages," *Speculum* 11 (1936), p. 91; and Finnegan, *Oral Poetry*, p. 20. Though Crosby published before Parry and Lord and assumes that the poets *wrote* the verses, she shows that they were composed primarily for oral delivery. Though most of these medieval singer poets were men, women also took on this role. See Meg Bogin, *The Women Troubadours* (New York, 1976).

13. Lord, *Singer of Tales*, p. 4, and Jean Rychner, *La chanson de geste, Essai sur l'art epique des jongleurs* (Geneva and Tille, 1955), p. 35.

14. Bede, *Historia Ecclesiastica*, bk. 4, chap. 22, sec. 24, completed in 731 A.D. See Frances P. Magoun, Jr., "Bede's Story of Caedmon: The Case History of an Anglo-Saxon Oral Singer," *Speculum* 30 (1955), pp. 49–63.

15. Magoun comments: "This is not how most oral singers learn their songs, since most songs . . . are based on old tradition which the singers have mastered during their period of absorption and learning." ("Bede's Story of Caedmon," p. 60.) For other documents relating to the transformation and adaptation of legend into verse and song, see C. R. Baskervill, "Mummers' Wooing Plays," pp. 225–272; and Baskervill, "Dramatic Aspects," pp. 28, 29, 78–79.

16. See Ruth Crosby, "Oral Delivery"; Lord, *Singer of Tales*; Brewer, "Gospels and Laws of Folktales," pp. 37–52; and Moses Gaster, *Studies and Texts* (1928; reprint New York, 1971) vol. 2, pp. 1113ff.

As in so many cases of orally transmitted legend or poetry, the transformed legend, handed down from generation to generation, was preserved by memory and practice rather than by written record. See Funk and Wagnalls, *Standard Dictionary of Folklore, Mythology, and Legend* (New York, 1949), pp. 398ff.

17. Lord, *Singer of Tales*, p. 4.

18. Reinsch, *Die Pseudo-Evangelien*, p. 60. The translation that follows is mine.

19. Reinsch, *Die Pseudo-Evangelien*, p. 63.

20. *Mimi*, or pantomimists, formed part of the nomadic group of entertainers in the Middle Ages that traveled from town to town or market to market. See Karl Young, *The Drama of the Medieval Church* (Oxford, 1933), pp. 9–10; and Tydeman, *Theatre in the Middle Ages*, p. 14.

21. See Chambers, *Mediaeval Stage*, vol. 1, pp. 26, 161–162, 192.

22. According to Baskervill, the mummers' plays reached this stage between the sixth and the tenth centuries. See "Dramatic Aspects," p. 20.

23. L. Douëss-d'Arcq, ed., *La chronique d'Enguerran de Monstrelet* (Paris, Société de l'Histoire de France, 1861), vol. 5, pp. 3–4.

24. Douëss-d'Arcq, *Chronique d'Enguerran de Monstrelet*, vol. 5, pp. 3–4. ". . . personnage, *sans parler*, de la Nativité Nostre-Dame, de son mariage, et l'Annunciacion, des Trois Rois, des Innocens, et *du bon homme qui semoit son bled. Et furent ces personnages très bien joués.*" Emphasis mine.

25. Young, *Drama of the Medieval Church*, p. 10; Baskervill, "Dramatic Aspects," p. 66.

26. The Flight into Egypt could have taken place at any time during the calendar year, but in the Infancy Cycle is generally placed after the Purification of the Virgin, a festival fixed on February 2.

For a discussion of ritualized observance that evolved into drama, see Baskervill, "Dramatic Aspects," pp. 19–87; Baskervill, "Mummers' Wooing Plays," pp. 225–272; and Tydeman, *Theatre in the Middle Ages*, pp. 1–21. For similar methods of dramatic presentation in ancient rituals, see Theodor Gaster, *Thespis* (Garden City, N.Y., 1961), pp. 401–405.

27. There is no Latin version of the tale and no evidence that it was ever used in *exempla*. Thus, as a primarily vernacular tale, it was not part of the ecclesiastical Latinate culture.

28. A decree of the Council of Rome in 826 is typical of church denunciation of what was viewed as pagan. People were accused of celebrating saint's days by dancing, singing shameful words, performing dances, and behaving "just like pagans." Quoted by Tydeman, *Theatre in the Middle Ages*, p. 16. See also Chapter V, "Daemon." Aberrant lower clergy sometimes participated in obviously pagan processional song-dances. The "Chronicle of Lanercost" gives

an account of a priest named John who, during Easter week in 1282, compelled the young women of his parish to join in a processional song-dance in honor of the pagan fertility figure Priapus. The priest led the procession, carrying a pole topped with a phallus. He participated in the dancing himself and by his mimed actions and shameless words stirred the spectators to participate. Though this is clearly an extraordinary case, pagan ceremonial continued, and so did ecclesiastical denunciation. See Tydeman, *Theatre in the Middle Ages*, p. 16.

29. For a bibliography, see Le Goff, "Rêves," pp. 299–306.

30. Emile Mâle, *Religious Art in France, The Twelfth Century* (Princeton, 1978, new ed. and trans.), pp. 365–372.

31. Mâle, *Religious Art in France*, pp. 365–372.

32. Le Goff, "Rêves," p. 306.

33. Brewer, "Gospels and Laws of Folktales," pp. 39–40.

34. Also called Robert du Mont, Abbot of Mont Saint Michele. See Ernest Rupin, *Roc-Amadour* (Paris, 1904), pp. 26–29; and E. Albe, "La vie et les miracles de S. Amator," *Analecta Bollandiana* 28 (1909), pp. 57–90.

35. Rupin, *Roc-Amadour*, p. 27.

36. The final verse of the Amadour section appears to indicate that the poet was familiar with a rather obscure Amadour tradition, stemming from a legend that scholars have until now thought was a seventeenth-century development. In reference to Saint Amadour, the poet repeats that Christ taught him to chant masses and that he chanted masses every day. Later texts indicate that particularly in Spain Saint Amadour was known to have "prayed" his parents out of purgatory by the recitation of numerous masses and that therefore the frequent saying of masses of Saint Amadour was a common practice. The poet's allusion to Saint Amadour's masses and his repetition of those words must indicate that the legend and perhaps even the practice was already known in thirteenth-century Europe.

37. Thomas Parry, *A History of Welsh Literature* (Oxford, 1955), pp. 40–42; Thomas Jones, *The Black Book of Carmarthen "Stanzas of the Graves"* (Oxford, 1968), p. 97.

38. A. O. H. Jarman, "Taliesin," in *A Guide to Welsh Literature*, ed. A. O. H. Jarman and G. R. Hughes (Swansea, 1976), vol. 1, p. 51. The dating of early Welsh poetry is very controversial. Some scholars say verses were first written down in the ninth century, but concede that verse in the Welsh language existed well before this time. See David Green, "Linguistic Considerations in the Dating of Early Welsh Verse," *Studia Celtica* 6 (1971), pp. 1–11; Proinsias Mac Cana, review of *The Gododdin*, by K. H. Jackson, *Celtica* 9 (1971), pp. 316–329; and David N. Dumville, "Palaeographical Considerations in the Dating of Early Welsh Verse," *The Bulletin of the Board of Celtic Studies* 27, pt. 2 (May 1977), pp. 246–251.

39. Brynley F. Roberts, "Tales and Romance," in Jarman and Hughes, *Guide to Welsh Literature*, vol. 1, p. 205. Scholars attribute the lack of coherence and structure of so many of the poems to the probability that those who actually wrote them down were not well versed in the tradition of early Welsh storytelling and had to rely on their own untrained memories for the content and progression of a tale.

40. Ceri W. Lewis, "The Historical Background of Early Welsh Verse," in Jarman and Hughes, *Guide to Welsh Literature*, vol. 1, p. 35.

41. The language in which the poem is cast poses many difficulties for scholars, and the translations contain several discrepancies. The earliest translation into a modern language is by W. F. Skene, *The Four Ancient Books* (Edinburgh, 1868), vol. 1, pt. 2, pp. 513–555. A more recent English translation of the Grain Miracle part of the poem is Ifor Williams, "Y Cynhaeaf Gwyrthiol," *Bulletin of Celtic Studies* 10 (1939), pp. 33–34. A French version, a direct translation of Williams's English version, is Joseph Vendryes, "Le miracle de la moisson en Galles," *Comptes rendus de l'Academie des Inscriptions*, 1948, pp. 74–75. I would like to thank Professor Michael J. Connolly of Boston College for helping to clarify some portions of the Welsh.

42. The text is cited from the translation by Williams, "Y Cynhaeaf Gwyrthiol," p. 34. The obscure text could also be read as implying that the "Trinity of Heaven" was speaking these words.

43. Williams, "Y Cynhaeaf Gwyrthiol," p. 34.

44. Kuno Meyer, ed., "Neue Mitteilungen aus Irischen Handschriften," *Archiv für Celtische Lexikographie* 3 (1907), pp. 244–246. Copies are found in the "Book of Hy Mane," the "Book of the Dean of Lismore," no. 8; the "Book of the O'Conor Don," and others. See K. Jackson, "A Note on the Miracle of the Instantaneous Harvest," *The Bulletin of the Board of Celtic Studies* 10, pt. 3 (Nov. 1940), p. 204. See also K. Jackson, "Some Fresh Light on the Miracle of the

Instantaneous Harvest," *Folk-lore* 51 (1940), pp. 206–207, n. 10. Edward O'Reilly attributes the poem to Donogh Mor O'Daly (died in 1244), but he also mentions the attribution to Gilla Brighde Mac ConMidhe, *A Chronological Account of Nearly Four Hundred Irish Writers* (Dublin, 1820; reprint Shannon, 1970), pp. lxviii, lxxxix.

45. 'Ga īarraid ar muin Muiri   darindi in mac mirbuili,
    a tāeb fīrbhān fa ferta   'na mīngrān cāemh cruithnechta.
    In[n]isid, is ē 'ga ar,   fer a faicsin tre adh——,
    in lā sin tre lorg a mbond   f āsaig a colg 's a colond.
    Tic in ūair sim tresin n-ar   muinter Irūa[i]th na n-adrad,
    ger prap sain da bās 'ga būain   ar f ās in air re hāenūair.
From Meyer, "Neue Mitteilungen," p. 245, lines 27–29.

46. Translation by Jackson, "Some Fresh Light," p. 207.

47. See Pagels, "What Became of God the Mother?" pp. 293–303.

48. Joshua Whatmough, *KELTIKA, Being Prolegomena to a Study of Ancient Gaul* (n.p., n.d.), pp. 72–73, 75–76. On the migration of tales among various language groups, see v. Sydow, "Folk-tale Oicotypes."

49. Ralegh Redford, "The Cultural Relations of the Early Celtic World," in *Proceedings of the Second International Congress of Celtic Studies* (Cardiff, 1966), pp. 22–25.

50. Lewis, "Early Welsh Verse," in Jarman and Hughes, *Guide to Welsh Literature*, vol. 1, pp. 39–40.

51. Lewis, "Early Welsh Verse," pp. 38–39.

52. Lewis, "Early Welsh Verse," p. 39.

53. For the similar transmission of lore and oral traditions, see Lewis, "Early Welsh Verse," p. 19.

54. Whittredge, *La Nativité*, pp. 30–88, 155–197; Achille Jubinal, *Mystères inédits du quinzième siècle* (Paris, 1837), vol. 2, pp. 79–138; Grace Frank, *Medieval French Drama* (Oxford, 1967), pp. 136–153. Paris, Bibliothèque Sainte Geneviève, MS. 1131, which contains "Le Geu des Trois Roys," belonged, as far as can be traced, to the abbey of Saint Geneviève. The nature of its contents suggests that the collection originated in or near Paris. The play is, for the most part, in octosyllabic couplets.

55. The Latin term *tropus* is used to denote any verbal or musical embellishments to the regular liturgical office. See Tydeman, *Theatre in the Middle Ages*, p. 34.

56. See Chambers, *Mediaeval Stage*, vol. 2, pp. 7–8.

57. Young, *Drama of the Medieval Church*, vol. 1, p. 109, vol. 2, pp. 102ff., 455; Tydeman, *Theatre in the Middle Ages*, pp. 33ff.

58. Chambers, *Mediaeval Stage*, vol. 2, p. 44; Young, *Drama of the Medieval Church*, vol. 2, pp. 29–124, esp. p. 101; Tydeman, *Theatre in the Middle Ages*, pp. 42–43.

59. Young, *Drama of the Medieval Church*, vol. 2, pp. 102–106. The Flight into Egypt was also performed in mime as part of the revels on Innocents' Day (December 28) in the cathedral at Padua. See Young, vol. 1, pp. 107–108.

60. The earliest known vernacular version of the Three Kings play is from the middle of the twelfth century. The Old Castilian play "Reyes Magos" exists only in fragmentary form. See Tydeman, *Theatre in the Middle Ages*, p. 64; and R. M. Pidal, "Disputa del Alma y el Cuerpo y Auto de Los Reyes Magos," *Revista de Archivos, Bibliotecas y Museos* 4 (1900), pp. 449–462. The surviving scenes include dialogues among the Three Kings; the kings and Herod; and Herod and the Wise Men.

61. By 1284 plays in the vernacular with religious themes were well established, though Latin liturgical plays continued to be performed in Europe for several centuries. See Tydeman, *Theatre in the Middle Ages*, pp. 43–45.

62. Tydeman, *Theatre in the Middle Ages*, p. 65. It is generally thought, however, that "Le Geu des Trois Roys" was produced on an indoor stage. See Whittredge, *La Nativité*, p. 65.

63. If this play was produced inside as has been suggested (Whittredge, *La Nativité*, p. 65), then the introduction of a live mule would have presented some difficulties. A sculpted wooden version on wheels, however, would have served nicely. Such life-size wooden donkeys do survive from the late Middle Ages. The miraculous growth of wheat would have presented another difficulty in the staging of the play. Perhaps it was represented by a knee-high painting that was lifted upright when the audience's attention was on an intermediary scene. Such a prop is suggested in the manuscript painting in the Morgan Library in New York from 1275 (figures 52–53).

64. A glaring example of the playwright's misinformation is the fact that in his other play, "La Nativité," he called Genesis an author (Whittredge, *La Nativité*, p. 34).

65. On the growing interest in appealing through sermons and other means to the "worthy" common people, see Meiss and Beatson, *Vie de Nostre Benoit Sauveur*, pp. xx–xxiii.

66. An important figure in this respect was Jean Gerson (friend of the Duke of Berry) whose "Doctrinal aux Simples Gens" and "A.B.C. des Simples Gens" are in the same spirit as the sower's dialogue and proverbs. Jean Gerson, *Oeuvres complètes*, ed. Mgr. Georieux (Paris, 1960–1973), vol. 7, pp. 154–157, vol. 10, pp. 295–321, esp. p. 305, under "Paresse."

See also "Vie de Nostre Benoit Sauveur" (probably also by Gerson, c. 1400—see Meiss and Beatson, *Vie de Nostre Benoit Sauveur*, p. xv), a free translation of Pseudo—Bonaventura's *Meditationes Vitae Christi*. In the "Vie," people living close to the land were even more prominent than they were in the *Meditationes*. The compilers made it clear that the work was intended for all ranks of the laity. Besides containing some of the same proverbs as used by the sower in "Le Geu des Trois Roys," the "Vie" contains a version of the Grain Miracle (the *Meditationes* does not), a version no doubt inspired by the Apocrypha (see Tischendorf, *Evangelia Apocrypha*, pp. 164–175), where it is Christ who does the sowing. See Meiss and Beatson, *Vie de Nostre Benoit Sauveur*, pp. 26–27, 40–41.

67. The sower says this in French (line 1616, Whittredge, *La Divinité*, p. 182), and in Latin (line 1075, Whittredge, *La Divinité*, p. 184). It is taken from Psalm 127, line 2.

68. "Cy voisent Josep et Marie tout bellement" (line 1255), Whittredge, *La Divinité*, p. 189.

69. The sower says, "Vray Diex que tu as grant puissance / Semé ay ce blé, maintenant, / Cuillir le fault incontinant, / Car je voy bien qu'il en est temps." (lines 1369–1373, Whittredge, *La Divinité*, p. 192.)

70. In A. H. Hoffmann von Fallersleben, *Horae Belgicae* (Hannover, 1854), pt. 10, pp. 22–23. The text was taken from a manuscript in Berlin, MS. 8185. See F. van Duyse, *Het Oude Nederlandsche Lied* (Antwerp, 1907), vol. 3, p. 2096. For later variations on this carol, see van Duyse, pp. 2091–2096; and A. Lootens and J. M. E. Feys, *Chants populaires flamands* (Brussels, 1879), pp. 32–34.

71. Hoffmann von Fallersleben, *Hôrae Belgicae*, verse 9: "Doe ic dit saide, dat ic nu made, / Doe sach ic noorbi ene joncfrou varen."

72. See "Early Welsh Legend," in this chapter, and also Chapter VII.

73. See Frazer, *New Golden Bough*, p. 569. In the Judaic tradition women likewise had to be purified after one birth and before they could recommence intercourse. Mary dutifully (though according to church fathers unneccessarily) underwent this repurification process, commemorated by the feast of the Purification of Mary, February 2. February was also the month of purification ceremonies in the Roman tradition. See A. W. J. Hollman, *Pope Gelasius and Lupercalia* (Amsterdam, 1974), pp. 11, 27.

VII: The Grain Miracle in Medieval Art

1. Johnny Roosval, *Die Steinmeister Gottlands* (Stockholm, 1918), pp. 65–99; Johnny Roosval, *Swedish Art* (Princeton, 1932), pp. 1–7.

2. J. Graham-Campbell and D. Kidd, *The Vikings* (New York, 1980), pp. 180–181.

3. For examples of Viking picture stones see Graham-Campbell and Kidd, *Vikings*, pp. 28, 91.

4. Roosval, *Die Steinmeister*, pp. 90, 96; Roosval, *Swedish Art*, p. 6.

5. British Museum, MS. Sloane 2593, f. 22b. See James Kinsley, ed., *The Oxford Book of Ballads* (Oxford, 1969), p. 3. The ballad is Child no. 22. See also, F. J. Child, *The English and Scottish Popular Ballads* (Boston, 1882), pt. 1, pp. 233–242, pt. 2, pp. 505–506.

6. Child, *Popular Ballads*, p. 235. On December 26, which is called Great Horse Day in Germany, it was the custom for horses to be bled to keep them well during the year following,

or raced to protect them from witches. In Sweden horses were watered on that day. See also Lucy Broadwood, *Journal of the Folk-Song Society* 4, p. 25; R. C. A. Prior, *Ancient Danish Ballads* (London, 1860), pp. 397–398; and Andreas Lindbloom, *La peinture gothique en Suède et en Norvège* (Stockholm, 1917), p. 217.

7. Chadwick, *Origin of the English Nation*, pp. 231–234; H. R. Ellis Davidson, *Scandinavian Mythology* (London, 1969), p. 92.

8. Frey and Freya seem to stem from the culture farming groups who were settled in Scandinavia before the Germans came. See P. Grappin, "Germanic Lands: The Mortal Gods," in *Larousse World Mythology* (New York, 1965), pp. 387–388.

9. Discussed by Chadwick, *Origin of the English Nation*, pp. 226–231. The journey is recounted in the "Saga of Olaf Tryggvason" (chap. 173). Cited by Chadwick.

10. Chadwick, *Origin of the English Nation*, pp. 231–238, esp. p. 240, and E. Sykes, *Dictionary of Non-Classical Mythology* (London, 1952), pp. 79–80.

11. Ellis Davidson, *Scandinavian Mythology*, p. 29.

12. Tacitus represents the Aestii (the ancient inhabitants of the coast of Prussia) as being more devoted to agriculture than any other people (*Germania* 45). Tacitus says that the Aestii "worshiped the mother of the gods. The distinguishing mark of their cult is that they wear the shapes of wild boars. This serves for armor and protection in all things, rendering the worshiper of the goddess safe even among foes." This boar symbol was widely used among the Celts and Germans. It often served as an ornament for helmet or shield and an insignia carried into battle. See Chadwick, *Origin of the English Nation*, p. 234. We may infer that the boar was very likely the totem of the deity, from which the tribe traced their descendancy, and that the deity was probably a mother goddess figure.

13. A French roman of the twelfth century has the roasted cock story, but it is attached to the Magi. *La Chevalerie*, Ogier de Danemarche, by Raimbert de Paris, *Poème du XIIe siècle*, vol. 2, p. 485, lines 11,606–11,627. Cited by Child, *Popular Ballads*, pt. 1, p. 239.

14. The ultimate source of the reanimated cock tale is an interpolation in two late Greek manuscripts of the Gospel of Nicodemus. See Tischendorf, *Evangelia Apocrypha*, p. 269, n. 3.

15. In the Wendish version of the cock miracle, the resurrection of the cock is specifically related to the resurrection of plant life. See Child, *Popular Ballads*, pt. 1, pp. 240ff.

16. Lindbloom, *Peinture gothique*, pp. 89–94, plates 16, 17.

17. See Jean Porcher, *French Miniatures from Illuminated Manuscripts* (London, 1960), pp. 48–49, plates 40, 42, 43, 44. The organization in roundels may have been influenced by stained-glass windows.

18. S. Grundtvig, *Danmarks gamle Folkeviser* (Copenhagen, 1856), vol. 2, pp. 521–527.

19. For a discussion of the early medieval and Romanesque models of these "Madonnas in majesty," see Ilene H. Forsyth, *The Throne of Widsom* (Princeton, 1972).

20. Madeleine Pré, "L'église d'Asnières-sur-Vègre et ses peintures murales," *Congrès archéologique de France*, 1961, pp. 153–162; Madeleine Pré, "Dernières découvertes de peintures murales en l'église d'Asnières-sur-Vègre," *Gazette des beaux arts*, 6th ser., 48 (July–Aug. 1956), pp. 1–10; and Paul Deschamps and Marc Thibout, *La peinture murale en France* (Paris, 1963), pp. 102–104, 126, plates IX, 3; XLVIII, 3.

21. Medieval churchmen from Bede to Durand de Mende in the thirteenth century saw the Christian processions and prayers of the feast of the Purification of the Virgin as a substitute for the pagan ceremonies of Lupercalia, an event that was directed at both increasing the fertility of women through flagellation and purifying the fields in February. See D. de Bruyne, "L'origine des processions de la chandeleur et des rogations à propos d'un sermon inédit," *Revue benedictine* 34 (1922), pp. 14–26.

22. Dorothy Shorr, "The Iconographic Development of the Presentation in the Temple," *Art Bulletin* 28 (1946), pp. 17–32.

23. Arnold van Gennep, *En Savoie, du berceau à la tombe* (Chambéry, 1916), p. 245; Brand, *Popular Antiquities of Great Britain* (London, 1873), pp. 43–45; R. Lecotté and J. Dubois, *Témoins de la vie quotidienne* (Paris, 1971), p. 138. See also the curious illustration of the Presentation/Purification accompanied by a scene of purifying the fields of toads in a manuscript in Lilienfeld (Austria), Stiftsbib., MS. 151, illustrated in *Reallexikon zur Deutschen Kunstgeschichte*, vol. 3, col. 1070.

24. For contemporary examples of the workingman's headgear and Jew's cap, see *Psautier de Saint Louis*, published by the Bibliothèque Nationale from MS. Lat. 10525, ed. H. Omont

166   THE GODDESS OBSCURED

(Paris, n.d.), plates 11, 12, and others. See also figures 46, 51, and 57 in this book for the Jew's cap worn by Joseph.

25. *Gospel of Pseudo-Matthew* 20, in M. R. James, *The Apocryphal New Testament* (Oxford, 1953), p. 75. Both trees can be seen in a photo in Deschamps and Thibout, *Peinture murale en France*, plate IX, 3.

26. J. Dechelette, "Découverte de peinture murale," *Bulletin de la Diana* 19 (1913), pp. 41–49; Emile Mâle, "Chronique," *Bulletin de la Diana*, 1921, and *Bulletin monumental*, 1923, p. 222; Deschamps and Thibout, *Peinture murale en France*, pp. 3, 22, 104, 143.

27. Hairstyles, head-coverings, and armor permit scholars to date these mural paintings to the last quarter of the thirteenth century. See Deschamps and Thibout, *Peinture murale en France*, p. 104.

28. Though the windows at Saint-Julien-du-Sault have been restored, the iconography is authentic. See Gabrielle Rheims, "L'église de Saint-Julien-du-Sault et ses verrières," *Gazette des beaux arts*, 1926, pp. 139–162; and Louis Grodecki, "De 1200 à 1260," in *La vitrail français*, Marcel Aubert et al. (Paris, 1958), p. 155.

29. Grodecki, "De 1200 à 1260," p. 155. The windows were restored in the nineteenth century. See Rheims, "Saint-Julien-du-Sault," pp. 139ff.

30. The scene is most frequently found in books of hours (often accompanying the text of vespers) and in northern Renaissance panel paintings. A listing of the numerous artworks depicting the Grain Miracle can be found in the following studies: H. Wentzel, "Die Kornfeld-legende," *Aachener Kunstblat*, 1965, pp. 131–143; Leopold Schmidt, "Die Kornfeld-legende," in *Die Kornfeldlegende* (Berlin, 1963); H. Wentzel, "Die Kornfeldlegende," *Festschrift Kurt Banck* (Munich, 1957), pp. 177–192; Louis Réau, *L'iconographie de l'art chrétien* (Paris, 1957), vol. 2, pt. 2, p. 277; L. Schmidt, "Die Kornfeld Legende," *Alte und neue Kunst* 4 (1955); Joseph Vendryes, "Le miracle de la moisson en Galles," *Comptes rendus de l'académie des Inscriptions*, 1948, pp. 64–76; Karl Vogler, *Die Iconographie der "Flucht nach Aegypten"* (diss., Heidelberg; Arnstadt, 1930); Emile Mâle, *L'art religieux du XIIIe siècle en France*, 4th ed. (Paris, 1925), p. 261.

31. New York, Pierpont Morgan Library, MS. 729, fols. 289v, 290r. It accompanies the text of Nones. It is in French and Latin, for use at Amiens, thus probably written and illuminated at Amiens. The hands of several artists are discernible. See Belle da Costa Greene and Meta Harrsen, *The Pierpont Morgan Library, Exhibition of Illuminated Manuscripts* (New York, 1933–1934), no. 57, pp. 29ff.; and K. Gould, "Illumination and Sculpture in Thirteenth-Century Amiens," *Art Bulletin* 59, no. 2 (June 1977), pp. 161–166.

32. See Raymond Koechlin, *Les ivoires gothique français* (Paris, 1924), plates 45 (no. 181b), 155 (no. 857). The box is in the Musée Archéologique at Dijon.

33. W. O. Hassall, *The Holkham Bible Picture Book* (London, 1954), facsimile.

34. Hassall, *Holkham Bible*, pp. 36–40.

35. Hassall, *Holkham Bible*, p. 38.

36. Hassall suggests that the groupings and poses of the figures as well as the costumes and props may reflect actual theatrical performances (*Holkham Bible*, pp. 34ff.).

37. Grace L. Christie, *English Medieval Embroidery* (Oxford, 1938), fig. 51. The cloak, technically called a pluvial, is housed in the church treasury at Anagni in Italy. Since photographs of the cloak were unavailable, an illustration was based on Christie's publication. My thanks to the illustrator, Luisa Granito.

38. Millard Meiss and Marcel Thomas, *The Rohan Master, A Book of Hours, Bibliothèque Nationale, Ms., Latin, 9471* (New York, 1973). The Rohan Master executed only three of these folios by himself. The rest he apparently designed and then assigned to members of his workshop for completion.

39. The Grain Miracle was designed, if not executed, by the Rohan Master. See Meiss and Thomas, *Rohan Master*, p. 16.

40. The horsemen are very much inspired by, if not directly copied from, the Magi and a knight in their entourage in the "Très Riches Heures" of the Duke of Berry. See Meiss and Thomas, *Rohan Master*, no. 53.

41. Another late medieval tradition has it that this young man represents Joseph's son by a previous marriage.

42. See Vincent Scully, *The Earth, the Temple and the Gods* (New York, 1969).

43. Proinsias Mac Cana, *Celtic Mythology* (London, 1970), pp. 88–89.

44. See note 30.

VIII: The Grain Miracle in Folklore

1. The main bibliographic sources for the folkloric texts of the legend are: Francis James Child, *The English and Scottich Popular Ballads* (Boston, 1886), vol. 2, pp. 7ff., edition of and notes to "The Carnal and the Crane," Carol no. 55; Oskar Dähnhardt, *Natursagen* (Leipzig and Berlin, 1909), vol. 2, pp. 52–53, 61–66; and Jackson, "Some Fresh Light," pp. 203–210.

2. For a discussion of the migration of tales, see v. Sydow, "Folk-tale Oicotypes," pp. 44–59, esp. p. 47; and Ditmas, "The Way Legends Grow," p. 245.

3. V. Sydow, "Folk-tale Oicotypes," p. 47; Ditmas, "The Way Legends Grow," p. 245.

4. V. Sydow, "Folk-tale Oicotypes," pp. 56ff.

5. Bob Stewart, *Pagan Imagery in English Folksong* (Atlantic Highlands, N.J., 1977), pp. 35–54.

6. Donatien Laurent, "Breton Orally Transmitted Folk Poetry," in *The European Medieval Ballad,* ed. Otto Holzapfel (Odense University, 1978), p. 25.

7. Francis James Child, ed., *The English and Scottish Popular Ballads* (Boston, 1882; Dover reprint, New York, 1965), vol. 2, pp. 7–10. The version quoted below is Child's. For text and tune variants, see B. H. Bronson, *The Traditional Tunes for the Child Ballads* (Princeton, 1959), vol. 2, pp. 15ff. For the tune family to which "The Carnal and the Crane" belongs, see B. H. Bronson, *The Ballad As Song* (Berkeley, 1969), pp. 107–109. As with folklore, the "beginnings" of a tune family are impossible to uncover. Close variants of the same tune may be found accompanying texts with quite diverse sense and spirit. See Bronson, *Ballad As Song,* p. 119. In the case of "The Carnal and the Crane," there are different tunes that go with slightly different versions of the text. See Bronson, *Traditional Tunes,* pp. 15ff.

8. David Buchan, "British Balladry: Medieval Chronology and Relations," in Holzapfel, *European Medieval Ballad,* p. 100.

9. On the problems of precise dating of particular ballads, see B. R. Jonsson, "The Ballad in Scandinavia: Its Age, Prehistory, and Earliest History," in Holzapfel, *European Medieval Ballad,* pp. 9–15. Jonsson believes that the ballad genre existed in Scandinavia in the late thirteenth century. E. E. Metzner ("The Problem of Ballad Origin," in Holzapfel, *European Medieval Ballad,* pp. 34–36) conjectures that popular ballads were composed as early as the eleventh century, and he rejects the idea that the oldest ballads came from the domain of the nobility. See also Buchan, "British Balladry," p. 104. In Britain the ballad genre had evolved possibly by the late thirteenth century and was certainly in existence by the mid-fifteenth century.

10. For a study of structure and meaning in folksong, see Roger de V. Renwick, *English Folk Poetry* (University of Pennsylvania Press, 1980).

11. C. Hole, *British Folk Custom* (London, n.d.), p. 168.

12. Given the similarity between the construction of many folksongs and liturgical chants, one might begin to suspect that some of the folksongs *are* liturgical chants, or ritual music, in a much altered form. See Stewart, *Pagan Imagery,* p. 18.

13. Recorded variants are in brackets.

14. The words "sprung from" came from the following Gypsy variant (Lucy E. Broadwood, "The Carnal and the Crane," *Journal of the Folk-Song Society* 1 (1902), p. 183.

> 1 King Pharim sat amusing
> A musing all alone
> There came a blessed Savior
> And all to him unknown.
> 2 "Say, where did you come from, good man,
> Oh, where did you then pass?"
> "It is out of the land of Egypt,
> Between an ox and an ass."
> 3 "Oh, if you come out of Egypt, man,

One thing I fain I known
Whether a blessed Virgin Mary
Sprung from an Holy Ghost?

4 "For if this is true, good man,
   That you've been telling to me,
   Make that the roasted cock do crow three times
   In the place where they [we] did stand."

5 Oh, it's straight away the cock [did, shall] fetch
   And feathered to your own hand,
   Three times a roasted cock did crow
   On the place where they did stand.

6 Joseph, Jesus, and Mary,
   Were travelling for the West,
   When Mary grew a-tired,
   She might sit down and rest.

7 They travelled further and further,
   The weather being so warm,
   Till they came unto some husbandman
   A-sowing of his corn.

8 "Come, husbandman," cried Jesus,
   "From over speed and pride,
   And carry home your ripened corn,
   That you've been sowing this day.

9 "For to keep your wife and family
   From sorrow, grief, and pain,
   And keep Christ in your remembrance
   Till the time comes round again."

15. The veneration of the Virgin Mary as herself immaculately conceived was a popular aspect of Marian devotion, because there was confusion about the meaning of the expression "immaculate conception of Mary." The monk Eadmer (c. 1060–c. 1130) wrote a well thought of theological treatise arguing that Mary's conception was immaculate; the discussion continued for many centuries. See A. W. Burridge, "L'Immaculée Conception dans la théologie de l'Angleterre médiévale," *Revue d'histoire ecclesiastique* 32 (1936), pp. 570–597; and *Butler's Lives of the Saints*, vol. 4, pp. 518–521. See also Marina Warner, *Alone of All Her Sex* (New York, 1976), pp. 236–254.

16. See Gypsy version, note 14, stanzas 2–5.

17. See note 14, stanzas 1–3.

18. The crane, a water bird, was sacred to northern hunting tribes throughout the prehistory of northern Europe. Gimbutas, *Goddesses and Gods*, pp. 134–135. Gimbutas hypothesizes that the origin of the divinity of such a water bird is that it was hunted as a source of food and thus as a giver of nourishment.

19. R. Steele, ed., *Mediaeval Lore from Bartholomew Anglicus* (London, 1905), p. 126; E. Armstrong, *The Folklore of Birds* (London, 1958), pp. 75, 81. The great Celtic god Lug was known as the crow or raven god (Armstrong, p. 93).

20. See Chapter VII. In one version, Saint Stephen convinces Herod that Christ is born by causing a roasted cock to cry three times "Christus natus est."

21. One source for the Miracle of the Cock is the Gospel of Nicodemus, in Tischendorf, *Evangelia Apocrypha*, p. 269, n. 3.

22. Frazer, *New Golden Bough*, pp. 237–251. Could the reference to the thousands of children slain by Herod (verse 29) allude to the human sacrifice of the old pre-Christian reign? There is a special plea not to forget "those little ones" and not to deny them. In fact, ritual human sacrifice appears to have taken place as late as the fourth century in Rome and until much later in the pre-Christian north. For Rome see Clyde Pharr, ed., *The Theodosian Code* (Princeton, 1952), p. 473, XVI, 10.

23. L. Broadwood, *English Traditional Songs and Ballads* (n.p., 1908), pp. 74–75. The folklorist gives a variant for the last line, "Till seed-time comes round again" (p. x). "There is never a 'correct' version of any folksong, only variants sung by folk-singers. Some variants are more 'right' than others, but any standards are arbitrary. . . ." Stewart, *Pagan Imagery*, p. 27.

24. The myth of the dying god-king rescued by the protection of the mother goes back to the earliest recorded history. The ancient roots of the myth continue to appear in parallel forms: Inanna/Dumuzi in Sumeria, Ishtar/Tammuz in Babylonia, Anath/Baal in Canaan, Isis/Osiris in Egypt. There are various versions, but it is generally the powerful mother goddess who rescues her son/lover from the powers of death and drought, conquers the dark forces, and raises her son/lover to kingship. See T. Gaster, *Ritual, Myth and Drama in the Ancient Near East* (New York, 1950).

25. J. A. Hild, "Lupercalia," in Daremberg and Saglio, *Dictionnaire des antiquités*, vol. 3, pt. 2, pp. 1398ff. And A. W. J. Holleman, *Pope Gelasius I and the Lupercalia* (Amsterdam, 1974), pp. 11, 27.

26. See the "Expulsion of poisonous frogs from a vineyard, in February" (juxtaposed to the Presentation of Christ in the Temple, a scene that came to symbolize Mary's Purification) in a fourteenth-century manuscript in Lilienfeld, Austria, Stiftsbib, MS. 151, illustrated in *Reallexikon zur Deutschen Kunstgeschichte*, vol. 3, col. 1070.

27. This very ancient theme dates back in written form to the Sumerian cuneiform tablets of the third millennium B.C. See Samuel Noah Kramer, *History Begins at Sumer* (Philadelphia, 1981). A young Sumerian god was doomed to cyclical death and resurrection (Kramer, p. 323). The theme is likewise manifest in the myth and cultic practices associated with Cybele and Attis. The Trista was observed to commemorate the sorrow of the death of Attis, and the Hilleria was the feast of joy following his resurrection. See Vermaseren, *Cybele and Attis*, pp. 92, 113–124. For the Hittites see O. R. Gurney, *The Hittites* (London, 1981, reprint), p. 139. The Phoenician Adonis was another dying and reviving god associated with a Great Mother.

28. Stewart, *Pagan Imagery*, p. 25.

29. For the other versions see note 32. The Swedish, Catalán, and Flemish versions seem to promise rich results from a careful analysis by those who have more than a superficial acquaintance with the language.

30. V. Sydow, "Folk-tale Oicotypes," pp. 50–51, 243, n. 15. See also Jackson, "Some Fresh Light."

31. V. Sydow, "Folk-tale Oicotypes," p. 52.

32. Apart from the Lithuanian, Livonian, and Moravian versions of the tale (which were not available to me or had not been translated into a language I could work with), all versions of the Grain Miracle tale published and recorded by 1984 were consulted in the preparation of this chapter: *Aramaic:* G. Bergsträsser, "Neuaramäische Märchen, *Abhandlungen für die Kunde des Morgenlandes* (Leipzig, 1915), vol. 13, no. 3, p. 46; Hans Schmidt and Paul Kahle, *Volkserzählungen aus Palästina* (Göttingen, 1930), pp. 8–11. *Catalán:* F. Maspons y Labrós, *Lo Rondallayre, quentos populars catalans* (Barcelona, 1871), pp. 28–30; F. P. Briz, *Canson de la Terra, Cants populars catalans* (Barcelona and Paris, 1874), vol. 4, pp. 61-71; D. M. Milá y Fontanals, *Observaciones sobre la poesía popular* (Barcelona, 1853), pp. 130–132; D. M. Milá y Fontanals, *Romancerillo Catalán* (Barcelona, 1882), pp. 6–9; V. Almirall, *Miscelanea Folk-Lórica* (Barcelona, 1887), pp. 115–117. *Danish:* Hans Wentzel, "Die Kornfeldlegende," *Aachener Kunstblättern*, 1965, p. 142. *English:* Francis James Child, *The English and Scottish Popular Ballads* (Boston, 1885), vol. 2, pp. 7–9; L. E. Broadwood, *Journal of the Folk-Song Society* 4, pp. 22–24. *Flemish:* A. Lootens and J. M. E. Feys, *Chants populaires flamands* (Brussels, 1879), pp. 32–34; F. van Duyse, *Het oude Nederlandsche Lied* (Antwerp, 1907), vol. 3, pp. 2090–2097 (includes four Flemish songs that contain the legend); M. L'Abbé Carnal, "Noëls dramatiques des Flamands de France," *Annales du Comité Flamand de France*, 1854–1855, pp. 70–82 (a play done in the mid-eighteenth century at a girls' school). *French (dialect of Velay and Forez):* Victor Smith, 'Chants populaires du Velay et du Forez," *Romania* 8 (1879), pp. 419–421. *French (dialect of Bas-Quercy):* E. Soleville, *Chants populaires de Bas-Quercy* (Paris, 1889). *French:* Adrienne Carnoy, "La Fuite en Egypte," *La Tradition* 7 (1893), p. 312; George Carnoy, "La Fuite en Egypte," *La Tradition* 4 (1890), p. 139; J. Daymard, *Vieux chants populaires* (Cahors, 1889), p. 333; Horace Chauvet, *Légende du Roussillon* (Paris and Perpignan, 1899), pp. 95–96. *Gypsy (in English):* Lucy E. Broadwood, "The Carnal and the Crane," *Journal of the Folk-Song Society* 1 (1902), p. 183. *Irish:* A. Smythe Palmer, "An Irish Folk-tale," *Folklore Journal* 1 (1883), pp. 256–257; E. Adams, "The Vernacular Names of Insects," *Transactions of the Philological Society*, London, 1859, pp. 94–95; *Notes and Queries*, 4th ser., vol. 10, p. 183. *Italian:* Angelo de Gubernatis, *La mythologie des plantes* (Paris, 1882), vol. 2, p. 153. *Maltese:* Oskar Dähnhardt, *Natursagen* (Leipzig and Berlin, 1909), vol. 2, pp. 61–62. *Portuguese:* Jose Leite de Vasconcellos, *Tradições Populares de Portugal* (Porto, 1882), vol. 1, p. 106. *Provençal:* D. Arbaud, *Chants populaires de la Provence* (Aix, 1864), vol. 1, pp. 33–39,

vol. 2, pp. 235–241. *Scottish:* Miss Dempster, "The Folk-lore of Sutherlandshire," *Folklore Journal* 6 (1888), pp. 161–162. *Sorbian:* Leopold Haupt and J. E. Schmaler, *Volkslieder der Sorben in der Ober- und Neider-Lausitz* (Berlin, 1841, 3rd ed.; reprint 1953), pp. 275–276. *Swedish:* Svend Grundtvig, *Danmarks gamle Folkeviser* (Copenhagen, 1862), vol. 3, pp. 882–883. *Wendish:* Wilibald von Schulenburg, *Wendische Volkssagen und Gebräuche* (Leipzig, 1880), pp. 49–50.

33. See Chapter IV, "Walpurga"; and Frazer, *New Golden Bough*, pp. 401–412. For folkloric accounts of Mary among the bushels of grain at harvest see Leopold Schmidt, *Gestaltheiligkeit im bauerlichen Arbeitsmythos* (Vienna, 1952), p. 177.

34. Milá y Fontanals, *Romancerillo Catalán*, p. 7 (translation mine).

35. These ecotypes are cataloged in Stith Thompson, *Motif-Index of Folk Literature* (Copenhagen, 1955–1958); B131.6, A2231.7.1, A2221.5.

36. Maspons y Labrós, *Lo Rondallayre*, p. 29.

37. "Gaitx ets y gaitx serás, / per tant que menjis, no engreixarás." Maspons y Labrós, *Lo Rondallayre*, p. 30.

38. Chauvet, *Légende du Roussillon*, p. 95.

39. Dähnhardt, *Natursagen*, p. 53.

40. Dähnhardt, *Natursagen*, p. 65.

41. See note 14 and Broadwood, "Carnal and the Crane," p. 183.

42. Schmidt and Kahle, *Volkserzählungen*, p. 9.

43. Vamberto Morais, *A Short History of Anti-Semitism* (New York, 1976), pp. 19–20.

44. Morais, *Anti-Semitism*, p. 22.

45. *Notes And Queries*, 4th ser., vol. 10, p. 183.

46. Von Schulenburg, *Wendische Volkssagen*, pp. 49–50.

47. Bergsträsser, "Neuaramäische Märchen," p. 46.

Conclusion

1. See in particular Ena Campbell, "The Virgin of Guadalupe and the Female Self-Image"; Joanna Hubbs, "The Worship of Mother Earth in Russian Culture"; Tullio Tentori, "An Italian Religious Feast"; James J. Preston, "New Perspectives on Mother Worship"; and other essays, all in *Mother Worship*, ed. James J. Preston (Chapel Hill, 1982).

2. For a short history of the research into popular culture, see Natalie Zemon Davis, "The Historian and Popular Culture," in *Popular Culture in France*, ed. J. Beauroy et al. (Anma Libri, for Stanford University, 1976), pp. 9–16. See also Carlo Ginzburg, *The Cheese and the Worm*, trans. John Tedeschi and Anne Tedeschi (Baltimore, 1980; Penguin reprint, 1982), introduction, pp. xiv ff.

3. Rosemary Radford Ruether, *Sexism and God-talk* (Boston, 1983).

Index

Printed in the United States
49365LVS00003B/30